HOUGHTON MIFFLIN
Reading
A Legacy of Literacy

Grade 4
Traditions
Teacher's Edition

Back to School

Theme 1 **Journeys**
Focus On **Mysteries**

Theme 2 **American Stories**
Focus On **Plays**

Theme 3 **That's Amazing**

Theme 4 **Problem Solvers**
Focus On **Poetry**

▶ **Theme 5** **Heroes**
Focus On **Pourquoi Tales**

Theme 6 **Nature: Friend and Foe**

LODGE LEARNING LAB

WITHDRAWN

D1469213

Senior Authors J. David Cooper, John J. Pikulski

Authors Patricia A. Ackerman, Kathryn H. Au, David J. Chard, Gilbert G. Garcia, Claude N. Goldenberg, Marjorie Y. Lipson, Susan E. Page, Shane Templeton, Sheila W. Valencia, MaryEllen Vogt

Consultants Linda H. Butler, Linnea C. Ehri, Carla B. Ford

HOUGHTON MIFFLIN
BOSTON • MORRIS PLAINS, NJ

California • Colorado • Georgia • Illinois • New Jersey • Texas

Literature Reviewers

Consultants: **Dr. Adela Artola Allen**, Associate Dean, Graduate College, Associate Vice President for Inter-American Relations, University of Arizona, Tucson, Arizona; **Dr. Manley Begay**, Co-director of the Harvard Project on American Indian Economic Development, Director of the National Executive Education Program for Native Americans, Harvard University, John F. Kennedy School of Government, Cambridge, Massachusetts; **Dr. Nicholas Kannellos**, Director, Arte Publico Press, Director, Recovering the U.S. Hispanic Literacy Heritage Project, University of Houston, Texas; **Mildred Lee**, author and former head of Library Services for Sonoma County, Santa Rosa, California; **Dr. Barbara Moy**, Director of the Office of Communication Arts, Detroit Public Schools, Michigan; **Norma Naranjo**, Clark County School District, Las Vegas, Nevada; **Dr. Arlette Ingram Willis**, Associate Professor, Department of Curriculum and Instruction, Division of Language and Literacy, University of Illinois at Urbana-Champaign, Illinois

Teachers: **Betty Barnes**, Burnside Academy, Chicago, Illinois; **Mary Jane Bowman**, Lummis Elementary School, Las Vegas, Nevada; **Maria Gregory**, Herds Ferry Elementary School, Atlanta, Georgia; **Carmen Martinez-Eoff**, Olive Street School, Porterville, California; **Tracey Tramult**, Barrick Elementary School, Houston, Texas

Program Reviewers

Supervisors: **Judy Artz**, Middletown Monroe City School District, Ohio; **James Bennett**, Elkhart Schools, Elkhart, Indiana; **Kay Buckner-Seal**, Wayne County, Michigan; **Charlotte Carr**, Seattle School District, Washington; **Sister Marion Christi**, St. Matthews School, Archdiocese of Philadelphia, Pennsylvania; **Alvina Crouse**, Garden Place Elementary, Denver Public Schools, Colorado; **Peggy DeLapp**, Minneapolis, Minnesota; **Carol Erlandson**, Wayne Township Schools, Marion County, Indianapolis; **Brenda Feeney**, North Kansas City School District, Missouri; **Winnie Huebsch**, Sheboygan Area Schools, Wisconsin; **Brenda Mickey**, Winston-Salem/Forsyth County Schools, North Carolina; **Audrey Miller**, Sharpe Elementary School, Camden, New Jersey; **JoAnne Piccolo**, Rocky Mountain Elementary, Adams 12 District, Colorado; **Sarah Rentz**, East Baton Rouge Parish School District, Louisiana; **Kathy Sullivan**, Omaha Public Schools, Nebraska; **Rosie Washington**, Kuny Elementary, Gary, Indiana; **Theresa Wishart**, Knox County Public Schools, Tennessee

Teachers: **Carol Brockhouse**, Madison Schools, Wayne Westland Schools, Michigan; **Eva Jean Conway**, R.C. Hill School, Valley View School District, Illinois; **Carol Daley**, Jane Addams School, Sioux Falls, South Dakota; **Karen Landers**, Watwood Elementary, Talladega County, Alabama; **Barb LeFerrier**, Mullenix Ridge Elementary, South Kitsap District, Port Orchard, Washington; **Loretta Piggee**, Nobel School, Gary, Indiana; **Cheryl Remash**, Webster Elementary School, Manchester, New Hampshire; **Marilynn Rose**, Michigan; **Kathy Scholtz**, Amesbury Elementary School, Amesbury, Massachusetts; **Dottie Thompson**, Erwin Elementary, Jefferson County, Alabama; **Dana Vassar**, Moore Elementary School, Winston-Salem, North Carolina; **Joy Walls**, Ibraham Elementary School, Winston-Salem, North Carolina; **Elaine Warwick**, Fairview Elementary, Williamson County, Tennessee

Student Writing Model Feature

Special thanks to the following teachers whose students' compositions appear as Student Writing Models: **Cindy Cheatwood**, Florida; **Diana Davis**, North Carolina; **Kathy Driscoll**, Massachusetts; **Linda Evers,** Florida; **Heidi Harrison**, Michigan; **Eileen Hoffman**, Massachusetts; **Julia Kraftsow**, Florida; **Bonnie Lewison**, Florida; **Kanetha McCord**, Michigan

Credits

Cover and Theme Opener
Chris Shinn/Tony Stone Images

Photography
p. 532B, courtesy of Patti Burnett
Larry Ulrich/Tony Stone Images
p. 532D
Evan Kafka/Liaison Agency
p. 558F

Acknowledgments

Grateful acknowledgment is made for permission to reprint copyrighted material as follows:

Theme 5
"Animals in Action," by Aline A. Newman, from *Boy's Life* magazine, March 1998. Copyright © 1998 by Aline A. Newman. Reprinted by permission of Aline A. Newman and Boy's Life, a publication of the Boy Scouts of America.

"Avalanche!" by Walter Roessing, from *Boy's Life* magazine, February 1998. Copyright © 1998 by Walter Roessing. Reprinted by permission of Walter Roessing and Boy's Life, a publication of the Boy Scouts of America.

"Kids Did It!," by Laura Daily, from the December 1999 issue of *National Geographic World* magazine. Copyright © 1999 by the National Geographic Society. Reprinted by permission of the National Geographic Society.

Lodge Textbook PE 1119 .H68 2001 Gr. 4 TE Th.5

Printed in the U.S.A.

ISBN: 0-618-06538-5

23456789-WC-06 05 04 03 02 01 00

HEROES

OBJECTIVES

Reading Strategies predict/infer; monitor/clarify; evaluate; phonics/decoding

Comprehension cause and effect; making judgments; fact and opinion

Decoding Longer Words prefixes and suffixes; changing final *y* to *i*; VCV pattern; vowel diphthongs; two sounds of *g*; two sounds of *c*

Vocabulary prefixes *re-, un-, dis-;* homophones; dictionary: word histories

Spelling words with a prefix or a suffix; changing final *y* to *i*; VCV pattern

Grammar subject pronouns; sentence combining with subject pronouns; object pronouns; using the correct pronouns; singular and plural possessive pronouns; proofreading for *its* and *it's*

Writing information paragraph; using facts; problem/solution paragraph; sentence combining with pronouns; magazine article; combining sentences with possessive pronouns; process writing: personal essay

Listening/Speaking/Viewing view and evaluate information sources; listen for different purposes; present an oral book report

Information and Study Skills newspapers/magazines; conduct an interview; collect data (tables and charts)

Theme 5

Heroes
Literature Resources

Theme Writing Process: Personal Essay

Student Writing Model
H*E*R*O
a personal essay by Amanda B.
page 556

Reading-Writing Workshop
Personal Essay
pages 556–557G

Leveled Books

See Cumulative Listing of Leveled Books.

Reader's Library

Theme Paperbacks

Very Easy

- **Thanks to Sandra Cisneros**
- **Duke Ellington: A Life in Music**
- **Mark McGwire: Home Run Hero**

Lessons, pages R2–R7

Easy

Sammy Sosa: He's the Man
by Laura Driscoll
Lesson, page 557I

On Level

Mrs. Mack
by Patricia Polacco
Lesson, page 557K

Challenge

The Wreck of the Ethie
by Hilary Hyland
Lesson, page 557M

Audiotape and Selection Summary Masters

Heroes

Happy Birthday, Dr. King!, Gloria Estefan, Lou Gehrig: The Luckiest Man

Houghton Mifflin Classroom Bookshelf

Level 4

SOAR to SUCCESS!

The Intermediate Intervention Program
Level 4

Theme 5

Bibliography

Leveled Books for Independent Reading

Key

 Science

 Social Studies

 Multicultural

 Music

 Math

 Classic

 Art

Very Easy

 China's Bravest Girl
by Charlie Chin
Children's 1997 (32p)
Hua Mu Lan persuades her father
to let her go to war.

Martha Speaks
by Susan Meddaugh
Houghton 1992 (32p)
Martha, a dog who can speak,
saves the day when a burglar
shows up. **Available in Spanish as
Martha habla.**

Home Run
by Robert Burleigh
Harcourt 1998 (32p)
A poetic account of Babe Ruth
preparing to hit a home run.

 **César Chávez: Labor
Leader**
by Clara Sánchez de Morris
Modern
Curriculm 1994
(28p)
Chávez brought
improvements to
the lives of migrant
workers.

 **Dinner at Aunt
Connie's House**
by Faith Ringgold
Hyperion 1996 (32p)
Melody discovers the portraits in
Aunt Connie's house are of heroic
African American women.

Easy

 Fair Ball!
by Jonah Winter
Scholastic 1999 (32p)
Stars of baseball's Negro Leagues
profiled here include Cool Papa
Bell and Josh Gibson.

---

* **One Giant Step: The Story
of Neil Armstrong**
by Don Brown
Houghton 1998 (32p)
Armstrong became the first person
to set foot on the moon.

Maria's Comet
by Deborah Hopkinson
Simon 1999
(32p)
A young girl fasci-
nated by the stars
becomes the first
woman to discover
a comet.

 **Marian Anderson: A
Great Singer**
by Patricia and Fredrick
McKissack
Enslow 1991
(32p)
Anderson over-
came prejudice to
become one of the
greatest singers in
the world.

**The Bravest Dog Ever: The
True Story of Balto**
by Natalie Standiford
Random House 1989 (48p)
Balto, a sled dog, saved Nome,
Alaska, from diphtheria.

The Babe and I
by David A. Adler
Harcourt 1999 (32p)
A young boy selling newspapers to
help out his family
gets some help
from Babe Ruth
himself.

On Level

 Sisters in Strength
by Yona Zeldis
McDonough
Holt 2000 (48p)
Helen Keller, Harriet Tubman, and
Amelia Earhart are among the
eleven women profiled.

* **Out of Darkness: A Story of
Louis Braille**
by Russell Freedman
Clarion 1997
(81p)
A blind boy's experi-
ments made it pos-
sible for the blind to
read.

 **My Heroes, My
People**
by Morgan Monceaux
Farrar 1999 (64p)
Painter/author Monceaux offers
portraits of African Americans and
Native Americans of the American
West.

 **The Riches of Oseola
McCarty**
by Evelyn Coleman
Whitman 1998 (48p)
McCarty never finished school, but
after working hard all of her life
and saving her money, she estab-
lished college scholarships at age
eighty-seven.

 **America's Champion
Swimmer**
by David A. Adler
Harcourt 2000 (32p)
Gertrude Ederle was the first
woman to swim the English
Channel.

---

* = Included in Houghton Mifflin Classroom Bookshelf, Level 4

Hugger to the Rescue
by Dorothy Hinshaw Patent
Cobblehill 1994 (32p)

Hugger and other Newfoundland dogs are trained to search for and rescue people who are lost or hurt.

Seven Brave Women
by Betsy Hearne
Greenwillow 1997 (48p)

Hearne relates the exploits of seven of her female ancestors.

Colin Powell: Straight to the Top
by Rose Blue and Corinne J. Naden
Millbrook 1997 (48p)
The authors examine the life of the former general who has become a hero to millions.

Heroes
by Ken Mochizuki
Lee & Low 1995 (32p) also paper
A Japanese American boy learns the meaning of heroism.

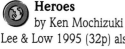
Challenge

Through My Eyes
by Ruby Bridges
Scholastic 1999 (64p)
Ruby Bridges, who integrated the schools of New Orleans as a six-year-old in 1960, tells her story.

* **Adventures of Greek Heroes**
by Mollie McLean
Houghton 1973 (192p)

The myths of Hercules, Perseus, Theseus, Orpheus, Meleager, and Jason are retold.

Pride of Puerto Rico: The Life of Roberto Clemente
by Paul Robert Walker
Harcourt 1981 (135p) also paper

The famous right fielder for the Pittsburgh Pirates was a hero on and off the field.

Books for Teacher Read Aloud

All by Herself
by Ann Whitford Paul
Harcourt 1999 (40p)
Heroic deeds of fourteen women and girls are presented in poetry.

Lives: Poems About Famous Americans
selected by Lee Bennett Hopkins
Harper 1999 (32p)
Poets salute sixteen American heroes, including Paul Revere, Langston Hughes, Babe Ruth, and Thomas Edison.

* = Included in Houghton Mifflin Classroom Bookshelf, Level 4

Technology

Computer Software Resources

- **Get Set for Reading CD-ROM**
  Heroes
  Provides background building, vocabulary support, and selection summaries in English and Spanish.

Video Cassettes

- **Johnny Appleseed.** *Filmic Archives*
- **John Henry** by Julius Lester. *Weston Woods*
- **A Picture Book of Martin Luther King, Jr.** *by David A. Adler. Live Oak Media*
- **Sadako and the Thousand Paper Cranes** *by Eleanor Coerr. Informed Democracy*
- **Brave Irene** *by William Steig. Weston Woods*

Audio Cassettes

- **Keep the Lights Burning, Abbie** *by Peter and Connie Roop. Live Oak Media*
- **A Picture Book of Martin Luther King, Jr.** *by David A. Adler. Audio Bookshelf*
- **A Picture Book of Rosa Parks** *by David A. Adler. Audio Bookshelf*
- **Kate Shelley and the Midnight Express** *by Margaret Wetterer. Live Oak Media*
- **John Henry.** *Rabbit Ears*
- **Johnny Appleseed.** *Rabbit Ears*
- **Audiotapes for *Heroes*.** *Houghton Mifflin Company*

Technology Resources addresses are on page R28.

Education Place
www.eduplace.com *Log on to Education Place for more activities relating to Heroes.*
Book Adventure
www.bookadventure.org *This Internet reading incentive program provides thousands of titles for students to read.*

Theme at a Glance

Theme Concept: *Making a difference with courage, dignity, and perseverance*

☑ **Indicates Tested Skills**
See page 526G for assessment options.

	Reading		Word Work
	Comprehension Skills and Strategies	**Information and Study Skills**	**Decoding Longer Words** *Structural Analysis/Phonics*
Anthology Selection 1: **Happy Birthday, Dr. King!** Social Studies Link	☑ Cause and Effect, *533D, 537, 555A* **Comprehension:** Sequence of Events, *539;* Story Structure, *543;* **Genre:** Realistic Fiction, *545;* **Writer's Craft:** Point of View, *547* **Strategy Focus:** Predict/Infer, *533C, 538, 548*	How to Take Notes, *552* Newspapers/Magazines, *555C*	☑ Structural Analysis: Prefixes and Suffixes, *555E* Phonics: Vowel Diphthongs, *555F*
Anthology Selection 2: **Gloria Estefan** Health Link	☑ Making Judgments, *559D, 575, 581A* **Comprehension:** Text Organization, *563;* Compare and Contrast, *567;* **Writer's Craft:** Sequence Words and Phrases, *569;* **Visual Literacy:** Photography, *573* **Strategy Focus:** Monitor/Clarify, *559C, 564, 568*	How to Follow a Recipe, *580* Conduct an Interview, *581C*	☑ Structural Analysis: Changing Final *y* to *i*, *581E* Phonics: Two Sounds of *g*, *581F*
Anthology Selection 3: **Lou Gehrig: The Luckiest Man** Math Link	☑ Fact and Opinion, *583D, 589, 607A* **Comprehension:** Making Judgments, *593;* Author's Viewpoint, *597;* **Visual Literacy:** Perspective, *595* ☑ Strategy Focus: Evaluate, *583C, 590, 594*	How to Read a Chart, *606* ☑ Collecting Data (Tables and Charts), *607C*	☑ Structural Analysis: VCV Pattern, *607E* Phonics: Two Sounds of *c*, *607F*
Theme Resources	Reteaching: Comprehension, *R8, R10, R12* Challenge/Extension: Comprehension, *R9, R11, R13*		Reteaching: Structural Analysis, *R14, R16, R18*

Special Theme Features

Test Preparation
Taking Tests: Writing an Answer to a Question
- Anthology, *608*
- Teacher's Edition, *608*
- Practice Book, *340–341*

Spelling
Additional Lessons:
- Frequently Misspelled Words
- Spelling Review/Assessment

<table>
<tr><td>

Pacing

- This theme is designed to take approximately 4 to 6 weeks, depending on your students' needs.

</td><td>

Multi–age Classroom

Related themes—

- **Grade 3:** *Off to Adventure!*
- **Grade 5:** *Give It All You've Got*

</td><td>

Technology

Education Place: www.eduplace.com Log on to Education Place for more activities relating to *Heroes*.
Lesson Planner CD-ROM: Customize your planning for *Heroes* with the Lesson Planner.

</td></tr>
</table>

Writing & Language

Cross-Curricular

Spelling	Vocabulary Skills, Vocabulary Expansion	Grammar, Usage, and Mechanics	Writing	Listening/ Speaking/Viewing	Content Area
✓ Words with a Prefix or a Suffix, *555G*	✓ Dictionary: Prefixes *re-, un-, dis-, 555I* Holiday Words, *555J*	✓ Subject Pronouns, *555K*	Writing an Information Paragraph, *555M* Using Facts, *555N*	View and Evaluate Information Sources, *555O*	**Responding:** Vocabulary, Listening and Speaking, *551* **Theme Resources:** *R26–R27*
✓ Changing Final *y* to *i*, *581G*	✓ Homophones, *581I* Musical Instruments, *581J*	✓ Object Pronouns, *581K*	Writing a Problem/Solution Paragraph, *581M* ✓ Sentence Combining with Pronouns, *581N*	Listen for Different Purposes, *581O*	**Responding:** Social Studies, Listening and Speaking, Internet, *579* **Theme Resources:** *R26–R27*
✓ VCV Pattern, *607G*	✓ Dictionary: Word Histories, *607I* Sports Terminology, *607J*	✓ Singular and Plural Possessive Pronouns, *607K*	Writing a Magazine Article, *607M* ✓ Combining Sentences with Possessive Pronouns, *607N*	Present an Oral Book Report, *607O*	**Responding:** Math, Viewing, Internet, *605* **Theme Resources:** *R26–R27*
	Challenge/Extension: Vocabulary Activities, *R15, R17, R19*	Reteaching: Grammar, *R20–R22*	Writing Activities, *R23–R25*		Cross-Curricular Activities, *R26–R27*

<table>
<tr><td>

- Teacher's Edition, *557F, 609*
- Practice Book, *306–308, 342–344*

</td><td>

Reading–Writing Workshop:
Personal Essay

- Anthology: Student Writing Model, *556–557*
- Practice Book, *304, 305*

</td><td>

- Teacher's Edition, *556–557G*
  Writing Process
  Main Idea and Details
  Introductions and Conclusions
  Pronoun Reference

</td></tr>
</table>

Planning for Assessment

Use these resources to meet your assessment needs. For additional information, see the *Teacher's Assessment Handbook.*

Diagnostic Planning

Leveled Reading Passages

Lexia Quick Phonics Assessment CD-ROM

- **Leveled Reading Passages** can be used to diagnose students' reading level and knowledge of skills and strategies.
- **Theme Skills Test** can be used as a pretest to determine what skills students know prior to instruction, and to plan levels of support for meeting individual needs.
- **Lexia Quick Phonics Assessment CD-ROM** can be used to identify students who need more help with phonics.

Ongoing Assessment

Comprehension Checks

Selection Tests

Reading-Writing Workshop

Comprehension
- Selection Comprehension Checks, **Practice Book,** pp. 291, 311, 326
- Selection Tests, **Teacher's Resource Book**

Writing
- Reading-Writing Workshop: Personal Essay, pp. 556–557G
- Other student writing samples for portfolios

Informal Assessment
- **Diagnostic Checks,** pp. 541, 549, 555B, 555F, 555L, 565, 577, 581B, 581F, 581L, 591, 603, 607B, 607F, 607L, R8–R22
- **Student Self-Assessment,** pp. 551, 557G, 579, 605
- **Reading Fluency,** p. 609A
- Observation Checklist, **Teacher's Resource Book**

End-of-Theme Assessment

Integrated Theme Test

Theme Skills Test

Integrated Theme Test
- Integrated test of reading and writing, matching many state test formats
- Comprehension strategies and skills, word skills, spelling, grammar, and writing

Theme Skills Test
- Tests discrete skills: Comprehension skills, word skills, spelling, grammar, writing, and information and study skills

Periodic Progress Assessment

Benchmark Test

Benchmark Test
- Assesses overall student progress in reading and writing, two to four times a year

National Test Correlation

✓ TESTED SKILLS for *Heroes*	Teacher's Notes	ITBS	Terra Nova (CTBS)	CAT	SAT	MAT
Comprehension Strategies and Skills						
• Strategies: Evaluate, Predict/Infer*, Monitor/Clarify*		O	O	O	O	O
• Skills: Cause and Effect, Making Judgments, Fact and Opinion, Sequence of Events*, Story Structure*, Compare/Contrast*, Text Organization*, Author's Viewpoint*		O	O	O	O	O
Information and Study Skills						
• Collecting Data (Tables, Charts)						
• Newspapers/Magazines*				O	O	O
Structural Analysis						
• VCV Pattern		O	O	O	O	
• Changing Final *y* to *i*		O	O	O		
• Words with a Prefix or Suffix (*re-, dis-, un-; -ness, -ment, -ful, -less*)		O	O	O	O	
Spelling						
• VCV Pattern		O	O	O	O	O
• Changing Final *y* to *i*		O	O	O		
• Words with a Prefix or Suffix (*re-, dis-, un-; -ness, -ment, -ful, -less*)		O	O	O	O	O
Vocabulary/Dictionary						
• Prefixes *re-, un-, dis-*		O	O	O	O	
• Homophones		O	O		O	
• Word Histories						
Grammar						
• Pronouns: Subject, Object, Singular Possessive and Plural Possessive		O	O		O	
Writing						
• Formats: Information Paragraph; Problem/Solution Paragraph; Magazine Article		O	O		O	O
• Sentence Combining with Pronouns			O	O		
• Sentence Combining with Possessive Pronouns			O	O		
• Reading-Writing Workshop: Personal Essay		O	O		O	O

READING | WORD WORK | WRITING & LANGUAGE

*These skills are taught, but not tested, in this theme.

KEY
ITBS Iowa Tests of Basic Skills
Terra Nova (CTBS) Comprehensive Tests of Basic Skills
CAT California Achievement Tests
SAT Stanford Achievement Test
MAT Metropolitan Achievement Tests

Meeting Individual Needs

Houghton Mifflin Reading includes a wide variety of resources for meeting the needs of all students. The chart below indicates features and components of the program and the students for whom they are most appropriate.

	On Level Students	English Language Learners	Challenge Students	Extra Support Students	Inclusion/Special Needs
Anthology					
• Get Set to Read	★	★	○	★	★
• Content Links	★	★	★	★	★
• Education Place	★	○	★	○	★
• Student Writing Model	★	★	○	★	★
• Taking Tests	★	★	○	★	★
Audiotape	○	★		★	★
Teacher's Edition					
• Teacher Read Aloud	★	★	○	★	★
• Meeting Individual Needs notes		★	★	★	★
• Theme Resources	★	★	★	★	★
• Selection Summaries	○	★		★	★
• Theme Project	★	○	★	○	○
• Reading-Writing Workshop	★	★	★	★	★
Practice Book	★	★	★	★	★
Leveled Books					
• Reader's Library *Very Easy*	○	○		★	★
• Theme Paperback *Easy*		★		★	★
• Theme Paperback *On Level*	★		○		
• Theme Paperback *Challenge*	○	○	★		
• Classroom Bookshelf	★	○	★	○	○
Challenge Handbook	○	○	★		
Extra Support Handbook		○		★	★

KEY: ★ = highly appropriate   ○ = appropriate

	On Level Students	English Language Learners	Challenge Students	Extra Support Students	Inclusion/Special Needs
Language Development Resources		★		○	○
Home/Community Connections	★	★	★	★	★
SOAR to SUCCESS		○		★	★
Phonics Intervention		○		★	★

Technology

	On Level Students	English Language Learners	Challenge Students	Extra Support Students	Inclusion/Special Needs
Education Place	★	○	★	○	○
Get Set for Reading CD-ROM	★	★	○	★	★
Lexia Quick Phonics Assessment CD-ROM				★	★
Lexia Phonics CD-ROM: Intermediate Intervention				★	★
Published by Sunburst Technology*					
• Tenth Planet™: Vowels Short and Long	○	○		★	★
• Tenth Planet™: Blends and Digraphs	○	○		★	★
• Tenth Planet™: Word Parts	○	○		★	★
• Reading Who? Reading You!	○	○		★	★
• EasyBook Deluxe	★	★		○	○
• Writer's Resource Library	★	★	○	○	○
• Media Weaver™ (Sunburst/Humanities Software)	★	★	★	○	

Launching the Theme
for *Heroes*

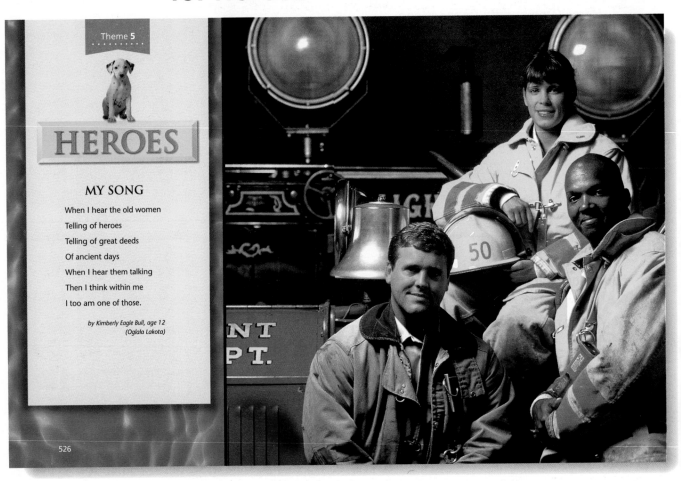

Read aloud the theme title and poem on Anthology page 526, pointing out that the author is a twelve-year-old student and a Native American. If necessary, tell students of the Native American tradition of oral history and oral storytelling. The "old women" would be telling the history of their people ("ancient days"). Use the following suggestions to prompt discussion:

- Who are some of your heroes? Why do you respect them? (Answers will vary.)
- In the poem "My Song," what do you think the line "I too am one of those" means? (She is also a hero; she is capable of achieving great things in her life; there is a connection formed between the poet and her ancestors who lived long ago.)
- What would make you feel like a hero? (You might ask some students to share a heroic experience they've had.)
- Why do you think firefighters were chosen to illustrate the *Heroes* theme? What qualities do they have that make them heroes? (They are brave, they help people, are hard workers.)

Multi-age Classroom

Related Themes:

Grade 5 . . . Give It All You've Got

Grade 4 . . . Heroes

Grade 3 . . . Off to Adventure!

▶ Theme Connections

Introduce Selection Connections on **Practice Book** pages 287–288. Have students do the first page. Explain that students will add to the second page after each selection and at the end of the theme to build their understanding of *Heroes*.

★ **Connecting/Comparing** questions in Responding (Anthology pages 550, 578, 604) help students focus on relationships among selections and to the theme overall.

Expressing Project

🖉 **Writing** Have students write a letter to one of their heroes. The hero may be someone they know or someone they have heard about, but it should be a real person. They should tell why they consider this person a hero, and explain why they respect him or her.

Challenge Ask students to think of a time, either real or fantasy, when they were a hero. Have them write a newspaper article about their heroic deed. Remind them to write an attention-getting headline. They should be sure to include the basic information about the situation, telling who, what, why, where, when, and how. They can add a picture to help show the people involved, the location, or any other pertinent details.

Terrence Saves the Day!

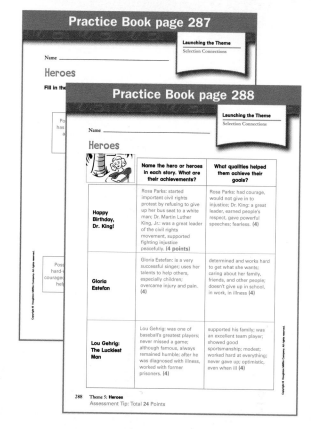

Practice Book page 287

Practice Book page 288

Technology

Education Place
www.eduplace.com
Log on to **Education Place** for more activities relating to *Heroes*.

Lesson Planner CD-ROM
Customize your planning for *Heroes* with the Lesson Planner.

Home Connection

Send home the theme letter for *Heroes* to introduce the theme and suggest home activities. See **Teacher's Resource Blackline Masters**.

For other suggestions relating to *Heroes*, see **Home/Community Connections**.

Happy Birthday, Dr. King!

Different texts for different purposes

Happy Birthday, **Dr. King!**

MULTICULTURAL CELEBRATIONS

by Kathryn Jones | Illustrated by Floyd Cooper

Anthology: Main Selection

Purposes

- strategy focus: predict/infer
- comprehension skill: cause and effect
- vocabulary development
- critical thinking, discussion

Genre: Realistic Fiction

Realistic characters and events come to life in a fictional plot.

Selection Summary

When Jamal's grandfather hears that the boy is in trouble for fighting to sit in the back of the bus, he tells Jamal about Rosa Parks, Martin Luther King, Jr., and the civil rights movement. Jamal responds with an idea for a skit for his school's King Day assembly.

Teacher's Edition: Read Aloud

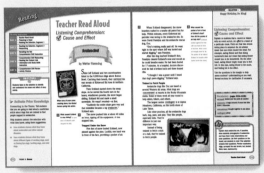

Purposes

- listening comprehension: cause and effect
- vocabulary development
- critical thinking, discussion

Anthology: Get Set to Read

Purposes

- background building: civil rights
- developing key vocabulary

Anthology: Content Link

Purposes

- content reading: social studies
- skill: how to take notes
- critical thinking, discussion

Leveled Books and Resources

See Cumulative Listing of Leveled Books.

Reader's Library

Very Easy

Thanks to Sandra Cisneros
by **Daniel Santacruz**

(Also available on blackline masters)

Purposes

- fluency practice in below-level text
- alternate reading for students reading significantly below grade level
- strategy application: predict/infer
- comprehension skill application: cause and effect
- below-level independent reading

Lesson Support

- Guided Reading lesson, page R2
- Alternate application for Comprehension Skill lesson on cause and effect, page 555A
- Reteaching for Comprehension Skill: cause and effect, page R8

Selection Summary Masters

Happy Birthday, Dr. King!
Teacher's Resource Blackline Masters

Audiotape

Happy Birthday, Dr. King!
Audiotape for *Heroes*

Theme Paperbacks

Easy

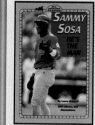

Sammy Sosa: He's the Man
by **Laura Driscoll**

Lesson, TE page 557I

On Level

Mrs. Mack
by **Patricia Polacco**

Lesson, TE page 557K

Challenge

The Wreck of the Ethie
by **Hilary Hyland**

Lesson, TE page 557M

Inclusion Strategy

Significantly Below-level Readers

Students reading so far below level that they cannot read *Happy Birthday, Dr. King!* even with the suggested Extra Support should still participate with the class whenever possible.

- Include them in the Teacher Read Aloud (p. 532A) and Preparing to Read (pp. 533C–533D).
- Have them listen to *Happy Birthday, Dr. King!* on the audiotape for *Heroes* and read the Selection Summary while others read Segment 1 of the selection.
- Have them read "Thanks to Sandra Cisneros" in the Reader's Library collection for *Heroes* while others read Segment 2 of *Happy Birthday, Dr. King!*.
- Have all students participate in Wrapping Up Segment 2 (p. 549) and Responding (p. 550).

Technology

Get Set for Reading CD-ROM

Happy Birthday, Dr. King!

Provides background building, vocabulary support, and selection summaries in English and Spanish.

Education Place

www.eduplace.com

Log on to Education Place for more activities relating to *Happy Birthday, Dr. King!*.

Book Adventure

www.bookadventure.org

This Internet reading incentive program provides thousands of titles for students.

Suggested Daily Routines

Instructional Goals	**Day 1**	**Day 2**

Reading
 	
Strategy Focus: Predict/Infer
 	
✓ *Comprehension Skill:* Cause and Effect
 	
Comprehension Skill Review: Sequence of Events; Story Structure
 	
Information and Study Skills: Newspapers/Magazines
	Teacher Read Aloud
	Avalanche!, 532A
	Preparing to Read ***Happy Birthday, Dr. King!***
	• Get Set: Background and Vocabulary, 533A
	• Key Vocabulary, 533B
	  Selection Vocabulary, *Practice Book, 289*
	• Strategy/Skill Preview, 533C
	  Cause and Effect Chart, *Practice Book, 290*
	Reading Segment 1
	Happy Birthday, Dr. King!, 534–541
	• Supporting Comprehension
	• Strategy Focus, 538
	Wrapping Up Segment 1, *541*
		Reading Segment 2
		Happy Birthday, Dr. King!, 542–549
		• Supporting Comprehension
		• Strategy Focus, 548
		
		Wrapping Up Segment 2, *549*
		Responding
		• Comprehension Questions: Think About the Selection, 550
		• Comprehension Check, *Practice Book, 291*
		Revisiting the Text
		• Comprehension: Cause and Effect, 537

Word Work ✓ *Spelling:* Words with a Prefix or a Suffix *Decoding Longer Words:* ✓ *Structural Analysis:* Prefixes and Suffixes *Phonics:* Vowel Diphthongs ✓ *Vocabulary:* Dictionary: Prefixes *re-, un-, dis-*	**Spelling** • Pretest, 555G • Instruction: Words with a Prefix or a Suffix, 555G • Take-Home Word List, *Practice Book: Handbook*	**Decoding Longer Words Instruction** • Structural Analysis: Prefixes and Suffixes, 555E • *Practice Book, 294* **Spelling** • *Practice Book, 295*
Writing & Language ✓ *Grammar:* Subject Pronouns *Writing:* Writing an Information Paragraph; Using Facts *Listening/Speaking/Viewing:* View and Evaluate Information Sources	**Daily Language Practice,** *555L* **Grammar Instruction** • Subject Pronouns, 555K **Writing** • Journal Writing, 535	**Daily Language Practice,** *555L* **Grammar Instruction** • Subject Pronouns, *Practice Book, 299* **Writing Instruction** • Writing an Information Paragraph, 555M • Journal Writing, 542

 = tested skills

📖 Leveled Books

See Cumulative Listing of Leveled Books.

Reader's Library
• **Very Easy** *Thanks to Sandra Cisneros, Lesson, R2*
Book Links: Anthology, 530
Bibliography: Teacher's Edition, 526C
Houghton Mifflin Classroom Bookshelf, Level 4

Theme Paperbacks, Lessons, 557H–557N
• **Easy** *Sammy Sosa: He's the Man*
• **On Level** *Mrs. Mack*
• **Challenge** *The Wreck of the Ethie*

Allow time every day for students to read independently from self-selected books.

Lesson Planner CD-ROM: Customize your planning for *Happy Birthday, Dr. King!* with the Lesson Planner.

Day 3

Revisiting the Text
• Genre: Realistic Fiction, 545
• Writer's Craft: Point of View, 547

Comprehension Skill Instruction
• Cause and Effect, 555A
• *Practice Book,* 292

Phonics Instruction
• Vowel Diphthongs, 555F

Spelling
• *Practice Book,* 296

Daily Language Practice, 555L

Grammar Instruction
• Let's Compare, 555K

 Writing
• Responding: Write a Scene, 550

Day 4

Comprehension Skill Instruction
• Reteaching Cause and Effect with Reader's Library, R8
• Independent Application, *Practice Book,* 293

Reading the Social Studies Link
• "Dear Mrs. Parks," 552–555

Information and Study Skills Instruction
• Newspapers/Magazines, 555C

Decoding Longer Words
• Reteaching Structural Analysis: Prefixes and Suffixes, R14
• Challenge/Extension Activities, R15

Spelling
• *Practice Book,* 297

Vocabulary Skill Instruction
• Dictionary: Prefixes *re-, un-, dis-,* 555I
• *Practice Book,* 298

Daily Language Practice, 555L

Grammar
• Reteaching, R20
• Let's Compare, *Practice Book,* 300

 Writing
• Using Facts, 555N
Listening/Speaking/Viewing
• View and Evaluate Information Sources, 555O

Day 5

Revisiting the Text: Comprehension Review Skill Instruction
• Sequence of Events, 539
• Story Structure, 543

Rereading for Fluency
Happy Birthday, Dr. King!, 534–549

Activity Choices
• Responding Activities, 551
• Challenge/Extension Activities, R9
• Cross-Curricular Activities, R26

Vocabulary Expansion
• Holiday Words, 555J

Spelling
• Posttest, 555H

Daily Language Practice, 555L

Grammar
• Sentence Combining with Subject Pronouns, 555L
• *Practice Book,* 301

Writing
• Sentence Combining with Subject Pronouns, 555L
• Writing Activities, R23
• Sharing Students' Writing: Author's Chair

Reading-Writing Workshop: Personal Essay

Based on the **Student Writing Model** in the Anthology, this workshop guides students through the writing process and includes skill lessons on—

• Main Idea and Details   See Teacher's Edition, *pages 556–557G.*
• Introductions and Conclusions
• Pronoun Reference

Allow time every day for students to write independently on self-selected topics.

Reading Instruction

DAY 1	• Teacher Read Aloud • Preparing to Read • Reading the Selection, Segment 1
DAY 2	• Reading the Selection, Segment 2 • Responding
DAY 3	• Revisiting the Text • Comprehension Skill Instruction
DAY 4	• Comprehension Skill Reteaching • Reading the Content Link • Information and Study Skills Instruction
DAY 5	• Comprehension Skill Review • Activity Choices

OBJECTIVES

Students listen to the selection to identify and understand the cause and effect of story events.

▶ Activate Prior Knowledge

Connecting to the Theme Tell students that you are going to read aloud a nonfiction article about dogs that are trained to find people trapped in avalanches.

Help students connect the selection with what they know, using these suggestions:

■ Have students discuss what they know about avalanches and other natural disasters.

■ Have students discuss what they know about different types of working dogs, such as Seeing Eye dogs, herding dogs, and sled dogs.

Teacher Read Aloud

Listening Comprehension:
✓ Cause and Effect

Avalanche!

by Walter Roessing

When tons of snow come crashing down, four-footed heroes spring into action.

1 What caused Eckland to stop falling? (A pine tree in Eckland's path stopped his fall.)

Skier Jeff Eckland and two snowboarders hiked to the 9,000-foot ridge above Button Bowl. Catching their breath, they <u>surveyed</u> the vast terrain of Kirkwood Ski Area in northern California.

Then Eckland started down the steep slope. As he carved his fourth turn in the heavy, windblown powder, the snow began sliding. Eckland fell and made a small snowslide. He wasn't worried—at first.

"Suddenly the entire slope gave way and that minislide became a *big* <u>avalanche</u>," Eckland says.

1 The snow pushed him at about 40 miles an hour, ripping off his equipment. A tree stopped him.

Trapped Under the Snow

Five feet of snow buried Eckland, now pinned against the pine. Luckily, one hand was in front of his face, providing a pocket of air.

2 When Eckland disappeared, the snow-boarders rushed to a nearby ski patrol hut for help. Within minutes, every Kirkwood ski patroller was racing to the avalanche site. So were David Paradysz and his avalanche rescue dog, Doc.

"Doc's training really paid off. He went right to the spot where Jeff was buried and started digging," says Paradysz.

After the dog reached Eckland's face, Paradysz cleared Eckland's nose and mouth so he could breathe easier. He had been buried for 17 minutes. At a hospital, doctors discovered he had a broken back and three busted ribs.

"I thought I was a goner until I heard that dog's paws digging," Eckland says.

Trained to Fetch People

Avalanche dogs like Doc are based at several Western ski areas. Most dogs are concentrated at resorts in the Rocky Mountain states. Some of them work all year round to help skiers, hikers, and others.

The largest canine contingent is at Alpine Meadows, California, on the north shore of Lake Tahoe.

Like other pooches, all the avalanche dogs bark, beg, pant, and play. They like people, especially kids. They're different in just one important way.

Instead of being trained to fetch a stick or a ball, they're trained to fetch people.

2 What caused the pocket of air in front of Eckland's face? How did the pocket of air help him? (Eckland landed against the tree with one hand in front of his face, which created enough room for air. The pocket of air helped Eckland to breathe while buried under the snow.)

Listening Comprehension: ✓ Cause and Effect

Explain to students that a *cause* is a reason why an event occurs. An *effect* is a result of a particular cause. Point out that two events taking place in sequence do not always mean that one event caused the other. For example, eating dinner and then doing homework does not mean that eating dinner caused you to do homework. On the other hand, eating dinner might cause you to feel full. In this case, eating dinner is the cause, and feeling full is the effect.

Use the questions in the margin to help assess students' understanding as you read. Reread sections for clarification if necessary.

Vocabulary *(pages 532A–532B)*

surveyed: looked over the parts of; studied

avalanche: a large amount of snow that falls down a mountain

concentrated: brought together in one place

contingent: group

MEETING INDIVIDUAL NEEDS

English Language Learners

Explain what avalanches are. If possible, show students photographs of avalanches and have them make observations and pose questions. List their questions on the board; ask students to note if the selection answers their questions. Preview vocabulary: *ridge, surveyed the vast terrain, hut, busted, fetch, keen, backcountry.*

(Teacher Read Aloud, continued**)**

Hasty the Hero

At Copper Mountain, in Colorado, a Golden Retriever named Hasty is a real hero. The dog has used its keen sense of smell to lead summer rescuers to dozens of lost hunters, hikers, and children in Colorado's backcountry. But Hasty is best known for saving a young woman's life.

A couple from Denver was skiing one quiet January morning at Copper Mountain. A wall of snow suddenly roared down the treeless terrain in an avalanche, burying the woman under three feet of snow. Luckily, some ski patrollers saw it happen. After radioing for help, they skied down to search for her.

At Copper's Patrol Headquarters, another patroller jumped onto a snowmobile with Hasty and rushed to the avalanche site. In this kind of accident, one well-trained dog with a sensitive sniffer can do the work of 30 people probing the snow with probe poles. A probe line was started where Hasty started digging, and the buried woman was located.

When rescuers cleared her face, she had a weak pulse and wasn't breathing.

"Suddenly her eyes opened," says Patti Burnett, Hasty's handler and patrol supervisor. "Thankfully, she survived and has made a full recovery."

Start Them Young

Dogs are born to want to use their noses, but they must be trained to rescue humans buried in the snow.

There were no avalanche dogs in the Copper Mountain area when Ms. Burnett brought in Hasty in 1986. The dog was only 2 months old, but Ms. Burnett immediately started training him for wilderness searching. Five

3 Why can dogs find a person buried under snow more quickly than humans can?

(Dogs have a strong sense of smell which helps them locate a buried person, while humans have to dig through the snow to find the person.)

Vocabulary *(page 532C)*

keen: very quick, sharp, or strong

backcountry: a rural area where few people live

ski patroller: a person who provides medical help to skiers and snowboarders

probing: poking, looking in

months later, Hasty first saw snow. And Burnett began training him as an avalanche rescue dog.

Pups are taught with simple tasks, says John Reller, who's 32 and an Eagle Scout. He owns Skadee (rhymes with Katie), an 8-year-old Golden Retriever that also works as an avalanche dog at Copper Mountain.

Hide-and-Seek in Real Life

"In training Skadee, we started out playing various hide-and-seek games," says Mr. Reller, a part-time volunteer patroller at Copper. "The games got more and more difficult. It takes an entire winter of constant training before a dog becomes skilled enough to find people buried in the snow."

After that first winter, dogs work out at least once a week to keep themselves—and their handlers—sharp.

Sometimes the handlers bury a volunteer in a small hole below the snow's surface. Patrollers walk around the site to throw off the victim's scent. Then Hasty, Skadee and the other dogs must answer to the command "search." It's easy to tell when the search is successful. "An avalanche dog starts digging like crazy and his tail changes from wagging to a fast circular motion," Mr. Reller says.

Skadee's reward is lots of praise and a glove to chew to pieces. A victim's reward is much greater.

▶ Discussion

Summarize After reading the story, discuss parts that students found interesting. Then ask them to summarize the selection.

Listening Comprehension:
✔ **Cause and Effect** Write the following chart headings on the board: *Cause, Effect.* Have students list pairs of events from the selection that fall into these categories.

Personal Response Ask students to describe an animal they know of that has done something heroic or special.

★ **Connecting/Comparing** Ask students to discuss how this selection fits in with the theme *Heroes.*

Get Set for Reading CD-ROM

Happy Birthday, Dr. King!
Provides background building, vocabulary support, and selection summaries in English and Spanish.

Preparing to Read

▶ Using *Get Set* for Background and Vocabulary

Connecting to the Theme Tell students they will be reading about people who have made a difference in the world. The first story, *Happy Birthday, Dr. King!,* is about Rosa Parks, Dr. Martin Luther King, Jr., and the advent of the civil rights movement.

Discuss with students what it means for everyone to have equal rights. Then use the Get Set to Read on pages 532–533 to explain how Rosa Parks and Dr. King helped change America.

n   Ask a student to read aloud "A Famous Bus Ride."

n   Have students discuss how the photographs show what the text talks about. Discuss how the events pictured show a nonviolent protest.

n   Ask students to explain the meaning of the boldfaced Key Vocabulary words: *fare, protest, boycott, stupendous,* and *civil rights.* Ask students to use these words as they talk about equal rights.

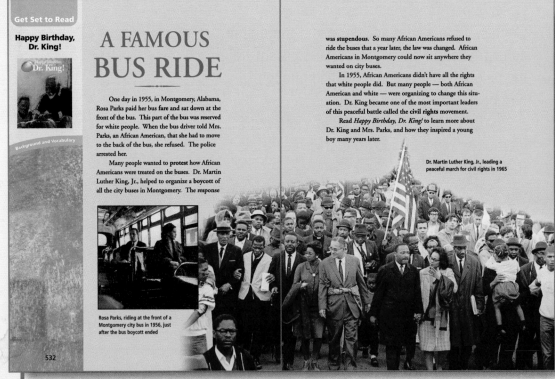

Get Set to Read

Happy Birthday, Dr. King!

A FAMOUS BUS RIDE

One day in 1955, in Montgomery, Alabama, Rosa Parks paid her bus fare and sat down at the front of the bus. This part of the bus was reserved for white people. When the bus driver told Mrs. Parks, an African American, that she had to move to the back of the bus, she refused. The police arrested her.

Many people wanted to protest how African Americans were treated on the buses. Dr. Martin Luther King, Jr., helped to organize a boycott of all the city buses in Montgomery. The response

was stupendous. So many African Americans refused to ride the buses that a year later, the law was changed. African Americans in Montgomery could now sit anywhere they wanted on city buses.

In 1955, African Americans didn't have all the rights that white people did. But many people — both African American and white — were organizing to change this situation. Dr. King became one of the most important leaders of this peaceful battle called the civil rights movement.

Read *Happy Birthday, Dr. King!* to learn more about Dr. King and Mrs. Parks, and how they inspired a young boy many years later.

Dr. Martin Luther King, Jr., leading a peaceful march for civil rights in 1965

Rosa Parks, riding at the front of a Montgomery city bus in 1956, just after the bus boycott ended

532

English Language Learners

Develop a list of heroic qualities that can be added to as students read the theme. Ask students what they know about Dr. King. Discuss the idea of a "peaceful battle."

▶ Developing Key Vocabulary

Use **Transparency 5–1** to introduce the Key Vocabulary from *Happy Birthday, Dr. King!*

■ Model how to figure out that civil rights belongs in the top oval.

■ For the boxes below, ask students to use what they know about the Key Vocabulary words to answer the questions. Have students share their strategies with the class.

Remind students that it's helpful to use the Phonics/Decoding Strategy when they read. For students who need more help with decoding, use the review below.

Practice/Homework **Practice Book** page 289.

Strategy Review
Phonics/Decoding

Modeling Write this sentence from *Happy Birthday, Dr. King!* on the board, and point to the word *arrested.*

> Rosa Parks wouldn't give her seat to a white man, and she got <u>arrested</u>.

Think Aloud

The first thing I notice about this word is the double consonant. If I split the word between the two r's, the first part probably says / ahr / as in the word argue. Then I see the shorter word rest and the -ed ending. When I put it all together I say, / ahr•rest•ehd /. Oh, it's / uh•REST•ehd /. I know what that word means and it makes sense with what I know about Rosa Parks.

Skill Finder
• Decoding Longer Words, pages 555E–555F

Key Concept
the beginning of the civil rights movement

Key Vocabulary

boycott: a refusal to buy from a company

civil rights (movement): referring to the legal privileges every American citizen is guaranteed

fare: the money a person must pay to travel, as on a bus or subway

protest: to express strong feelings against something

stupendous: amazing

See Vocabulary notes on pages 536, 538, 540, and 546 for additional words to preview.

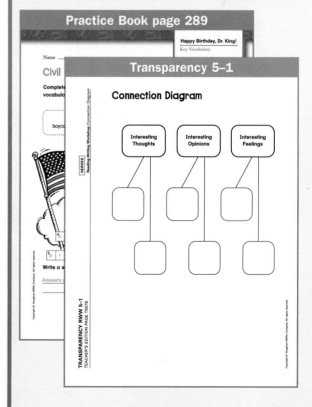

Practice Book page 289

Transparency 5–1

Connection Diagram

Interesting Thoughts | Interesting Opinions | Interesting Feelings

Strategy/Skill Preview

▶ **Strategy Focus:**
Predict/Infer

Strategy Focus

In this story, a boy learns a valuable lesson when his grandfather tells him about an important time in history. As you read, **predict** what will happen next.

Teacher's Note

Strategy/Skill Connection For a better understanding of *Happy Birthday, Dr. King!*, students can use the

• Predict/Infer Strategy

• Cause and Effect Comprehension Skill

Predicting events in the story will help students be able to determine which events are causes and which are effects.

As students fill in their Cause and Effect Charts (**Practice Book** page 290 and **Transparency 5–2**), they can use their answers to decide if their predictions were correct or need to be revised.

Ask students to turn to page 535 as you read the title and author of the story. Ask a student to read the Strategy Focus. Give students a few minutes to review the illustrations and to think about the Strategy Focus question. Then ask students to make predictions about the story and record their responses.

Teacher Modeling Review how to make a good prediction or inference. (Think of a possibility based on text clues and personal information.) Then model the strategy.

Think Aloud

From the title and cover, I predict that this story will concern the famous civil rights leader Dr. Martin Luther King, Jr. Since I know that Dr. King's birthday is a national holiday, I can make an inference that the story will be about celebrating his birthday.

Ask students to work in pairs or individually to make predictions and inferences about the importance of Dr. King to the characters. Have students record their predictions and inferences in their journals. Then remind students to keep their predictions and inferences in mind and to change them or make new ones as they read the story.

✓ Comprehension Skill Focus: *Cause and Effect*

Cause and Effect Explain to students that they will focus on *why* things happen (the *causes*) and the results, or *effects.* To develop the skill, students will complete a cause and effect chart by analyzing story events and their effects. Display **Transparency 5–2,** and model how to use the graphic organizer.

■ Begin by having a student read aloud the first three paragraphs of page 536, ending with *Maybe Mom won't ask me about school.*

■ Ask a student to read aloud the first event in the *Cause* column. Ask another student for the effect of that event that is given in those paragraphs. Model how to fill this in on the chart.

■ Have students to complete the same line on **Practice Book** page 290 with the same answer.

■ Tell students that sometimes they will need to write in the cause and other times the effect. Make sure they understand that, though effects come after causes in the order of time, effects are usually first to be identified in a story.

■ Have students complete their charts as they read. Monitor their progress.

Graphic Organizer: Cause and Effect

Cause	Effect
page 536 (Jamal gets a note from the pricipal.)	(Jamal is afraid he is in trouble and tries to sneak quietly into the house.)
page 539 (Jamal tells Grandpa Joe about the fight.)	(Grandpa Joe gets angry at Jamal.)

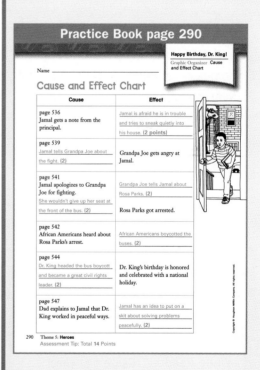

Options for Reading

▶ **Reading in Segments** Students can read *Happy Birthday, Dr. King!* in two segments (pages 534–541 and 542–549) or in its entirety.

▶ **Deciding About Support** Important historical events and appealing, realistic, fictional characters make this story interesting to read.

- Because of the familiar genre (realistic fiction) and conventional plot structure, most students should be able to follow On Level reading instruction.

- Students who might have difficulty with understanding events will benefit from Extra Support.

- Significantly below-level readers can listen to the Audiotape and read the Selection Summary for *Happy Birthday, Dr. King!* and then read "Thanks to Sandra Cisneros" in the **Reader's Library**.

▶ **Meeting Individual Needs** Use the notes at the bottom of the pages.

Meet the Author
Kathryn Jones

Her birthday: November 4
Where she lives: Dorchester, Massachusetts
Another place she's lived: Guyana (a country in South America)
Other jobs she's done: Worked at the Children's Museum in Boston, taught elementary school
Advice for students who want to become authors: Pay attention in English class, read a lot, and use your imagination when you write.
Other books: *Carnival*

Meet the Illustrator
Floyd Cooper

His first job as an artist: Working at a greeting card company
Why he became a children's book illustrator: He wanted to be creative and make the art he loved. He also wanted to create art for children that made them feel good.
Other work he does: He also writes some of the children's books he illustrates, such as *Mandela*.
Other books: *Grandpa's Face* by Eloise Greenfield, *Meet Danitra Brown* by Nikki Grimes, *I Have Heard of a Land* by Joyce Carol Thomas

Internet
If you want to find out more about Kathryn Jones and Floyd Cooper, visit Education Place.
www.eduplace.com/kids

534

Classroom Management

On Level
Reading Card 2

While Reading: Cause and Effect Chart (**Practice Book** page 290); Literature Discussion (p. 540, Reading Card 2); generate questions

After Reading: Literature Discussion (page 548); Wrapping Up Segment 1 (page 541) and Segment 2 (page 549)

Challenge
Reading Cards 1–3

While Reading: Cause and Effect Chart (**Practice Book** page 290); Irony (p. 537, Reading Card 1); Flashback (p. 545, Reading Card 3)

After Reading: Literature Discussion (Page 548); Wrapping Up Segment 1 (page 541) and Segment 2 (page 549)

English Language Learners

Intermediate and Advanced Fluency Have students read with an English-speaking partner. Then review each segment and make predictions. Have students check whether predictions were correct. For English language learners at other proficiency levels, see **Language Development Resources**.

Selection 1

Beginning
of Segment 1:
pages 534–541

Happy Birthday,
Dr. King!

by Kathryn Jones   Illustrated by Floyd Cooper

Strategy Focus

In this story, a boy learns a valuable lesson when his grandfather tells him about an important time in history. As you read, **predict** what will happen next.

535

Reading Segment 1

pages 534–541

Purpose Setting Have students read the title of the selection and skim the illustrations. Then have students predict what they think the story will be about. Remind students that they should confirm or change their predictions as they read.

 Journal Writing Students can record their original predictions in their journal and add new ones.

Reinforcing Comprehension and Strategies

- Remind students to use Predict/Infer and other strategies as they read and add to their Cause and Effect Chart (**Practice Book** page 290).

- Use the Strategy Focus notes on pages 538 and 548 to reinforce the Predict/Infer strategy.

- Use Supporting Comprehension questions beginning on page 536 to help students develop higher-level understanding of the text.

Extra Support: Previewing the Text

Before each segment, preview the text, using the notes below and on page 542. **While** reading, model strategies (pp. 538 and 548). **After** reading, review each segment (pp. 540 and 548) before students join the Wrapping Up discussion.

pages 536–537 When and where do you think the story takes place? Why?

pages 538–539 Jamal is carrying a note from the principal. Look at the illustration. How can you tell that he's afraid the note will make his family angry?

pages 540–541 Grandpa Joe tells Jamal how it was illegal for him to sit in the front of the bus when he was young. Why might Grandpa share this?

Reading

▶ Supporting Comprehension

1 Why does Jamal assume he's in trouble when he gets a pink slip even though he hasn't read it? (because in his school the pink slip must be the way a student's misbehavior is communicated from the principal to the student's parents)

2 How is Jamal's arrival home from school that day different from other days? (Usually he likes having his mom home from work but today he wishes she wasn't home yet.)

Vocabulary *(page 536)*

assignment: homework

assembly: big meeting

slip: small piece of paper

slush: watery snow

"Class, don't forget your assignment for tonight. Think about the Martin Luther King, Jr., assembly. His birthday is almost here," Mrs. Gordon said to her fourth grade class.

"Jamal, Arthur, you two wait. You have another assignment. Please take these notes from the principal home for your parents."

1 "A pink slip! I'm really in trouble now!" Jamal thought to himself walking home through the January slush. "Maybe Mom won't ask me about school."

Jamal decided to go in the front door and quietly upstairs to his room. Usually, he liked that his mother was home from her job at the hospital before he got home from school. Today was

2 different.

"Jamal, is that you? Is Alisha with you?" Mrs. Wilson called from the kitchen.

"It's just me, Mom," Jamal answered.

536

Extra Support

Strategy Modeling

Phonics/Decoding Use this example to model the strategy.

When I look at the word h-o-s-p-i-t-a-l, *I see a* VCCV *pattern* o-s-p-i, *so I'll split the word into smaller parts between the* s *and the* p. *The first part probably has a short vowel sound,* / hahs /. *Next I see the shorter word* pit. *The end probably sounds like* / al /. *I'll say* / hahs•pit•al /. / HAHS•pih•tuhl /. *That word makes sense.*

English Language Learners

Understanding Setting Help students correlate all of the clues in the story into understanding the place and time of the setting. Have students think about the date of Martin Luther King, Jr.'s birthday and the expression *January slush* on page 536. Then have them look at the illustration on page 537. Also, ask students to decide if Jamal lives in a city; review the names of the rooms in his house. Have volunteers name the rooms in their homes.

---

536 THEME 5: **Heroes**

537

Comprehension Skill Lesson
Cause and Effect

OBJECTIVES

Students identify the relationship between causes and effects.

Remind students that an effect is a description of an event and a cause is an explanation for why the event happened. Readers can ask questions to identify causes and effects:

- What happened? (to determine an effect or result)

- Why did it happen? (to determine a cause)

Sometimes, clue words help signal cause-effect relationships. Put the following sentences describing events from page 536 on the board. Tell students that *as a result* are clue words.

> *Dr. Martin Luther King Jr.'s birthday is coming soon.*
> *As a result, the class must think about the assembly for homework.*

- Point out the *cause:* Dr. King's birthday is coming soon.

- Point out the *effect:* the class must think about the assembly for homework.

Have students find another cause and effect on page 536. (Cause: Jamal gets a note from the principal; effect: He is afraid he is in trouble and so he sneaks into the house.)

Skill Finder

• **Instruction,** pp. 555A–555B
• **Reteaching,** p. R8
• **Review,** Themes 1, 2, 3, and 6

MEETING INDIVIDUAL NEEDS

Challenge

Reading Card 1

Irony *Irony* occurs when something happens that is different from what was expected. It can be a contrast between what is stated and what is suggested or a contrast between what a character believes and what the reader knows. Irony can also occur when an event reverses what the readers or characters expected. Have students discuss the irony in Jamal's sneaking in but his mother's hearing him anyway. Later have students consider why it is ironic that Jamal gets in trouble for wanting to sit in the back of the bus.

538

▶ Strategy Focus: Predict/Infer

Teacher/Student Modeling Discuss story clues on page 539 to predict a key event in the story.

Grandpa Joe is very angry at Jamal—the capital letters tell me that he is shouting. I predict that Grandpa will use this incident to teach Jamal a lesson. Since the story is called Happy Birthday, Dr. King! *I can infer that the lesson will have something to do with Dr. King.*

Ask students to read the last two paragraphs on page 539 and make a prediction or inference about the story. Guide students to include the photo of Dr. King at the bottom of the page in their inference.

▶ Supporting Comprehension

3 How does the author show that Jamal is afraid to tell his mother about the pink slip from the principal? (He tries to make light of the situation by saying *"It's no big deal."*)

4 What detail does the author use to show that Jamal is truthful and honest? (He tells his mother the complete story about the fight.)

Vocabulary *(page 539)*
<u>crumpled</u>: wrinkled

⊖ Cross-Curricular Connection

Social Studies Dr. Martin Luther King, Jr. (1929–1968), one of the leaders in the American civil rights movement, advocated nonviolent resistance to injustice. King was the pastor of a Baptist Church in Montgomery, Alabama, when he organized the 381-day bus boycott. Building on his success, King adopted Gandhi's principles of nonviolent protest to lead a massive civil rights campaign, including desegregation and black voter registration drives. In 1964, King was awarded the Nobel Peace Prize for his work in the civil rights movement.

"How did your day go?" she asked.

"Well, we're planning Dr. King's birthday cele-bration and I have some math and . . ." Jamal pulled the crumpled pink slip out of his pocket.

"A pink slip? Did you get into trouble?" she asked looking him straight in the eye. Grandpa Joe came into the kitchen.

"What's this I hear about trouble — and Dr. King?" he asked. "What's the pink paper?"

"It's just a note from the principal. It's no big deal," Jamal said. "Yesterday I got into a fight with another kid on my bus. We both wanted to sit in the back seat."

Grandpa Joe's smile disappeared.

"FIGHTING to sit at the BACK of the bus! I can't believe what I'm hearing!" Grandpa Joe said in that voice — that voice that tells the family to sit up and listen.

"Why would you want to fight over some-thing like that?" he said, walking toward the basement door. "I just can't believe it."

"Why is Grandpa Joe so angry?" Jamal asked his mother. "It's no big deal."

"It is a very big deal — especially to your grandfather. Why don't you go and talk to him about it?"

3

4

539

Extra Support

Strategy Modeling

Predict/Infer Use this example to model the strategy.

I can use clues from what I read now to help figure out what might happen later in the story. On page 539, I learn that Jamal doesn't understand why Grandpa Joe is so upset about the school fight. Jamal's mother knows why and sends Jamal to talk to his grandfather. I predict that Grandpa Joe's anger must have something to do with his own experiences on a bus.

Comprehension Skill Lesson
Sequence of Events

OBJECTIVES

Students identify

- the sequence (or order) of story events
- words that signal the sequence of events

Review sequence of events by writing these events from page 539 on the board:

> *First Jamal took out the crumbled pink slip, and then Mama asked if he had gotten into trouble.*

■ Underline the words *first* and *then* in the sen-tences. Point out how they signal when each of the two events happened.

■ Ask students to name other story events from pages 536–539. List them in random order on the board. Have students rearrange the events to show the correct sequence of events. Note any words that students add to signal sequence, such as *first, then, next, before, after, last,* and *finally.*

Have students create a time line to track the events in the story. Encourage students to use clue words to further indicate the sequence of events.

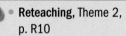

- **Instruction,** Theme 2, pp. 181A–181B
- **Reteaching,** Theme 2, p. R10
- **Review,** Theme 1, p. 67

Reading

▶ Supporting Comprehension

5 How does the author show that Jamal is a polite, considerate child? (He apologizes for fighting and vows not to fight again.)

6 Why do you think the author includes Grandpa Joe's memories of life in Montgomery, Alabama, in the 1950s? (to help readers understand, through a first person account, what life was like for African Americans in the 1950s)

7 Why does the author describe Rosa Parks' actions? (to make sure that readers understand Rosa Parks' bravery and contribution to the civil rights movement)

> ### Vocabulary *(page 541)*
> **celebration:** a party in honor of someone or something
>
> **fare:** the money a person must pay to travel, as on a bus or subway

540

Extra Support

Segment 1: Review

Before students join the whole class for Wrapping Up on page 541, have them

- check predictions
- take turns modeling Predict/Infer and other strategies they used
- check and revise their Cause and Effect Chart on **Practice Book** page 290, and use it to summarize

On Level   Challenge

Reading Card 2

Literature Discussion

In mixed-ability groups of five or six, students can discuss their own questions and the discussion prompts on Reading Card 2.

- How do you know that Grandpa Joe is a reasonable man even though he initially gets very angry at Jamal?
- Do Jamal and his family seem like real people to you? Why or why not?

"Grandpa Joe, I'm sorry that I got into trouble for fighting. I won't do it again."

"Jamal, you are ten years old and old enough to understand. It's almost Martin Luther King, Jr.'s birthday. What are you doing for the celebration this year?"

"What does Dr. King's assembly have to do with a little fight?"

Grandpa Joe took a deep breath and began . . .

"A long time ago I was raising my family in Montgomery, Alabama. This is what used to happen when African Americans wanted to ride the city buses.

"First, we'd get on at the front of the bus, pay our fare, and get off. Then we'd get back on again at the rear of the bus. We didn't like it, but that's how things were. It was the law. Then one day, in 1955, a lady named Rosa Parks . . ."

"Rosa Parks," Jamal interrupted, "we read about her. She sat in the front of the bus and wouldn't give her seat to a white man, and she got arrested."

5

6

7

End of Segment 1:
pages 534–541

English Language Learners

Understanding Cause-Effect Discuss cause-effect relationships. Ask a volunteer to provide an example from another selection. Explain that the pink slip Jamal received is an effect. Tell students to consider Jamal's remark and feelings as he walked home from school and as he describes the cause of the pink slip to his family. Discuss disciplinary policies in your school.

Wrapping Up Segment 1
pages 534–541

First, provide Extra Support for students who need it (p. 540). Then bring all students together.

■ **Review Predictions/Purpose** Discuss which predictions were accurate and which needed to be revised. Record any changes and new predictions.

■ **Model Strategies** Refer students to the **Strategies Poster** and have them take turns modeling Predict/Infer and other strategies they used as they read. Provide models if needed (page 539).

■ **Share Group Discussions** Have students share their questions and literature discussions.

■ **Summarize** Help students use the transparency and their Cause and Effect Chart to summarize what has happened to Jamal so far.

Comprehension/Critical Thinking

1 Using Grandpa Joe's experiences, describe his feelings about sitting in the back of the bus. (When he was raising his family in Montgomery, Alabama, they had no choice about where to sit on a bus. He was unhappy and frustrated about it, but he didn't want to break the law.) **Drawing Conclusions**

2 Do you think Jamal will use Grandpa Joe's experiences in the Martin Luther King, Jr., assembly? Explain. (Yes, because he now has a more personal connection to Dr. King and should be able to create a fitting tribute.) **Predicting Outcomes**

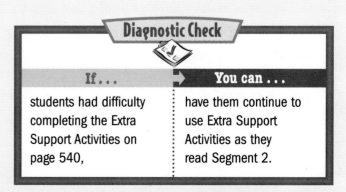

Diagnostic Check

If . . .	You can . . .
students had difficulty completing the Extra Support Activities on page 540,	have them continue to use Extra Support Activities as they read Segment 2.

Reading

Reading Segment 2

pages 542–549

Purpose Setting Have students summarize the story so far and predict what Jamal will do to honor Dr. King's birthday at the school assembly. Then have students read pages 542–549 to check their predictions.

Journal Writing Students can record any revisions they made to their original predictions and explain what made them change their mind.

Vocabulary *(page 542)*

protest: to express strong feelings against something

boycott: a refusal to buy or deal with a company

"But, Jamal, there is more to the story. When African Americans heard about her arrest, many of us stopped riding the buses. We wanted to protest her arrest and get the same rights that white people had. That was the Montgomery Bus Boycott. And the boycott worked. We finally won — without fighting.

"Now, you go think about that bus boycott. Maybe you can figure out why I'm so unhappy about your pink slip."

"Jamal. Your sister's home. Come and set the table," Mrs. Wilson called. Jamal hurried up the stairs. He had some hard thinking to do.

"Heard you got into trouble," Alisha said to her brother.

"Oh, be quiet."

"Okay you two," said Jamal's dad coming in. "Jamal knows he did something wrong. How is your homework going?"

542

Extra Support: Previewing the Text

Before reading Segment 2, preview the text, using the notes below. **While** reading, model strategies (p. 548). **After** reading, review the segment (p. 548) before students join the Wrapping Up discussion.

pages 542–543 In 1955, African Americans refused to ride the buses in Montgomery, Alabama, to protest unfair treatment.

pages 544–545 Over dinner, the family talks about Dr. King. Why is everyone part of the discussion?

pages 546–547 Jamal's dad once heard Dr. King speak in person. How do you think this memory will help Jamal think of a way to honor Dr. King at the assembly?

pages 548–549 What do you think Jamal will do at the school assembly?

543

Revisiting the Text

Review/Maintain

Comprehension Skill Lesson
Story Structure

OBJECTIVES

Students

- identify characters, setting, and plot

- describe how a change in story structure can alter a story

Review the following definitions:

characters: main people or animals in a story around whom the story events revolve

setting: the time and place of the story

plot: the sequence of story events

Divide the class into three groups and have each group identify either the characters, setting, or plot of *Happy Birthday, Dr. King!* Reconvene the class to discuss their findings. (main characters: Jamal, Grandpa Joe; setting: a present-day city; plot: Jamal needs to find a way to celebrate Dr. King's birthday at the school assembly; also, Jamal has a fight with another student over the right to sit at the back of the bus) Ask students how the story might change if Jamal had not gotten into a fight on the bus. (Grandpa Joe would not have told his story about Dr. King and the bus boycott. As a result, Jamal wouldn't have created the skit.) Ask the groups what might change in the story if no one in Jamal's family ever saw Dr. King speak.

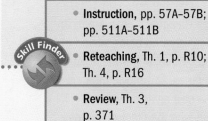

Skill Finder

- **Instruction,** pp. 57A–57B; pp. 511A–511B

- **Reteaching,** Th. 1, p. R10; Th. 4, p. R16

- **Review,** Th. 3, p. 371

English Language Learners

Point out the two instances in which the tone of a character's voice is described (*that voice that tells the family to sit up and listen* on page 539 and *I couldn't believe the power of his speech* on page 544). Ask students to describe each tone of voice, and have volunteers demonstrate and explain the message the tone carries.

Reading

▶ Supporting Comprehension

8 Why do you think the author has Alisha mention Dr. King's "I Have a Dream Speech"? (because it is famous and important)

9 What does the author mean in the phrase *the power of his speech*? (Dr. King's words had the ability to move his listeners to action or belief.)

Vocabulary *(page 544)*

civil rights: referring to the legal privileges every American citizen is guaranteed

---

Cross-Curricular Connection

Social Studies After the success of the Montgomery Bus Boycott, nonviolent civil rights protests spread across the South. In 1960 in Greensboro, North Carolina, African American college students insisted on being served at a local lunch counter. Soon, department stores, supermarkets, libraries, and movie theaters were desegregated. The civil rights movement reached its climax in 1963 with the great march on Washington, DC. A year later, President Johnson passed the Civil Rights Bill, outlawing discrimination in public places.

"Well . . . we have to think of something to do for the Martin Luther King, Jr., assembly."

8 "Everyone in my class is learning parts of his 'I Have a Dream' speech," Alisha chimed in.

"I'll think of something. Grandpa Joe and I were talking about the bus boycotts."

"That should give you some ideas," his dad said. "Did you know that Grandpa Joe took me to hear Dr. King speak when I was your age?"

"You heard Martin Luther King, Jr., yourself?" Jamal asked.

"I sure did. It was during the boycott, too. Grandpa Joe took me to a meeting at a church one night. This man went up to the front and suddenly everyone stood and clapped. Then, he started talking. I couldn't believe the power of

9 his speech.

"That man was Dr. King. He told us why to boycott the buses, and how we needed to help each other. Dr. King became a great leader of the civil rights movement."

"I know about that part," Jamal said. "That's why we celebrate his birthday. But *how* to celebrate is the problem."

544

English Language Learners

Discuss the reference to the "I Have a Dream" speech, and make sure students understand Dr. King's dream. If possible, get a recording of Dr. King's speeches from a library so students can listen to his words and his voice. Discuss what your school does to celebrate Dr. King's birthday.

545

Genre Lesson
Realistic Fiction

OBJECTIVES

Students identify elements of realistic fiction.

Explain the characteristics of realistic fiction:

- The story problem is true-to-life. The story problem could have really happened, even though the author created it.

- The characters are also realistic. They look, think, feel, and act like people we may know.

- The setting seems familiar. Readers can identify with the time and place.

Point out that Jamal's fight on the bus and his inability to understand why it upsets his grandfather make him seem like a real person. Then ask students to identify other details that make *Happy Birthday, Dr. King!* realistic fiction. (Examples: Jamal sneaking inside, Jamal and his sister squabbling, his school honoring a real person)

Have small groups of students create a chart showing examples of ways that Jamal acts like a real person. Allow sufficient time for students to work and then share their conclusions.

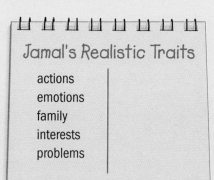

Jamal's Realistic Traits

actions
emotions
family
interests
problems

Challenge

Reading Card 3

Flashback

Writers sometimes use flashbacks to fill in missing information, explain the characters' actions, and advance the plot. A *flashback* is a scene that breaks into the story to show an earlier part of the action. Rewrite Jamal's dad's memories of hearing Dr. King speak as a flashback. The flashback might begin like this:

I'm tired of walking everywhere. Why can't we ride the bus again? Dad says I'll understand when I hear Dr. King speak.

▶ Supporting Comprehension

10 Why does the author include the word *peaceful* so often in the first few paragraphs? (to show that Jamal's dad admires Dr. King's belief in nonviolent protests and that he also believes in finding peaceful solutions to problems)

11 Why does Jamal's dad stop Jamal when he starts to list his ideas for the assembly? (to make Jamal slow down and think about his ideas; to teach Jamal that thought should precede actions and not vice versa)

Vocabulary (page 547)
skit: a brief play

stupendous: amazing

546

"Then remember, Dr. King always spoke out about peaceful ways to make things happen. Does that help?"

"Peaceful . . ." Jamal said slowly, thinking. "You mean like not fighting? And those peaceful ideas worked back then?"

"Jamal, peaceful ideas work today, too," his dad answered.

"Peaceful," Jamal said again and his face brightened. "That's it! Our class could do something to show that fighting is not the way to get things done. Maybe we could do a skit. Everyone could have a part and we could have costumes and I could be the star and . . ." **10**

"Whoa," his dad said. "First you'd better eat your dinner. Then you can write down your ideas for Mrs. Gordon." **11**

"Grandpa Joe," Jamal asked as his grandfather joined them. "When you were a kid, did you ever do something *really* stupid that turned out to be *stupendous* instead?"

Grandpa Joe's smile returned and he nodded his head.

547

Writer's Craft Lesson
Point of View

OBJECTIVES

Students

- identify point of view
- explore how the story changes with a shift in point of view

Explain that point of view is the position from which a story is told. Describe each point of view:

- **first-person point of view:** The narrator is a character in the story who explains the events through his or her own eyes, using the pronouns *I* and *me.*

- **third-person point of view:** The narrator looks through the eyes of some or all of the characters using the pronouns *he, she,* and *they.*

Have students identify the point of view on page 547. (third-person) Discuss the advantages and disadvantages of the third-person point of view. (Advantage: Readers see what all the characters see. Disadvantage: We don't closely identify with one of the characters.) Read the fourth paragraph on page 547 aloud, and recast it from Jamal's point of view. Have small groups of students rewrite another passage from Jamal's point of view.

Reading Fluency

- **Rereading for Fluency:** Have students choose a favorite part of the story to reread to a partner, or suggest they read the first half of page 547. Encourage students to read with feeling and expression.

- **Assessing Fluency:** See the guidelines in the Theme Assessment Wrap-Up, page 608–609A.

Reading

"All right children, settle down now. We have a lot of work to do today," Mrs. Gordon said. "Let's start with the Martin Luther King, Jr., birthday assembly. Who has an idea for what our class can do? Oh — Jamal?"

12

Jamal stood proudly. "I have an idea for a skit. It's about these two dopey boys who don't understand about Martin Luther King, Jr. They get into a fight over a seat in the back of the bus . . ."

13

▶ Strategy Focus: Predict/Infer

Student Modeling Have students model their predictions about what Jamal will do for the Dr. King birthday celebration. If necessary, use the following prompt:

What does the illustration suggest that Jamal will do to honor Dr. King at the school assembly?

Remind students that setting predictions and making inferences helps them focus on the main ideas and details in the story.

▶ Supporting Comprehension

12 How does the author let you know that the Dr. King celebration is important? (The teacher deals with it first in class that day.)

13 How has the author solved the story problem that Jamal has? (Thanks to Grandpa Joe's story about Dr. King, Jamal learns a lesson and comes up with a way to honor Dr. King.)

 Extra Support

Segment 2 Review

Before students join in Wrapping Up on page 549, have them

- review and discuss the accuracy of their predictions
- take turns modeling the reading strategies they used
- help you complete **Transparency 5–2** and their Cause and Effect Charts (**Practice Book** page 290)
- summarize the whole story

 On Level Challenge

Literature Discussion

Have small groups of students discuss the story, using their own questions or the questions in Think About the Selection on page 550.

Wrapping Up Segment 2
pages 542–549

Provide extra support for students who need it (p. 548). Then bring all students together.

- **Review Predictions/Purpose** Have students compare their predictions with the selection itself and discuss reasons why students' predictions were or were not accurate.

- **Model Strategies** Have students take turns modeling Predict/Infer and discuss where they used the strategy as they read. Provide models if needed (pages 538 and 548).

- **Share Group Discussions** Have students discuss what we learn from reading realistic fiction.

- **Review** Have students use their Cause and Effect Charts to summarize the main events of the story.

Comprehension/Critical Thinking

1 How does Jamal's family help him create a meaningful skit for the Martin Luther King, Jr., birthday assembly? (By sharing their memories of Dr. King, his family leads Jamal to think of a skit.) **Cause and Effect**

2 In your opinion, what purpose do heroes serve? (They lead us, inspire us, and improve our lives.) **Making Generalizations**

End of Segment 2: *pages 542–549*

English Language Learners

Point out that the events in the passage on page 548 and the illustration on page 549 are different. Encourage students to use the illustration to decide what the author wants the readers to believe happens. Guide students to explain how both what Jamal tells his teacher about his skit ideas, and the illustration, help readers understand the ending.

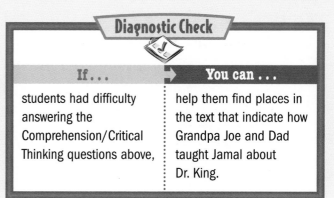

Diagnostic Check

If . . .	You can . . .
students had difficulty answering the Comprehension/Critical Thinking questions above,	help them find places in the text that indicate how Grandpa Joe and Dad taught Jamal about Dr. King.

Responding

 Think About the Selection

Discuss or Write Have students discuss or write their answers. Sample answers are provided; accept reasonable responses that are supported with evidence from the story.

1. **Drawing Conclusions** Jamal's grandfather and all African Americans had to fight for the right to sit in the front of the bus and he's unhappy that his grandson fought for the opposite.

2. **Making Inferences** Jamal learns about the civil rights movement. He now appreciates the legal, social, and economic rights Dr. King and his supporters won for all Americans.

3. **Cause and Effect** Jamal explains the irony in his fight to sit in the back of the bus in light of Dr. King's achievements.

4. **Drawing Conclusions** Jamal means that from the fight on the bus and his grandfather's story he was able to come up with a great idea for Dr. King's assembly.

5. **Compare and Contrast** Answers will vary.

6. **Connecting/Comparing** Making Judgments Answers will vary. Students are likely to cite Dr. King for his brave, nonviolent protest and accomplishments.

Responding

Think About the Selection

1. Why is Jamal's grandfather so unhappy that Jamal fought to sit at the back of the bus?

2. What does Jamal learn from talking with his grandfather? How is he different after the talk?

3. How does Jamal use what he learns from his grandfather in his skit?

4. Jamal says that he did something "really stupid that turned out to be stupendous instead." What do you think he means?

5. What would you like to do for a school celebration of Dr. King's birthday?

6. **Connecting/Comparing** Who do you think are the heroes in this story? What makes them heroic?

 Creating

Write a Scene

Jamal has an idea for a skit to honor Dr. King. Write the opening scene for the skit. Use the style for writing a play described in Focus on Plays (pages 278–291). Give your scene to other students so they can act it out.

Tips
- Review the story to decide what to include.
- Write lines that sound like real people talking.
- Before you revise, test your ideas by acting out your scene with a partner.

550

 English Language Learners

Beginning/Preproduction Ask students to describe the illustrations on pages 543 and 549. Then help them talk about the connection between the two.

Early Production and Speech Emergence Use questions to guide a discussion about what Jamal learns.

Intermediate and Advanced Fluency Ask students to describe the sequence of events from Jamal receiving the pink slip to the skit.

Vocabulary

Make Posters of Peaceful Ideas

Write MARTIN, LUTHER, and KING, JR., in capital letters down the left side of a big sheet of paper. With a group, choose words or phrases that begin with each letter and that are about solving problems peacefully. Write the words beside each letter. Look at your poster and discuss your ideas for peace.

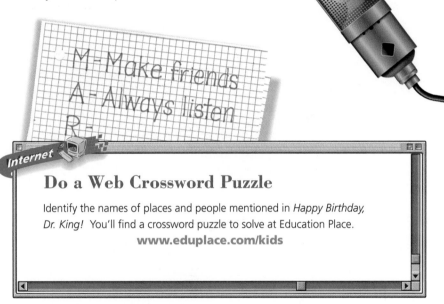

Internet

Do a Web Crossword Puzzle

Identify the names of places and people mentioned in *Happy Birthday, Dr. King!* You'll find a crossword puzzle to solve at Education Place.

www.eduplace.com/kids

551

Listening and Speaking

Listen to a Speech

Listen to a recording of Dr. King's "I Have a Dream" speech. Discuss your reactions to the speech with two or three other students. Talk about the ideas and how Dr. King expressed them. Also discuss how he used his voice to make the speech effective.

English Language Learners

Review the style for writing a play. Then have students brainstorm characters that should appear in the skit and ideas for their dialogue. Have the students work with English-speaking partners or in small mixed groups to write the new opening scenes.

✏ Personal Response

Invite students to share their personal responses to *Happy Birthday, Dr. King!* As an alternative, ask students to write in their journals or to respond in their own way.

▶ Comprehension Check

Assign **Practice Book** page 291 to assess students' understanding of the selection.

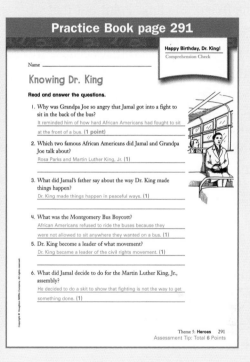

Practice Book page 291

> Happy Birthday, Dr. King!
> Comprehension Check
>
> Name _____
>
> **Knowing Dr. King**
>
> **Read and answer the questions.**
>
> 1. Why was Grandpa Joe so angry that Jamal got into a fight to sit in the back of the bus?
> It reminded him of how hard African Americans had fought to sit at the front of a bus. **(1 point)**
>
> 2. Which two famous African Americans did Jamal and Grandpa Joe talk about?
> Rosa Parks and Martin Luther King, Jr. **(1)**
>
> 3. What did Jamal's father say about the way Dr. King made things happen?
> Dr. King made things happen in peaceful ways. **(1)**
>
> 4. What was the Montgomery Bus Boycott?
> African Americans refused to ride the buses because they were not allowed to sit anywhere they wanted on a bus. **(1)**
>
> 5. Dr. King become a leader of what movement?
> Dr. King became a leader of the civil rights movement. **(1)**
>
> 6. What did Jamal decide to do for the Martin Luther King, Jr., assembly?
> He decided to do a skit to show that fighting is not the way to get something done. **(1)**
>
> Theme 5: **Heroes** 291
> Assessment Tip: Total 6 Points

End-of-Selection Assessment

Selection Test Use the test in the **Teacher's Resource Blackline Masters** to assess selection comprehension and vocabulary.

Student Self-Assessment Have students assess their reading with additional questions such as

• What parts of the selection were easy for me? Why?

• What parts of the selection were difficult for me? What strategies did I use to help me?

• Would I recommend this story to my friends? Why or why not?

Reading

Social Studies Link

pages 552–555

▶ Skill: How to Take Notes

Read aloud the title of the link. Point out that "Dear Mrs. Parks" is a series of letters taken from a book of the same title. Explain that because there are several letters—all containing a great deal of information—students might want to write down key facts, details, and examples as they read.

Before You Read Have students read and discuss the tips in the left column on page 552.

■ Help students scan the letters, pointing out how to find the main idea in the topic sentence of each letter.

■ Guide students to write key words and phrases rather than complete sentences as they take notes.

While You Read Encourage students to look for details in each of Mrs. Parks' letters that answer the questions *Who? What? When? Where? Why?* and *How?* Have students take notes as they read "Dear Mrs. Parks."

Vocabulary *(page 553)*

theme: topic

stand: an opinion about an important issue

oppression: unfair treatment

endure: to put up with

Social Studies Link

Skill: How to Take Notes

① To begin, write the **title** at the top of a piece of paper.

② As you read, look for important **ideas, facts,** and **opinions**.

③ Write a **heading** for each main idea.

④ List important **details** and **key words** below each heading.

Dear Mrs. Parks

Rosa Parks Answers Letters from Young People

by Rosa Parks

> **Dear Mrs. Parks,**
>
> **How old are you? (If you can't tell me, I'll understand.)**

I'm glad to answer that. I am thankful for each day that I'm alive. This year (1996) I turned 83. I was born February 4, 1913.

552

 Classroom Management

All Students

Reading the Letters Most students will be able to read the letters independently. Have all students complete the activities under How to Take Notes, Outline, and Comprehension Check. For students needing extra reading support, pair them with more proficient partners to read the letters.

Dear Mrs. Parks,

The sixth graders are doing a history project. We chose you. The theme is "Taking a stand in history." We have some questions. Can you answer them? How did you feel when you were on the bus?

Jennifer and Jamie
La Puente, California

Your theme is a good one. A person should not take a stand to make history. Taking a stand for what is right is most important.

When I sat down on the bus on the day I was arrested, I decided I must do what was right to do. People have said over the years that the reason I did not give up my seat was because I was tired. I did not think of being physically tired.

My feet were not hurting. I was tired in a different way. I was tired of seeing so many men treated as boys and not called by their proper names or titles. I was tired of seeing children and women mistreated and disrespected because of the color of their skin.

I thought of the pain and the years of oppression and mistreatment that my people had suffered. I felt that way every day. December 1, 1955, was no different. Fear was the last thing I thought of that day. I put my trust in the Lord for guidance and help to endure whatever I had to face. I knew I was sitting in the right seat.

553

▶ Outline

Draw a simple outline on the board. Explain that an outline is a written plan of information found in a piece of writing. Tell students that an outline contains main ideas and supporting details. Discuss how making an outline can help you organize your notes in a logical and easy-to-read way.

Have students help you complete the outline to take notes on "Dear Mrs. Parks."

■ Begin by writing the title of the link at the top of the outline.

■ After Roman numeral I, write the main idea "Letter 1: Mrs. Parks' age."

■ Below the main idea, write capital letters, beginning with A, followed by periods and details that support the main idea.

■ Continue the process with Roman numerals for each of Mrs. Parks' letters and supporting details below each one.

■ Explain that as students read the link, they can complete the outline with their notes. Remind students to follow the directions for taking notes.

Purpose Setting Have students read "Dear Mrs. Parks" to learn more advice from Rosa Parks. Remind them to take notes and look for the main ideas and supporting details of each letter.

INDIVIDUAL NEEDS **Extra Support**

Understanding Text Organization

Help students who need extra support by previewing the link as a class. Start with the title. Point out that titles are designed to get the reader's attention while also suggesting the topic of the whole piece. Guide students to see how the title, "Dear Mrs. Parks," ties into the idea of a series of letters and responses. Have students point out which are the children's letters to Rosa Parks and which are her responses.

Social Studies Link continued
pages 552–555

Vocabulary (pages 554–555)

aerobics: a type of exercise with a lot of movement

wisdom: knowledge that comes from experience

dignity: self-respect

treasure: care a lot about

Dear Mrs. Parks,

In school and when I am around certain people, I want to ask questions, but I am having trouble doing this. What would you do, Mrs. Parks?

Jimmy
Cleveland, Ohio

You can never learn very much if you do not ask questions. Many times questions are more important than answers. A person should never be afraid to admit he or she does not know an answer. Once you do this, then you are on the path of learning.

I am 83 years of age, and I am still learning. I am fascinated by the computer age, and I am still learning how to use some of the new technology. I just started taking water aerobics and swimming lessons last year. I ask a lot of questions during my swimming lessons. Take a deep breath! You can drown yourself with problems if you do not ask questions.

Dear Mrs. Parks,

It seems that my grandparents are always right, and they always want to help someone. Why do older people seem to be smarter than young people?

James
Highland Park, Michigan

554

English Language Learners

Ask a volunteer to recall Rosa Parks from the selection and describe her role in the Civil Rights Movement. Explain that the first question on page 552 hints that asking an adult about her age is inappropriate. Help students identify the main points of each of Rosa's responses. Model how to take notes.

It is true that with age comes wisdom. Yet we never stop learning. From the moment we are born, we begin to learn. The longer you live, the more you understand this basic truth: All people want self-respect and the chance to use their gifts and talents. You should treat people as you would want them to treat you. We should show each other respect and help others to keep their dignity.

Your grandparents understand that adults are needed to reach out and help the younger generation. You and many young people are waiting to benefit from our wisdom and experience. There is still work to do.

Dear Mrs. Parks,

My teacher told us that you just celebrated your 83rd birthday. My great-grandmother is 85 years old. She talks about the old days all the time. Sometimes I wonder what the old days have to do with me.

Adrienne
Vienna, Virginia

When your great-grandmother talks to you about those days, you must listen, listen, listen. When she talks to you that way, she is trying to keep history alive. She seeks to inspire you by sharing stories of the past, of good times and bad times. There is no better way for us to learn from the mistakes of the past than through stories handed down from people who have lived through those times.

Listen to your great-grandmother and her stories from the past. She is preparing you to take your place in the world of tomorrow. Treasure her stories, and remember them so that you can share them with future generations.

555

▶ **Comprehension Check**

Outline   Finish the outline by having volunteers fill in the remaining details.

Comprehension/Critical Thinking   Ask students to use their notes, outlines, and the letters to answer these questions.

1 Why would people write to Mrs. Parks? (She is a hero to many Americans. They respect her bravery and wisdom.) **Making Inferences**

2 Why did Mrs. Parks sit down on the bus the day she was arrested? (She was taking a stand against injustice.) **Drawing Conclusions**

3 Why do you think photographs of Mrs. Parks were included in the link? (They help readers visualize Mrs. Parks and make her words come alive.) **Text Organization**

4 **Connecting/Comparing** How is Mrs. Parks like Dr. Martin Luther King, Jr.? How is she different? (Both Mrs. Parks and Dr. King were important figures in the civil rights movement. Mrs. Parks took a courageous stand and served as an inspiration, while Dr. King became a leader for the civil rights movement.) **Compare and Contrast**

Challenge

Social Studies

Have volunteers use on-line resources, reference books, and magazines to find out more about the major figures and events in the civil rights movement of the 1950s and 1960s. These might include Rosa Parks, Martin Luther King, Jr., the "Freedom Riders," and the Supreme Court decision *Brown v. the Board of Education of Topeka, Kansas.*

Comprehension Skills

✔ Cause and Effect

OBJECTIVES

Students

- identify causes and effects
- understand how one cause can lead to multiple effects
- learn which clue words can signal causes and effects

Practice Book page 290

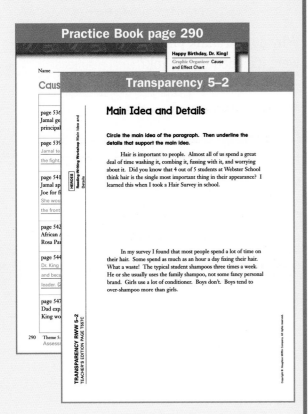

▶ Teach

Use **Transparency 5–2** to review different cause and effect relationships in *Happy Birthday, Dr. King!* and to discuss

■ the cause of the Montgomery Bus Boycott

■ the effects of the boycott

■ how the entire story began with the pink slip from the principal

Students can refer to the selection and to **Practice Book** page 290.

Graphic Organizer: Cause and Effect Guide

Cause	Effect
Page 542 (African Americans heard about Rosa Parks arrest.)	(African Americans boycotted the buses.)
Page 544 (Dr. King headed the bus boycott and became a great civil rights leader.)	(Dr. King's birthday is honored and celebrated with a national holiday.)
Page 547 (Dad explains to Jamal that Dr. King worked in peaceful ways.)	(Jamal has an idea to put on a skit about solving problems peacefully.)

Modeling Tell students that it is possible for a cause to have multiple effects, even if the effects aren't clearly numbered or ordered. Sometimes authors will use clue words such as *because, since, when,* and *as a result* that allow readers to easily identify causes and effects. Yet, if these words aren't used, readers can still use them to help make sense of a story. Have students refer to their charts on **Practice Book** page 290 as you use the Think Aloud below to model what you mean.

Think Aloud

What I find incredible is that the simple action of one person started the whole chain of events that became the civil rights movement. Since Rosa Parks refused to sit at the back of the bus, she was arrested. This resulted in a boycott of the buses. This led to a rise in popularity for Dr. King, who organized the boycott. And it's because of his organization of peaceful protests that every American today is guaranteed equal rights. All of this happened because one woman didn't want to give up her seat. Amazing!

Explain how clue words such as *because, when,* and *since* can signal a cause and words such as *if* and *as a result* can signal an effect.

▶ Practice

Have students work in pairs or in small groups to identify causes and effects. Ask students to refer to the letters people wrote Mrs. Parks that appear on pages 552–555. Write the following questions on the board and have students answer them based on the letters.

- **page 552: Why is Mrs. Parks happy to tell her age?** (She is thankful for every day she is alive.)

- **page 553: What is the reason Jennifer and Jamie write to Mrs. Parks?** (They are doing a history project on her.)

- **page 553: What happened to make Mrs. Parks not want to give up her seat?** (She had grown tired of the mistreatment.)

Make sure students label each of their answers with either *Cause* or *Effect.* Remind students that a cause is why something happened and an effect is what happened.

▶ Apply

Use **Practice Book** pages 292–293 to diagnose whether students need Reteaching. Students who do not need Reteaching may work on Challenge/Extension Activities, page R9. Students who need Extra Support may apply the skill to an easier text using the **Reader's Library** selection "Thanks to Sandra Cisneros" and its Responding activity.

Skill Finder

• Revisiting, p. 537	• Review, Themes 1, 2, 3, and 6	• Reteaching, p. R8

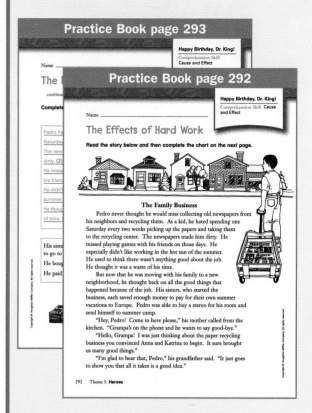

Practice Book page 293

Practice Book page 292

Name _____

The Effects of Hard Work

Read the story below and then complete the chart on the next page.

The Family Business

Pedro never thought he would miss collecting old newspapers from his neighbors and recycling them. As a kid, he hated spending one Saturday every two weeks picking up the papers and taking them to the recycling center. The newspapers made him dirty. He missed playing games with his friends on those days. He especially didn't like working in the hot sun of the summer. He used to think there wasn't anything good about the job. He thought it was a waste of his time.

But now that he was moving with his family to a new neighborhood, he thought back on all the good things that happened because of the job. His sisters, who started the business, each saved enough money to pay for their own summer vacations to Europe. Pedro was able to buy a stereo for his room and send himself to summer camp.

"Hey, Pedro! Come in here please," his mother called from the kitchen. "Grampa's on the phone and he wants to say good-bye."

"Hello, Grampa! I was just thinking about the paper recycling business you convinced Anna and Katrina to begin. It sure brought us many good things."

"I'm glad to hear that, Pedro," his grandfather said. "It just goes to show you that all it takes is a good idea."

292 Theme 5: Heroes

Extra Support

- Reteaching, page R8

- **Reader's Library:** *Heroes* Selection 1, "Thanks to Sandra Cisneros"

Diagnostic Check

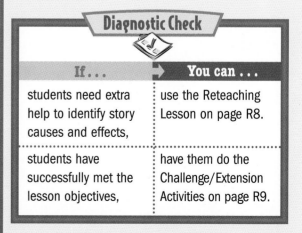

If...	▶ You can ...
students need extra help to identify story causes and effects,	use the Reteaching Lesson on page R8.
students have successfully met the lesson objectives,	have them do the Challenge/Extension Activities on page R9.

Information & Study Skills
Newspapers/Magazines

▶ Teach

Newspapers Explain to students that newspapers and magazines are sources of many different kinds of information. Most newspapers cover a large variety of topics. Some may be more specific, such as those that mainly feature information on business, sports, or the entertainment industry.

Magazines Point out that there are many different kinds magazines, some of which are general in nature and cover many areas. Others concentrate on a specific kind of information, such as news, sports, television, nature, computers, business, cooking, or fashion. Libraries usually carry a selection of different kinds of magazines.

Old issues Most libraries keep back copies of recent newspapers and magazines. They also keep older issues on microfilm or microfiche. Library users can read these on special viewing machines.

Web sites Many newspapers and magazines now have their own Web sites. Internet users can read certain articles on-line. These may be the same as in the printed newspaper or magazine or they may include other material as well. There are even webzines, magazines that appear only on-line.

Modeling Demonstrate for students how to use back issues of newspapers as a source of information.

> **Think Aloud**
>
> *I'm doing a social studies project and have to find out what kinds of jobs are available in this area. I know that most jobs are advertised in the Classified section of the newspaper. So I go to the library and find back copies for the last two weeks. I look under "Help Wanted" and make a list of the jobs and count how many openings there are for each kind.*

Practice

Suggest that students probably already know something about where to find different kinds of information in newspapers. Ask these questions:

- **In what section can you find the baseball scores?** (sports)

- **What is the funniest part of the newspaper?** (the comics page)

- **What parts of the newspaper have the biggest print?** (the front page, headlines, advertisements)

- **What would you learn from the Local News section?** (what's happening in my local area)

 Apply

Ask students to work in small groups. Have one or more groups look through a local newspaper and list the different kinds of information it provides. Have another group look in the local library to see what types of magazines are on the shelves. Another group can search the Internet for on-line children's magazines. Allow time for groups to share their findings with the class.

Word Work Instructions

DAY 1	• Spelling Pretest • Spelling Instruction
DAY 2	• Structural Analysis Instruction • Spelling Practice
DAY 3	• Phonics Instruction • Spelling Practice
DAY 4	• Structural Analysis Reteaching • Vocabulary Skill Instruction • Spelling Game
DAY 5	• Expanding Your Vocabulary • Spelling Test

OBJECTIVES

Students

• read words with prefixes and suffixes

• read words and syllables with vowel diphthongs

• use the Phonics/Decoding strategy to decode longer words

Teacher's Note

Tell students that they will recognize many of the word parts and vowel sounds they learn about in this lesson. Explain that good readers use what they know about sounds and word parts to help them decode new words they come across in their reading.

Decoding Longer Words

✓ Structural Analysis: Prefixes and Suffixes Spelling Connection

▶ Teach

Write these sentences: *Grandpa's smile <u>disappeared</u> when he was <u>unhappy</u>, but it <u>returned</u> later. Jamal had an extra <u>assignment</u> because of his <u>thoughtless</u> behavior on the bus.* Remind students that prefixes and suffixes can change a word's meaning. Name the prefixes (dis-, un-, re-) and suffixes (-ment, -less) in these sentences. Explain that *re-* means "again" or "back to." If Grandpa's smile *returned,* it came back. *Dis-* and *un-* are prefixes that mean "not" or "the opposite of." If Grandpa's smile *disappeared,* it "did not appear." If he was *unhappy,* he was "not happy." Explain that the suffix *-ment* makes a word a noun, as in *assignment.* The suffix *-less* means "without." Jamal's *thoughtless* behavior means he acted "without thought." Have students review the Phonics/Decoding strategy.

Modeling Write the following sentence and model how to decode *kindness* and *peaceful: Dr. King spoke about <u>kindness</u> and <u>peaceful</u> ways to make things happen.*

Think Aloud

The base words are kind *and* peace. Kind *is an adjective, but the suffix* -ness *makes it into a noun,* kindness. *The suffix* -ful *might mean "full of" because it looks like the word* full. Peaceful *would then mean "full of peace."*

▶ Practice

Display these sentences and have students copy the underlined words. *Many people <u>disagreed</u> with the <u>unequal</u> treatment of African Americans. The civil rights <u>movement</u> taught us that individuals are not <u>powerless</u> to stop <u>unfairness</u>.* Have students circle the prefixes and suffixes and to decode the words.

▶ Apply

Have students complete **Practice Book** page 294.

Skill Finder	• Strategy Review: Phonics/ Decoding, p. 533B	• Reteaching, p. R14

Phonics: Vowel Diphthongs

▶ Teach

Tell students that understanding vowel diphthongs will help them use the Phonics/Decoding strategy to decode unfamiliar words. Explain that

- the spelling patterns *oi* and *oy* can have the /oi/ sound as in *coin*
- the spelling patterns *ow* and *ou* can have the /ow/ sound as in *clown*

Modeling Write this sentence and model how to decode *proudly: Jamal stood* <u>*proudly*</u> *to tell his idea to the class.*

Think Aloud

I notice the spelling pattern o-u in the middle of this word. I know that pattern can have the /ow/ sound as in the word round. Next I'll blend that sound with the letters around it. /prowd/ When I add on the -ly ending, the word is /PROWD•lee/. I know if you feel proud it means you feel happy about something you've done. It makes sense that Jamal would be proud of his idea for a skit.

▶ Practice

Write these sentences on the board and have students copy the underlined words: *African Americans were not <u>allowed</u> to sit at the front of the bus. Many people made the <u>choice</u> to walk <u>around</u> <u>town</u> rather than ride the bus. During his <u>boyhood</u>, Jamal's father went to hear Dr. King speak.* Tell students to circle the /oi/ and /ow/ spellings and decode each word. Call on students to model the Phonics/Decoding strategy at the board.

▶ Apply

Tell students to decode the following words from *Happy Birthday, Dr. King!* and discuss their meanings: *voice,* page 539; *power, boycott,* page 544; and *joined,* page 547.

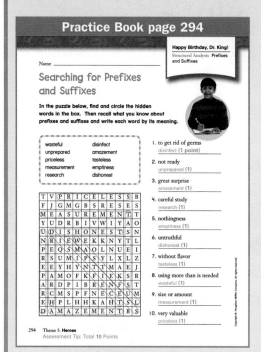

Practice Book page 294

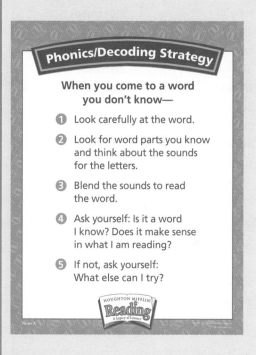

Phonics/Decoding Strategy

When you come to a word you don't know—

1. Look carefully at the word.
2. Look for word parts you know and think about the sounds for the letters.
3. Blend the sounds to read the word.
4. Ask yourself: Is it a word I know? Does it make sense in what I am reading?
5. If not, ask yourself: What else can I try?

Diagnostic Check

If . . .	You can . . .
students need help reading words with prefixes or suffixes,	use the Reteaching Lesson on page R14.

Word Work

OBJECTIVES

Students write spelling words that have a prefix or a suffix.

Spelling Words

Basic Words

redo*	reread*
treatment	unsure*
rebuild	movement*
discolor	peaceful*
careless	unpaid
dislike*	distrust
sickness	kindness
beautiful	useless*
unlucky	displease*
awful	powerful*

Review Words

hopeful
remake*
rewrite*
useful
unfair

Challenge Words

unusual*
rearrange
appointment
discontinue
resourceful

Forms of these words appear in the literature.

Extra Support

Basic Word List You may want to use only the left column of Basic Words with students who need extra support.

Spelling

✓ Words with a Prefix or a Suffix

Day 1   Teaching the Principle

Pretest Use the Day 5 Test sentences. Say each underlined word, read the sentence, and then repeat the word. Have students write only the underlined word.

Teach Write *rebuild, dislike, unlucky, sickness, treatment, beautiful,* and *careless* on the board, say the words, and have students repeat them. Tell the class that each word contains a prefix, a word part added to the beginning of a word, or a suffix, a word part added to the end of a word. Also mention that prefixes and suffixes add meaning. Underline the prefixes and suffixes and explain their meanings: *re-* ("again"), *dis-* ("not"), *un-* ("not" or "opposite of"), *-ness* ("quality of being"), *-ment* ("act of"), *-ful* ("full of"), and *-less* ("without"). Circle the *i* in *beautiful;* explain that when a suffix is added to a base word that ends in *y,* the *y* is changed to *i.*

Add *awful* to the board, say it, and have students repeat it. Note that the final *e* of this word's base word *(awe)* was dropped when *-ful* was added.

List the remaining Basic Words on the board, say each one, and have students repeat it. Underline the prefix or suffix in each word.

Practice/Homework Assign **Practice Book** page 423. Tell students to use this Take-Home Word List to study the words they missed on the Pretest.

Day 2   Reviewing the Principle

Practice/Homework Review the spelling principle and assign **Practice Book** page 295.

Day 3   Vocabulary

Switching Prefixes and Suffixes List these Basic Words on the board: *redo, discolor, careless, dislike, movement, unpaid.* Then add these affixes in another column: *un-, re-, -ness, -ful, -less.* Ask small groups to find each Basic Word's base word, and then write as many *new* words as they can by adding the listed prefixes or suffixes to those base words. (Students can make *undo, colorful, colorless, careful, unlike, likeness, remove, repaid.*) Next, list the remaining Basic Words on the board. Have students use each word orally in a sentence. (Sentences will vary.)

Practice/Homework For spelling practice, assign **Practice Book** page 296.

Day 4 Base Words Plus

Ask students to form groups of three: two players and a caller. Tell each group to write the lesson's seven prefixes or suffixes, and their meanings (e.g., *-ness*, "quality of being"), on separate index cards. The caller keeps the cards and also needs a list of Basic and Review Words.

To play, the caller draws a card and chooses a list word that has the prefix or suffix noted on the card. Then he or she uses the list word's base word and the meaning of the prefix or suffix to define the list word (e.g., "the quality of being kind"). The caller states the meaning for Player 1, who earns a point by guessing the correct word and spelling it correctly. Player 2 then takes a turn, and afterward, the caller and a player switch roles. The player with the highest score at the end of the game wins.

Practice/Homework For proofreading and writing practice, assign **Practice Book** page 297.

Day 5 Spelling Assessment

Test Say each underlined word, read the sentence, and then repeat the word. Have students write only the underlined word.

Basic Words

1. You cannot <u>redo</u> your own work.
2. What <u>treatment</u> do you have for a cold?
3. We can <u>rebuild</u> your house after the flood.
4. Will the sun <u>discolor</u> the curtain?
5. It was <u>careless</u> of me to forget my hat.
6. I <u>dislike</u> the chore of washing dishes.
7. The doctor cured his <u>sickness</u>.
8. We danced to the <u>beautiful</u> music.
9. I do not win when I feel <u>unlucky</u>.
10. The heavy rains were <u>awful</u>.
11. I had to <u>reread</u> the page five times.
12. She feels <u>unsure</u> of what to do next.
13. Jay threw the ball in a swift <u>movement</u>.
14. This quiet room is so <u>peaceful</u>.
15. Will five dollars cover the <u>unpaid</u> bill?
16. The dogs <u>distrust</u> any stranger.
17. Sending a card is an act of <u>kindness</u>.
18. Is the broken tool <u>useless</u>?
19. Cold steak will <u>displease</u> the chef.
20. Horses are <u>powerful</u> animals.

Challenge Words

21. This food is <u>unusual</u>.
22. She helped me <u>rearrange</u> the chairs.
23. I made an <u>appointment</u>.
24. The company will <u>discontinue</u> that model.
25. He was <u>resourceful</u> in finding facts for his report.

Technology

Spelling Spree!™

Students can use the **Spelling Spree!™** for extra practice with the spelling principles taught in this lesson.

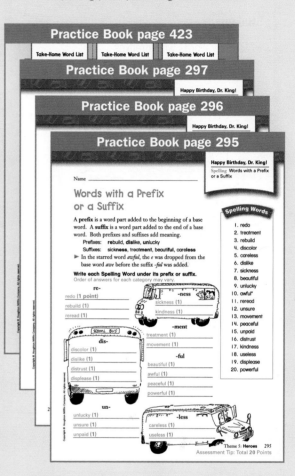

··· Houghton Mifflin Spelling and Vocabulary ···
Correlated instruction and practice

Challenge

Challenge Word Practice Tell students to use the Challenge Words to create crossword puzzles. Have them draw the puzzle, write clues, and then trade puzzles with a partner.

OBJECTIVES

Students

- identify words with prefixes
- use dictionary definitions of prefixes along with sentence context to define new words

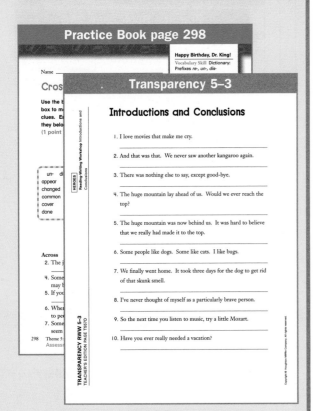

Practice Book page 298

Transparency 5–3

Introductions and Conclusions

1. I love movies that make me cry.
2. And that was that. We never saw another kangaroo again.
3. There was nothing else to say, except good-bye.
4. The huge mountain lay ahead of us. Would we ever reach the top?
5. The huge mountain was now behind us. It was hard to believe that we really had made it to the top.
6. Some people like dogs. Some like cats. I like bugs.
7. We finally went home. It took three days for the dog to get rid of that skunk smell.
8. I've never thought of myself as a particularly brave person.
9. So the next time you listen to music, try a little Mozart.
10. Have you ever really needed a vacation?

Vocabulary Skills

✔ *Dictionary: Prefixes re-, un-, dis-*

▶ Teach

Display **Transparency 5–3,** blocking out all but the definition for *prefix.*

Read aloud the definition. Explain that the dictionary definition of a particular prefix, along with the sentence context, can help students figure out the meaning of a new word.

On the transparency, uncover the dictionary definitions of *re-, dis-,* and *un-.* Read each definition aloud. Point to a prefix and suggest words that begin with the prefix. Apply the dictionary definition to those examples. Repeat the steps with each of the prefixes.

Display words 1 through 7 on the transparency and identify the words with prefixes. (numbers 2, 4, 5, and 7) Remind students that prefixes are added to the beginning of a word.

Modeling On the transparency, display sentences 8 through 10. Point to the underlined word in sentence 8, *disagreed,* and model how to use prefixes to figure out its meaning.

Think Aloud

When I look at the word disagreed, *I see the prefix* dis- *at the beginning. I know what the word* agreed *means. From the definition, I know that the prefix* dis- *changes a word to mean the opposite. That means that* disagree *is the opposite of* agree. *So I know that this sentence means that Dr. King did not agree with what the police did.*

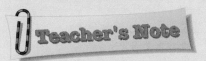

► Practice

In pairs or small groups, have students copy sentences 9 and 10. Have students figure out the meanings of the underlined words using dictionary definitions of the prefixes and the sentence context.

► Apply

Have students complete **Practice Book** page 298.

Expanding Your Vocabulary
Holiday Words

Remind students that Dr. King's birthday is in January. Point out that some of the words associated with the celebration are *civil rights, boycott,* and *overcome.* Discuss the meaning of each word with students. Then point out that other holidays are associated with special words. For example, the Fourth of July is officially called Independence Day. Discuss other vocabulary that is associated with particular holidays. (Possibilities include Memorial Day, Veterans Day, Flag Day, Presidents Day, Thanksgiving.)

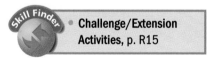

Challenge/Extension
Activities, p. R15

Word Histories The word *boycott* comes from the name of a real person. Captain Charles Cunningham Boycott (1823–1897) was a British soldier who became a farmer. He was also manager of a rich farmer's property. Relations were tense between poor farmers and the wealthy landlords who owned the farms. One day, an Irish leader named Charles Steward Parnell told farmers to pay less rent to their landlords. The farmers agreed that they would not speak to anyone who turned down the lower rents. When Boycott refused to accept lower rents, the other farmers stopped talking to him. Within months, Boycott's name became synonymous with the refusal to deal with a person or a business.

··· **Houghton Mifflin Spelling and Vocabulary** ···
Correlated instruction and practice

English Language Learners

Introduce prefixes *re-, dis-, un-* to English language learners orally with simple examples such as *view / review, like / dislike,* and *comfortable / uncomfortable.* Write these examples on the board for students to repeat. Talk about how the meaning changes with the addition of the prefix. Ask for other examples from students.

Grammar Skills

✓ Subject Pronouns

	Writing and Language Instruction
DAY 1	• Daily Language Practice • Grammar Instruction • Journal Writing
DAY 2	• Daily Language Practice • Writing an Information Paragraph • Journal Writing • Grammar Practice
DAY 3	• Daily Language Practice • Grammar Instruction • Write a Scene
DAY 4	• Daily Language Practice • Listening/Speaking/Viewing • Writing: Improving Your Writing • Grammar Practice
DAY 5	• Daily Language Practice • Grammar: Improving Your Writing

OBJECTIVES

Students

- identify subject pronouns
- use subject pronouns in sentences
- proofread and correct sentences with grammar and spelling errors
- combine sentences with subject pronouns to improve writing.

Wacky Web Tales

Students may use the **Wacky Web Tales** floppy disk to create humorous stories and review subject pronouns.

Day 1

Display the chart at the top of **Transparency 5–4.** Go over the chart with examples of subject pronouns. Then display the sentences below the chart.

Have students read the sentences, and ask volunteers to choose the correct subject pronoun to replace the underlined words in each sentence. Write the subject pronoun on the line provided. Then go over the following rules and definitions:

- A pronoun is a word that replaces one or more nouns.

- *I, you, he, she, it, we,* and *they* are subject pronouns.

> **Singular subject pronouns:** I, you, he, she, it
>
> **Plural subject pronouns:** we, you, they

Ask students to look at *Happy Birthday, Dr. King!* to find examples of subject pronouns. Have them share the examples they find. Then have students correct the Day 1 Daily Language Practice sentences on **Transparency 5–6.**

Day 2

Practice/Homework Have students correct the Day 2 Daily Language Practice sentences. Then assign **Practice Book** page 299.

Day 3 · Let's Compare

Divide the class into groups of four or five students. Ask each group to write down four sentences with noun subjects. Remind students that their subjects may have more than one word. Then have groups exchange sentences. Ask one group to read the sentences they have been given, one by one. Then have each member of the group go to the board and rewrite one of the sentences using subject pronouns. Repeat the exercise for each of the other groups. Then have students correct the Day 3 Daily Language Practice sentences.

Day 4

Practice/Homework Have students correct the Day 4 Daily Language Practice sentences. Assign **Practice Book** page 300.

Day 5 Improving Your Writing

Sentence Combining with Subject Pronouns Point out that when two sentences have different subjects but the same predicate, students can combine them into one sentence having a compound subject. Have students read the sentences on **Transparency 5–5.** Then ask students to use the joining word in parentheses to combine the subjects in each pair of sentences into one sentence with compound subject pronouns. Write the new sentence on the lines below each pair of sentences.

Then have students review a piece of their own writing to see if they can improve it by using combining sentences with different subject pronouns but the same predicate.

Practice/Homework Have students correct the Day 5 Daily Language Practice sentences. Then assign **Practice Book** page 301.

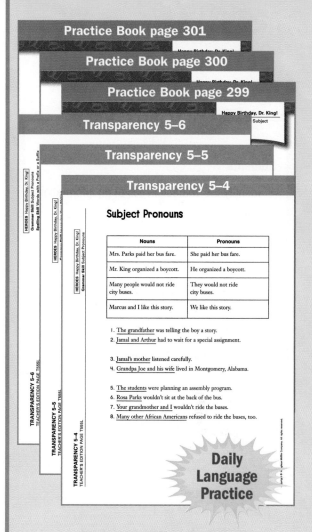

Practice Book page 301
Practice Book page 300
Practice Book page 299
Transparency 5–6
Transparency 5–5
Transparency 5–4

Subject Pronouns

Nouns	Pronouns
Mrs. Parks paid her bus fare.	She paid her bus fare.
Mr. King organized a boycott.	He organized a boycott.
Many people would not ride city buses.	They would not ride city buses.
Marcus and I like this story.	We like this story.

1. The grandfather was telling the boy a story.
2. Jamal and Arthur had to wait for a special assignment.
3. Jamal's mother listened carefully.
4. Grandpa Joe and his wife lived in Montgomery, Alabama.
5. The students were planning an assembly program.
6. Rosa Parks wouldn't sit at the back of the bus.
7. Your grandmother and I wouldn't ride the buses.
8. Many other African Americans refused to ride the buses, too.

Daily Language Practice

·········· **Houghton Mifflin English** ··········
Correlated instruction and practice

Diagnostic Check

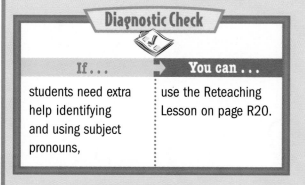

If...	You can...
students need extra help identifying and using subject pronouns,	use the Reteaching Lesson on page R20.

Grammar Skills 555L

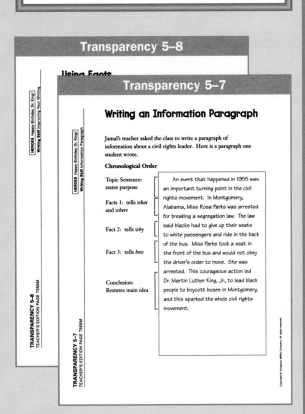

Transparency 5–8

Using Facts

Transparency 5–7

Writing an Information Paragraph

Jamal's teacher asked the class to write a paragraph of information about a civil rights leader. Here is a paragraph one student wrote.

Chronological Order

Topic Sentence: states purpose	An event that happened in 1955 was an important turning point in the civil rights movement. In Montgomery, Alabama, Miss Rosa Parks was arrested for breaking a segregation law. The law said blacks had to give up their seats to white passengers and ride in the back of the bus. Miss Parks took a seat in the front of the bus and would not obey the driver's order to move. She was arrested. This courageous action led Dr. Martin Luther King, Jr., to lead black people to boycott buses in Montgomery, and this sparked the whole civil rights movement.
Facts 1: tells *what* and *where*	
Fact 2: tells *why*	
Fact 3: tells *how*	
Conclusion: Restates main idea	

Writing Skills
Writing an Information Paragraph

▶ Teach

In *Happy Birthday, Dr. King!*, Jamal learns about who Dr. Martin Luther King, Jr., and Rosa Parks were and why they were important to the civil rights movement.

Tell students that an information paragraph presents a main idea and includes facts that support it and tell what, how, and why. The paragraph begins with a clearly stated topic sentence. The body of the paragraph presents facts that explain and develop the main idea. The paragraph ends with a concluding sentence that restates the main idea.

▶ Practice

Display **Transparency 5–7.** Have students read the paragraph about Rosa Parks. Ask:

- **What is the main idea?** (Rosa Parks' arrest was a turning point in the civil rights movement.)
- **What information is contained in sentence 2?** (what happened, when, and where)
- **What information is given in sentence 3?** (the basis for the action)
- **What information is given in sentences 4 and 5?** (what Miss Parks did to protest a law and what resulted)

Discuss with students the guidelines for writing an information paragraph.

Guidelines for
Writing an Information Paragraph

- Begin an information paragraph with a topic sentence that clearly states the main idea.
- Organize the facts and details in a way that is easy to follow, such as chronological or time order.
- All details and facts must support the main idea in the topic sentence.
- Write a concluding sentence, if necessary.

Technology

▶ Apply

Students can use **Practice Book** page 302 to help them plan and organize their writing. Have them use this graphic organizer to plan an information paragraph. Ask them to write about a leader they admire. Have them explain who they chose, what the leader did, and why they chose that person.

Improving Your Writing
Using Facts

Teach Tell students that facts can be organized in different ways. Explain that chronological order can be used to put facts in time order: what happened first, what happened next, and so on. Facts can also be arranged in order of importance from most important to least or least important to most. Facts can also be arranged spatially. Spatial order describes how something looks from the inside to the outside, or from top to bottom.

Practice Assign **Practice Book** page 303. Then have students review their information paragraphs. Ask them to describe how they organized the facts, chronologically, spatially, or in order of importance. Discuss why one organizational method makes more sense than another for different kinds of facts.

Apply Model turning a group of facts into an information paragraph, using **Transparency 5–8.**

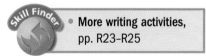
• More writing activities, pp. R23–R25

The Writer's Resource Library

Students may use this set of reference tools as they work on their own writing.

©Sunburst Technology Corporation, a Houghton Mifflin Company. All Rights Reserved.

Type to Learn™

Students may use **Type to Learn™** to learn proper keyboarding technique.

©Sunburst Technology Corporation, a Houghton Mifflin Company. All Rights Reserved.

·········· **Houghton Mifflin English** ··········
Correlated instruction and practice

Portfolio Opportunity

Save students' information paragraphs as samples of their writing development.

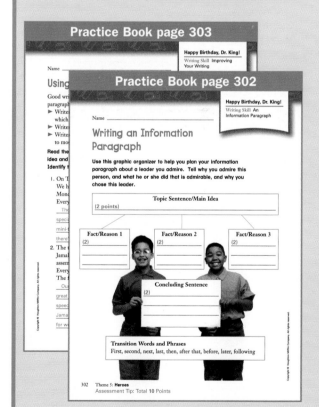

Practice Book page 303

Happy Birthday, Dr. King!
Writing Skill Improving Your Writing

Name _____

Practice Book page 302

Happy Birthday, Dr. King!
Writing Skill An Information Paragraph

Name _____

Writing an Information Paragraph

Use this graphic organizer to help you plan your information paragraph about a leader you admire. Tell why you admire this person, and what he or she did that is admirable, and why you chose this leader.

| Topic Sentence/Main Idea |
| (2 points) |

| Fact/Reason 1 (2) | Fact/Reason 2 (2) | Fact/Reason 3 (2) |

| Concluding Sentence (2) |

Transition Words and Phrases
First, second, next, last, then, after that, before, later, following

302 Theme 5: **Heroes**
Assessment Tip: Total **10** Points

Students

- establish standards for evaluating information sources

- apply their standards while researching a specific question

Listening/Speaking/Viewing
View and Evaluate Information Sources

▶ Teach

Explain to students that many people call the present period in our history the Information Age. By that they mean that there is more information available now than there has ever been in history. Point out that this information comes to us in a variety of forms, including radio and television broadcasts, books, magazines, newspapers, CD-ROMs, and the Internet. Internet material itself comes from a wide variety of sources, including colleges, businesses, public and private organizations, and individuals. Explain to students that just because information is printed or appears on the Internet does not guarantee that it is accurate. Tell students that it is important to always verify, or double-check, information.

Ask students to suggest what steps they should take to evaluate information they find, for example, on the Internet. Write their ideas on the board. Guide them to understand the following:

- Be aware of the source. Is it an official site, such as a university, museum, or scientific institution, or someone's class project or personal site?

- Look for links to other sites. They might give supporting information.

- Look for a bibliography, a list of sources that the writer of the piece used when researching the work.

- Check what you find against sources you trust, such as encyclopedias or periodicals with reputations for accuracy.

- If you use a print source to check the information, compare the copyright date to the date on the Internet material.

- Don't be fooled by appearances. Just because a site looks good doesn't necessarily mean that it's reliable. On the other hand, spelling mistakes and typos may be signs of other factual errors.

English Language Learners

With students, make a list of the sources they have used in the past both in and out of school. Survey the students to see which sources are in their first language and which are in English. Show examples of each type of source you talk about as well as those mentioned in Practice. Then have students work in mixed groups to complete the activity.

Practice

Have students evaluate which of the following would be likely to have the fairest and most up-to-date information about civil rights in an Asian country you are researching:

- an e-mail message, forwarded to you by a friend

- a two-year-old almanac

- the encyclopedia your father used when he was your age

- a web site operated by that country's government

- a CD-ROM encyclopedia that the library just received

- an article in a recent issue of a major news magazine

Ask students to explain their choices.

Apply

Ask students to use three different sources, including the Internet, to find the answer to a question that interests them. Have them share their questions and tell how they evaluated the information and answers they found.

Improving Viewing Skills

- Learn by speaking with a reference librarian which sources of information you can rely on.

- Be aware of the difference between facts you can check and opinions.

- If two sources have totally different points of view, that suggests that there is a difference in opinion rather than facts. Try to find a better source, or try to verify the information offered by the two sides.

Reading-Writing Workshop

Personal Essay

What Makes a Great Personal Essay?

Review with students these characteristics of a personal essay.

A personal essay is an article that shares a writer's thoughts, opinions, reflections, or feelings on a topic of great personal importance.

When you write a personal essay, remember to

- open with an interesting beginning that makes your reader want to read on
- write in your own natural voice
- share your thoughts, impressions, opinions, or feelings with your reader
- state a main idea or theme that you would like to share with your audience
- bring your main idea to life using vivid, lively details
- use pronouns correctly
- conclude with an ending that highlights the main focus of your personal essay

Have students read the Student Writing Model. Then discuss with them what the student writer did to make her writing interesting to read.

Student Writing Model

A Personal Essay

A personal essay explains the writer's opinion and gives reasons to support the opinion. Use this student's writing as a model when you write a personal essay of your own.

H*E*R*O

> A good **opening** draws the reader into the essay.

My Dad is a hero to me, and I want to tell everyone about him. My Dad has brown hair with golden blond streaks. He usually wears shorts and a golf shirt, or a suit. He is about 5'8" tall, and when he is angry his face is like a cherry red rose that just opened up, and his voice is like a lion that is right on your trail.

> A good essay stays with the main point, or **focus**.

> **Examples** clarify ideas in an essay.

My Dad also has a sweet side, like when we make cut-and-bake cookies, or when he makes his famous smores pie with hot pudding and melted marshmallows.

556

Theme Writing Skills

- **Using Facts,** p. 555N
- **Sentence Combining with Pronouns,** p. 581N
- **Sentence Combining with Possessive Pronouns,** p. 607N

Theme Grammar Skills

- **Sentence Combining with Subject Pronouns,** p. 555L
- **Using the Correct Pronoun,** p. 581L
- **Proofreading for** *its* **and** *it's,* p. 607L

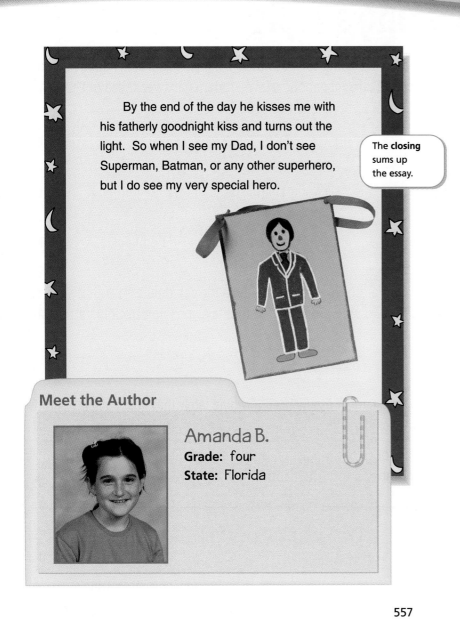

By the end of the day he kisses me with his fatherly goodnight kiss and turns out the light. So when I see my Dad, I don't see Superman, Batman, or any other superhero, but I do see my very special hero.

The **closing** sums up the essay.

Meet the Author

Amanda B.
Grade: four
State: Florida

557

Reading as a Writer

1. Where does the writer tell the reader about the main focus on this personal essay? (in the first sentence)

2. How does the writer interest the reader in her topic? (She calls her Dad her hero and then says she will tell you why.)

3. What details help the reader to see what Dad looks like? (Answers will vary. Possible responses: Descriptive details about how her father looks; what he wears; what his voice sounds like.)

4. What details help the reader to know what Dad is like as a person? (Answers will vary. Possible responses: what his face looks like when he's angry; what he bakes with the writer; his goodnight kiss.)

5. How does the writer close this personal essay? (by restating that she sees her Dad as her hero)

Reading-Writing Workshop

Personal Essay,
continued

Type to Learn™

Students may use **Type to Learn™** to learn proper keyboarding technique.

©Sunburst Technology Corporation, a Houghton Mifflin Company. All Rights Reserved.

The Writer's Resource Library

Students may use this set of reference tools as they work on their own writing.

©Sunburst Technology Corporation, a Houghton Mifflin Company. All Rights Reserved.

Choosing a Topic

Tell students they are going to write their own personal essay about a point of view that they feel strongly about. Have students answer these questions, either in a writing journal or on a sheet of paper:

■ What audience are you writing for: people who share your point of view? friends and family? essay readers?

■ What do you see as your writing purpose: to amuse or entertain? to connect with other people? to reveal the truth about something?

■ How do you plan to publish your essay: as an illustrated booklet? on an Internet web site? by giving a reading with an audience?

Have students generate three or more ideas for personal essays that they could write. Offer the following prompts if students are having trouble getting started.

■ Are there any people in your life who are really special to you?

■ What things make your life rich?

■ Has you seen, heard, or experienced anything lately that was: thrilling? surprising? greatly disappointing? just plain wonderful?

Have students work with a partner or in small groups to decide which topic would be the best one to write about.

Tips for
Getting Started

* Look at titles of other essays. Which ones look interesting?
* What is the best thing that's happened in your life lately? The most disappointing thing?
* Are you misunderstood? In what way? How might you clear up this misunderstanding?
* What is your strongest opinion? Why is it so strong?
* Who is your favorite person?
* Imagine yourself as a talk show host for one night. What would be the theme of your show?

Organizing and Planning

Point out that a successful personal essay often shares the writer's thoughts, feelings, and opinions on a topic. Go over these points for organizing a personal essay.

- Sort thoughts, opinions, and feelings separately.
- Look for connections between your thoughts, opinions, and feelings.
- Plan your essay around the connections you find. Let one item lead to the next.

Use a diagram on **Transparency RWW5–1** to model exploring a topic for a personal essay.

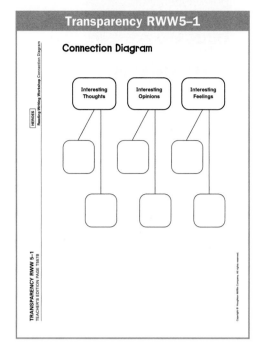

Graphic Organizer: Connection Diagram

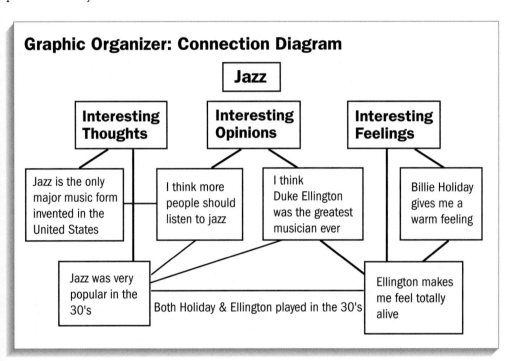

Discuss some of the connections on the sample chart in class. Then distribute Transparency RWW5–1 for students to use to organize and plan their personal essays.

Tips for
Organizing a Personal Essay

- List thoughts, opinions, and feelings.
- Find connections between thoughts, opinions, and feelings.
- Organize the essay around the connections you find.

Reading-Writing Workshop

Personal Essay, *continued*

Main Idea and Details

Remind students that top-notch writers structure each paragraph they write around a strong main idea that is supported by solid, meaningful details. Review these points for main idea and details.

- The main idea typically comes early in the paragraph. It is often the first sentence in the paragraph, but it doesn't need to be.

- Think of the paragraph as a tower. The main idea is the top of the tower. The details are the foundation that supports the tower.

- Just like the supports of a tower, the details work together to support the main idea. Each detail should be interesting and to the point. Inappropriate details can make the whole structure wobbly and unstable.

Display **Transparency RWW5–2.** Read the directions together, and go over the first two items, if necessary. Then have students complete Transparency RWW5–2. Encourage students to use details as a solid foundation for the main ideas they write in their own personal essays.

Transparency RWW5–2

Main Idea and Details

Circle the main idea of the paragraph. Then underline the details that support the main idea.

Hair is important to people. Almost all of us spend a great deal of time washing it, combing it, fussing with it, and worrying about it. Did you know that 4 out of 5 students at Webster School think hair is the single most important thing in their appearance? I learned this when I took a Hair Survey in school.

In my survey I found that most people spend a lot of time on their hair. Some spend as much as an hour a day fixing their hair. What a waste! The typical student shampoos three times a week. He or she usually uses the family shampoo, not some fancy personal brand. Girls use a lot of conditioner. Boys don't. Boys tend to over-shampoo more than girls.

Tips for
Main Idea and Details

- Think of each paragraph as a tower with details serving as a foundation for a main idea.
- Make sure that details work together.
- Make sure each detail is interesting and to the point.

Introductions and Conclusions

Remind students that introductions and conclusions have a powerful impact on the reader because they are the first and last things the reader sees. Go over these characteristics of introductions and conclusions:

■ The function of the introduction is to pull the reader in.

■ A good introduction may ask a question, issue a challenge, pose a mystery, or deliver a surprise. Anything that stimulates the reader to keep reading is acceptable.

■ The function of the conclusion is to sum up the essay and bring it to a close.

■ Good conclusions may look back to the beginning, offer a chuckle, give a final bit of evidence to clinch the case, or present a moral that sums up the meaning of the essay.

Model the first two exercises in **Transparency RWW5–3.** Ask students to identify each example as an introduction or a conclusion. Discuss the students' responses. Go over additional examples, if necessary. Then have students complete Transparency RWW5–3. After finishing the page, encourage students to evaluate the openings and closings of their own personal essays.

Transparency RWW5–3

Introductions and Conclusions

1. I love movies that make me cry.

2. And that was that. We never saw another kangaroo again.

3. There was nothing else to say, except good-bye.

4. The huge mountain lay ahead of us. Would we ever reach the top?

5. The huge mountain was now behind us. It was hard to believe that we really had made it to the top.

6. Some people like dogs. Some like cats. I like bugs.

7. We finally went home. It took three days for the dog to get rid of that skunk smell.

8. I've never thought of myself as a particularly brave person.

9. So the next time you listen to music, try a little Mozart.

10. Have you ever really needed a vacation?

Tips for
Writing Introductions and Conclusions

• Challenge, question, or surprise the reader in the introduction.
• In the conclusion, bring the essay to a close.
• Take a look back at the beginning as you end the essay.

Reading-Writing
Workshop

Personal Essay,
continued

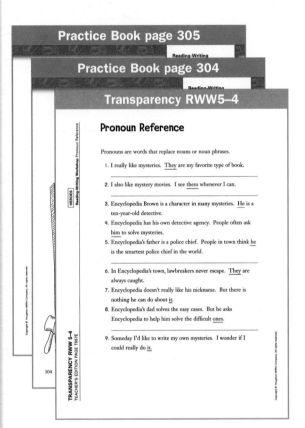

Practice Book page 305

Practice Book page 304

Reading-Writing

Transparency RWW5–4

Pronoun Reference

Pronouns are words that replace nouns or noun phrases.

1. I really like mysteries. <u>They</u> are my favorite type of book.

2. I also like mystery movies. I see <u>them</u> whenever I can.

3. Encyclopedia Brown is a character in many mysteries. <u>He</u> is a ten-year-old detective.
4. Encyclopedia has his own detective agency. People often ask <u>him</u> to solve mysteries.
5. Encyclopedia's father is a police chief. People in town think <u>he</u> is the smartest police chief in the world.

6. In Encyclopedia's town, lawbreakers never escape. <u>They</u> are always caught.
7. Encyclopedia doesn't really like his nickname. But there is nothing he can do about <u>it</u>.
8. Encyclopedia's dad solves the easy cases. But he asks Encyclopedia to help him solve the difficult <u>ones</u>.

9. Someday I'd like to write my own mysteries. I wonder if I could really do <u>it</u>.

304

TRANSPARENCY RWW 5–4
TEACHER'S EDITION PAGE T557E

PREWRITING   DRAFTING   **REVISING**   PROOFREADING   PUBLISHING

Revising

Have students evaluate their finished drafts, using Evaluating Your Personal Essay on **Practice Book** page 304. Students may want to evaluate their drafts with a partner in a Writing Conference.

Once students have evaluated and discussed their drafts, have them go back and revise any parts they feel still need work.

Improving Your Writing
GRAMMAR LINK ▸ **Pronoun Reference**

Remind students that good writers use pronouns correctly, which gives their writing a smooth, easy-to-read quality. Define a *pronoun* as a word that takes the place of a noun or word that functions as a noun. Go over these characteristics of pronouns.

- Examples of pronouns include: I, me, you, yourself, he, she, they, them, it, we, us.

- Pronouns refer to the person or thing that they replace. Example: I like peanuts. <u>They</u> are crunchy. In these sentences, the word *they* replaces *peanuts.*

- When you write, be clear about the words that pronouns replace. For example: Maxine and Ted have three beagles. <u>They</u> are very smart. In these sentences, it isn't clear whether *They* refers to the beagles or to Maxine and Ted.

- Add words to make situations clear. Example: Maxine and Ted have three beagles. <u>They</u> are very smart dogs. Now the situation is clear. The word *They* refers to the dogs, not to Maxine and Ted.

Model the use of pronouns, using **Transparency RWW5–4.** In each case, ask students: *What word or words does this pronoun replace?* When students can reliably identify the words that the pronouns refer to, have them complete Transparency RWW5–4 on their own.

Assign **Practice Book** page 305. Encourage students to review their personal essays to make sure they have used pronouns correctly.

Proofreading

Have students proofread their papers carefully to correct capitalization, punctuation, and spelling errors. Students can use the chart on **Practice Book** page 433 to help them with their proofreading marks.

Practice Book

Spelling Practice: pp. 306–308
Take-Home Word List: p. 425

5-Day Spelling Plan

See p. 555G

Improving Your Writing

Spelling Connection   Frequently Misspelled Words

Write the Spelling Words on the board, or distribute the Take-Home Word List on **Practice Book** page 425. Read the words aloud, and have students repeat them. Help students identify the part of the word likely to be misspelled.

Spelling Assessment

Pretest

1. My aunt <u>brought</u> me the cards.
2. Will <u>enough</u> people want to play?
3. We don't have to <u>buy</u> the game.
4. You have to <u>guess</u> the next word.
5. Let's go to my house <u>Saturday</u>.
6. In <u>January</u> we put up the calendar.
7. By <u>February</u> I'm tired of winter!
8. What is your <u>favorite</u> kind of meal?
9. The cat is <u>lying</u> in a sunny spot.
10. Kyla was <u>tying</u> her sister's scarf.
11. Dad parked just <u>around</u> the corner.
12. I enjoy <u>swimming</u> in the pool.
13. Have you <u>heard</u> the news?
14. Consuela danced and <u>also</u> sang.
15. I <u>tried</u> to answer her question.

Test: Use the Pretest sentences.

Challenge Words

16. Each player must <u>choose</u> a number.
17. I <u>chose</u> a card from Leah's hand.
18. The lid on that bottle is <u>loose</u>.
19. Don't <u>lose</u> your train ticket.
20. The seed was one <u>millimeter</u> long.

Challenge Word Practice

Have students use the Challenge Words to write five sentences about how to play a board game.

Pretest

brought	swimming
enough	heard
buy	also
guess	tried
Saturday	
January	**Challenge Words**
February	choose
favorite	chose
lying	loose
tying	lose
around	millimeter

··· **Houghton Mifflin Spelling and Vocabulary** ···
Correlated instruction and practice

Personal Essay,
continued

Publishing and Evaluating

Have students make a final copy of their personal essays. Then have students look back at the publishing ideas note they made when they were choosing a topic for their personal essays. Tell them to decide if that's still the way they want to share their writing. If students need help deciding how to share what they have written, here are some ideas:

■ Publish your essay as an article in a student newspaper.

■ Use your essay to accompany an exhibit of your photos or drawings.

The Scoring Rubric is based on the criteria in this workshop, and reflects the criteria students used in Evaluating Your Personal Essay on **Practice Book** page 304. A six-point rubric can be found in the **Teacher's Assessment Handbook.**

Portfolio Opportunity
Save students' final copies of their personal essays as examples of the development of their writing skills.

Student Self-Assessment

- How interesting was your personal essay? Did you communicate your thoughts, opinions, or insights effectively to your readers?

- How engaging was your introduction? Did it do a good job of attracting your readers' attention?

- How well written was your essay? Did you write in your own voice? Did you write paragraphs with clearly stated main points that were supported by strong details?

- Did you use pronouns correctly in your essay?

- How did you end your essay? Did your conclusion effectively close matters?

- Overall, how would you rate your essay? What was the best part? What part of your essay did your readers enjoy most?

Scoring Rubric

4

The work meets all evaluation criteria. The introduction is attention grabbing. The writer effectively communicates ideas and impressions. The main focus of the essay is well supported by interesting and vivid details. The conclusion sums up the essay effectively. There are almost no usage, mechanics, or spelling errors.

3

The essay is strong in many respects but contains some flaws. The introduction is adequate but could have been improved. The main focus is well supported in some cases but not in others. The conclusion restates the main focus of the essay but not in a very effective way. The essay contains some pronoun errors. There are some usage, mechanics, and spelling errors.

2

The writing minimally meets the criteria for a personal essay. The introduction and conclusion are weakly presented. The main focus is poorly supported. The work has a large number of pronoun errors. There are many usage, mechanics, and spelling errors.

1

The work does not meet the standards for a personal essay. The writing does not state a main focus. The writing is difficult to follow. Many errors in usage, mechanics, and spelling interfere with comprehension.

Using Leveled Books

Paperbacks for *Heroes*

Leveled **Theme Paperbacks** provide varying levels of reading difficulty—Easy, On Level, and Challenge—to meet all students' needs.

Options for Reading
Students may

- begin reading the Theme Paperbacks at the start of the theme, after the class has read the first Anthology selection, or at any point in the theme;

- read the books at their levels independently or with appropriate teacher support;

- finish an Easy or On Level book before the completion of the theme and move on to the next difficulty level;

- move to an easier book if appropriate, based on your observation. If a student is struggling with the Easy book, have that student read the Very Easy Reader's Library book for this theme.

Theme Paperbacks

Easy	On Level	Challenge

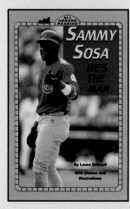

See **Cumulative Listing of Leveled Books.**

Reader's Library   Very Easy

Reader's Library books offer stories related by skill and topic to the Anthology stories at a difficulty level approximately two grades below grade level.

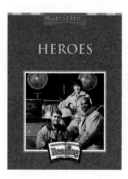

Reader's Library

Houghton Mifflin Classroom Bookshelf

The **Houghton Mifflin Classroom Bookshelf** provides theme-related books for independent reading.

Houghton Mifflin Classroom Bookshelf

 Sammy Sosa: He's the Man

by Laura Driscoll

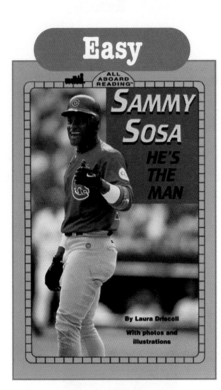

Easy

Selection Summary

The nonfiction book *Sammy Sosa: He's the Man* tells of this baseball great's career beginning in the Dominican Republic and takes him to the "canyon of heroes" in New York City.

Key Vocabulary

flocking, p. 11: gathering together in a crowd

canvas, p. 15: heavy, coarse cloth of cotton, hemp, or flax

slump, p. 20: an extended period of poor performance, especially in a sport

mature, p. 27: having grown or gained experience

humble, p. 31: marked by meekness or modesty in behavior, attitude, or spirit

deeds, p. 48: actions

▶ Preparing to Read

Building Background Ask students what they know about Sammy Sosa and his bid to topple the home-run record. As they read, have students note the sequence of events and make inferences about Sammy Sosa.

Developing Key Vocabulary Call students' attention to the baseball terms and colloquial phrases. Preview the Key Vocabulary words listed at the left for each segment of the book, pages 1–24 and pages 25–48.

▶ Guided Preview

Sammy Sosa may be read in its entirety or in two segments, pages 1–24 and pages 25–48. Before they begin the book, have students read the chapter titles, look at the illustrations, and recall what they know about Sammy Sosa and the 1998 baseball season. Encourage students to stop periodically as they read and ask questions about the events and people in the text.

▶ Guiding the Reading

pages 1–24

■ Explain to students that the phrase "his bat has been on fire" means that a batter has been very successful at hitting the ball.

■ Why do fans enjoy watching Sammy Sosa play baseball? (He knows how to have fun and engages the fans when he is on the field. He is also an excellent hitter.)

■ Why does the author choose to tell Sammy Sosa's story out of sequence? (Answers will vary but could include that the first chapter describing Sammy's outstanding 1998 baseball season will capture the reader's attention.)

■ How does Sammy Sosa become a major-league player? (He grew up poor playing baseball with makeshift equipment on the streets of San Pedro in the Dominican Republic. He is spotted by an American baseball scout and is brought to the United State to play minor-league ball. He is successful and moves up to the majors—the Chicago Cubs.)

■ **What changes does Sosa make to become a better hitter?** (He changes his stance and grip on the bat and shortens his swing. As a result, he has more time to see the ball before he swings. Sosa works hard and learns how to be more patient and wait for a good pitch before swinging.)

pages 25–48

■ **Why is the 1998 baseball season so exciting for fans?** (Mark McGwire and Sammy Sosa are in a race to break Roger Maris's home-run record of 61. Each man is a competitor and a good sport, and each is respectful of the other and his achievements.)

■ **Explain to students that the term "neck and neck" means very close, as in a race.**

■ **What does Sosa's statement about Mark McGwire reveal about him as a person?** (Answers will vary.)

■ **Who breaks the home-run record? Explain how the season ends.** (Mark McGwire breaks the record in his last two games of the season. He beats Sosa by four runs. The Cubs reach the playoffs in part because of Sosa's hits during the season. He is voted the National League's Most Valuable Player.)

■ **Why does the author end the book with Sosa's comment, "I'd rather have people remember me one day for being a good person first, and a good ballplayer second"?** (Answers will vary.)

▶ Responding

Using details from the book, have students discuss their reactions to the story about Sammy Sosa. Have students discuss their reading strategies. Finally, have students discuss and summarize the main events of this book.

Activity Discuss with students their definition of a hero and then discuss whether they think Sosa is such a person.

English Language Learners

Some students may need additional explanations of the baseball terms and colloquial phrases used throughout the book. Encourage students to use the illustrations to help them follow the sequence of events.

Mrs. Mack
by Patricia Polacco

On Level

MRS. MACK
PATRICIA POLACCO

▶ Preparing to Read

Building Background Have students discuss experiences they (or someone they know) have had riding a horse. Encourage students to think about what might happen next as they read each chapter.

Developing Key Vocabulary Call students' attention to the specialized equine vocabulary and point out that most terms are defined in context. Preview with them the Key Vocabulary words listed at the left for each segment of the book, pages 5–23 and pages 24–38.

▶ Guided Preview

Mrs. Mack may be read in its entirety or in two segments, pages 5–23 and pages 24–38. Have students read the chapter titles and look through the illustrations before they begin reading. As they read, encourage them to stop and ask questions about the characters and plot. Have students make predictions about what will happen to Patricia during her summer at Dogpatch. Encourage students to reread any passages they find confusing or difficult.

▶ Guiding the Reading

pages 5–23

 Why is Patricia disappointed when she arrives at Mrs. Mack's stable? (It is in the roughest part of town and is shabby and rundown. The other students appear unfriendly and tough, and the horses look old and tired. Patricia doesn't think that she will fit in.)

 What attracts Patricia to Penny? (Penny is beautifully shaped and colored and looks strong and intelligent.)

■ What steps does Patricia take to learn how to ride? (First, she has to clean up the stalls and groom the horses. Next, she learns how to bridle and saddle a horse. Then she rides around the corral on a gentle horse. Eventually she graduates to riding more difficult horses and leaving the corral.)

■ Ask students to explain the meaning of the phrase "crippled up inside." (Mrs. Mack uses it in reference to Hap. He has a difficult time being with other people because he is depressed. He feels guilty and thinks he is responsible for his brother's death in the circus.)

Selection Summary
In the fiction book *Mrs. Mack*, a young girl spends a summer fulfilling her dream—to learn how to ride a horse. She learns much about herself and others in the process.

Key Vocabulary
filly, p. 5: a young female horse

contours, p. 11: the outline of a figure, body, or mass

curry down, p. 14: to groom a horse with a currycomb, a comb with metal teeth

bridle, p. 16: a harness consisting of straps, a bit, and reins, fitted around a horse's head and used to control the animal

canter, p. 20: a slow, easy gallop

mount, p. 25: a horse or other animal for riding

■ **Why do you think the author ends the chapter with Patricia leaving a gift for Hap?** (The author wants to show that Patricia's attitude has begun to change.)

pages 24–38

■ **Why does the author explain how Donnie, Nancy, and Patricia are alike?** (Answers will vary but may include that the author wants the reader to understand that although they seem different, they are alike in their love of horses.)

■ Point out that *withers* is the highest part of the back of a horse or similar animal.

■ **Describe everyone's reaction to Patricia's first ride on Penny.** (Patricia is ecstatic, and everyone shares in her joy and pride of accomplishment. Although she is reluctant and afraid to ride Penny after her fall, she does it anyway. Mrs. Mack is confident that Patricia will succeed. Even Hap is pleased with her efforts.)

■ **Who is the hero in the story? Explain your answer.** (Answers will vary.)

▶ **Responding**

Have students discuss how Patricia changes and matures during her summer at Dogpatch. Ask what they think is the most important lesson she learns and have them explain who or what helps her learn it. Have students discuss the reading strategies they used. Finally, ask them to discuss and summarize the main events of the book.

MEETING INDIVIDUAL NEEDS

English Language Learners

Be sure students understand that *shugah* is a term of endearment used by Mrs. Mack, and that it is a version of the word *sugar*. Also point out and explain as needed the expressions *taste the fear* and *swallowed the fear*.

The Wreck of the Ethie

by Hilary Hyland

Challenge

Selection Summary

In December 1919, a terrible storm hit the western coast of Newfoundland, and the captain of the steamship *Ethie* tried to run the ship aground in order to save the lives of those aboard. Based on actual events, this fictionalized narrative tells the incredible story of how one dog saved all ninety-two crew members and passengers.

Key Vocabulary

plumed, p. 1: feathered or feather-like in shape

frigid, p. 9: extremely cold

accommodations, p. 31: compartments or rooms; lodgings

desolate, p. 37: deserted; dismal

incessant, p. 50: continuing without pause; never-ending

destiny, p. 85: predetermined fate or course of events

succumbed, p. 96: yielded to an overpowering force

▶ Preparing to Read

Building Background Have students share what they know about the dangers ships face when they are at sea during a bad storm. Briefly discuss the qualities of heroism. Ask students to think about ways in which animals can perform heroic acts. Remind students to use their reading strategies as they read this book.

Developing Key Vocabulary Point out that a glossary of nautical terms can be found at the end of *The Wreck of the Ethie.* Preview with students the meanings of the Key Vocabulary words listed at the left for each segment of the book, pages 1–57 and pages 59–102.

▶ Guided Preview

The Wreck of the Ethie may be read in its entirety or in two segments: chapters 1–7, pages 1–57; and chapters 8–13, pages 59–102. Invite students to look at the map of the Newfoundland area and read the author's preface. Encourage students to make predictions about what will happen in the story.

▶ Guiding the Reading

pages 1–57

■ Based on what you learn about Skipper in chapters 1 and 2, how would you describe the dog and his strengths? Why do you think the author includes this information? (Skipper is unusually strong, helpful, determined, and loyal. The author probably provides this information so that the reader will understand the dog's abilities and actions later in the story.)

■ On page 31, the author writes that "the air was full of commotion." What descriptions does the author use to support the meaning of this phrase? (The sounds of the scene are described by words and phrases such as *"the ship's bell clanged"*; the sailors are singing as they *"noisily"* load the cargo; bagpipes are playing Christmas carols.)

- What clues in chapter 6 suggest that this trip may not be an easy one? (The appearance of the white gulls, the drop in air pressure, the deep red band on the horizon, and the shifting winds all signal that a storm may be approaching.)

- Why does the crew jettison the herring barrels? (The barrels are very heavy, and the ice forming on them would make them even heavier; their weight could cause the ship to roll over.)

pages 59–102

- What is the predicament the *Ethie* is in, and why does Captain Flannery describe it as *dire* on page 62? (The captain knows that the ship and everyone aboard is in serious danger. Even if they can beach the *Ethie*, which will destroy the ship, he can't be certain that everyone will survive.)

- Do you think Captain Flannery's decision to beach the *Ethie* is wise? Why do you think Mr. Warren opposes it so strongly? (Answers will vary, but students should support their opinions with evidence from the story.)

- How do Skipper's actions save the people aboard the *Ethie*? (Skipper does what no human could do—he swims out to grab the rope and brings it ashore, so that it can be anchored to a tree. The passengers and crew can then be brought over on the breeches buoy.)

- On page 100, what does Colleen mean when she reflects that the wreck changed everyone on the *Ethie* forever? (Answers will vary.)

▶ Responding

Have students use the Evaluate strategy to think about why the author chose Coleen and Patrick as main characters in the book. Then have students share their reactions to the book. Finally, ask them to summarize the main events of the book.

Bonus Have students research the Newfoundland breed and other types of dogs that help people in their everyday lives.

English Language Learners

Help students understand the meaning of the verse on page 22: "Mackerel skies and mare's tails/Make tall ships carry short sails." Explain that this saying is included to foreshadow what will happen to the *Ethie*.

Gloria Estefan

Different texts for different purposes

REAL-LIFE READER BIOGRAPHY

GLORIA ESTEFAN

Grammy Award–Winning Recording Artist

Anthology: Main Selection

Purposes

- strategy focus: monitor/clarify
- comprehension skill: making judgments
- vocabulary development
- critical thinking, discussion

Genre: Biography

A true story of the life of a real person.

Selection Summary

The Cuban-born singer helped care for her ailing father and finished college before joining Emilio Estefan's band. Theirs was the first band with hits on both the Latin and pop charts. After recovering from a serious accident, Gloria used her continued success for charitable causes.

Teacher's Edition: Read Aloud

Purposes

- listening comprehension: making judgments
- vocabulary development
- critical thinking, discussion

Anthology: Get Set to Read

Purposes

- background building: music business
- developing key vocabulary

Anthology: Content Link

Purposes

- content reading: health
- skill: how to follow a recipe
- critical thinking, discussion

Leveled Books and Resources

See Cumulative Listing of Leveled Books.

Reader's Library

Very Easy

Duke Ellington: A Life in Music
by Erick Montgomery

(Also available on
blackline masters)

Purposes

- fluency practice in below-level text
- alternate reading for students reading significantly below grade level
- strategy application: monitor/clarify
- comprehension skill application: making judgments
- below-level independent reading

Lesson Support

- Guided Reading lesson, page R4
- Alternate application for Comprehension Skill lesson on making judgments, page 581A
- Reteaching for Comprehension Skill: making judgments, page R10

Selection Summary Masters

Audiotape

Gloria Estefan
Audiotape for
Heroes

Gloria Estefan
Teacher's Resource Blackline Masters

MEETING INDIVIDUAL NEEDS

Inclusion Strategy

Significantly Below-level Readers

Students reading so far below level that they cannot read *Gloria Estefan* even with the suggested Extra Support should still participate with the class whenever possible.

- Include them in the Teacher Read Aloud (p. 558E) and Preparing to Read (pp. 559A–559D).

- Have them listen to *Gloria Estefan* on the audiotape for *Heroes* and read the Selection Summary while others read Segment 1 of the selection.

- Have them read "Duke Ellington: A Life in Music" in the Reader's Library collection for *Heroes* while others read Segment 2 of *Gloria Estefan.*

- Have all students participate in Wrapping Up Segment 2 (p. 577) and Responding (p. 578).

Theme Paperbacks

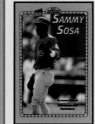

Easy

Sammy Sosa: He's the Man
by Laura Driscoll

Lesson, TE page 557I

On Level

Mrs. Mack
by Patricia Polacco

Lesson, TE page 557K

Challenge

The Wreck of the Ethie
by Hilary Hyland

Lesson, TE page 557M

Technology

Get Set for Reading CD-ROM
Gloria Estefan

Provides background building, vocabulary support, and selection summaries in English and Spanish.

Education Place
www.eduplace.com

Log on to Education Place for more activities relating to *Gloria Estefan*.

Book Adventure
www.bookadventure.org

This Internet reading incentive program provides thousands of titles for students to read.

Suggested Daily Routines

Instructional Goals	Day 1	Day 2

Reading
 	
Strategy Focus: Monitor/Clarify
 	
☑ *Comprehension Skill:* Making Judgments
 	
Comprehension Skill Review: Text Organization; Compare and Contrast
 	
Information and Study Skills: Conduct an Interview
	Teacher Read Aloud
	Kids Did It! Real-Life Heroes, 558E
	
	Preparing to Read *Gloria Estefan*
	• Get Set: Background and Vocabulary, 559A
	• Key Vocabulary, 559B
	   Selection Vocabulary, *Practice Book, 309*
	• Strategy/Skill Preview, 559C
	   Judgments Chart, *Practice Book, 310*
	
	Reading Segment 1
	Gloria Estefan, 560–565
	• Supporting Comprehension
	• Strategy Focus, 564
	
	Wrapping Up Segment 1, *565*
		Reading Segment 2
		Gloria Estefan, 566–576
		• Supporting Comprehension
		• Strategy Focus, 568
		
		Wrapping Up Segment 2, *577*
		
		Responding
		• Comprehension Questions: Think About the Selection, 578
		• Comprehension Check, *Practice Book, 311*
		
		Revisiting the Text
		• Comprehension: Making Judgments, 575

Word Work ☑ *Spelling:* Changing Final *y* to *i* *Decoding Longer Words:* ☑ *Structural Analysis:* Changing Final *y* to *i* *Phonics:* Two Sounds of *g* ☑ *Vocabulary:* Homophones	**Spelling** • Pretest, 581G • Instruction: Changing Final *y* to *i*, 581G • Take-Home Word List, *Practice Book: Handbook*	**Decoding Longer Words Instruction** • Structural Analysis: Changing Final *y* to *i*, 581E • *Practice Book, 314* **Spelling** • *Practice Book, 315*
Writing & Language ☑ *Grammar:* Object Pronouns ☑ *Writing:* Writing a Problem/Solution Paragraph; Sentence Combining with Pronouns *Listening/Speaking/Viewing:* Listen for Different Purposes	**Daily Language Practice,** *581L* **Grammar Instruction** • Object Pronouns, 581K ✏️ **Writing** • Journal Writing, 561	**Daily Language Practice,** *581L* **Grammar Instruction** • Object Pronouns, *Practice Book, 319* ✏️ **Writing Instruction** • Writing a Problem/Solution Paragraph, 581M • Journal Writing, 566

 = tested skills

 Leveled Books

See Cumulative Listing of Leveled Books.

Reader's Library
• **Very Easy** *Duke Ellington: A Life in Music,* Lesson, R4

Book Links: Anthology, *530*
Bibliography: Teacher's Edition, *526C*
Houghton Mifflin Classroom Bookshelf, Level 4

Theme Paperbacks, Lessons, *557H–557N*
• **Easy** *Sammy Sosa: He's the Man*
• **On Level** *Mrs. Mack*
• **Challenge** *The Wreck of the Ethie*

Allow time every day for students to read independently from self-selected books.

Technology

Lesson Planner CD-ROM:
Customize your planning for *Gloria Estefan* with the Lesson Planner.

Day 3

Revisiting the Text
- Writer's Craft: Sequence Words and Phrases, *569*
- Visual Literacy: Photography, *573*

Comprehension Skill Instruction
- Making Judgments, *581A*
- *Practice Book, 312*

Phonics Instruction
- Two Sounds of *g*, *581F*

Spelling
- *Practice Book, 316*

 Daily Language Practice, *581L*

Grammar Instruction
- What's the Object?, *581K*

✏ **Writing**
- Responding: Write a Book Jacket Summary, *578*

Day 4

Comprehension Skill Instruction
- Reteaching Making Judgments with Reader's Library, *R10*
- Independent Application, *Practice Book, 313*

Reading the Health Link
- "¡Sabroso!, A Recipe from Gloria Estefan's Restaurant," *580–581*

Information and Study Skills Instruction
- Conduct an Interview, *581C*

Decoding Longer Words
- Reteaching Structural Analysis: Changing Final *y* to *i*, *R16*
- Challenge/Extension Activities, *R17*

Spelling
- *Practice Book, 317*

Vocabulary Skill Instruction
- Homophones, *581I*
- *Practice Book, 318*

 Daily Language Practice, *581L*

Grammar
- Reteaching, *R21*
- What's the Object?, *Practice Book, 320*

✏ **Writing**
- Sentence Combining with Pronouns, *581N*

Listening/Speaking/Viewing
- Listen for Different Purposes, *581O*

Day 5

Revisiting the Text: Comprehension Review Skill Instruction
- Text Organization, *563*
- Compare and Contrast, *567*

Rereading for Fluency
Gloria Estefan, 560–577

Activity Choices
- Responding Activities, *579*
- Challenge/Extension Activities, *R11*
- Cross-Curricular Activities, *R26*

Vocabulary Expansion
- Musical Instruments, *581J*

Spelling
- Posttest, *581H*

 Daily Language Practice, *581L*

Grammar
- Using the Correct Pronouns, *581L*
- *Practice Book, 321*

✏ **Writing**
- Using the Correct Pronouns, *581L*
- Writing Activities, *R23*
- Sharing Students' Writing: Author's Chair

✏ **Reading-Writing Workshop: Personal Essay**

Based on the **Student Writing Model** in the Anthology, this workshop guides students through the writing process and includes skill lessons on—

- Main Idea and Details   See Teacher's Edition, *pages 556–557G.*
- Introductions and Conclusions
- Pronoun Reference

Allow time every day for students to write independently on self-selected topics.

Reading Instruction

DAY 1	• Teacher Read Aloud • Preparing to Read • Reading the Selection, Segment 1
DAY 2	• Reading the Selection, Segment 2 • Responding
DAY 3	• Revisiting the Text • Comprehension Skill Instruction
DAY 4	• Comprehension Skill Reteaching • Reading the Content Link • Information and Study Skills Instruction
DAY 5	• Comprehension Skill Review • Activity Choices

OBJECTIVES

Students listen to the selection to make judgments about events and the characters' responses to events.

⏵ **Activate Prior Knowledge**

Connecting to the Theme Tell students that you will be reading aloud true stories about young people who were able to help out in emergency situations.

Help students connect the selection with what they know, using these suggestions:

■ Have students discuss different types of emergencies that could occur.

■ Ask students to describe any skills that might be necessary to help out in an emergency.

Teacher Read Aloud

Listening Comprehension:
 ## Making Judgments

Kids Did It! Real-Life Heroes

by Laura Daily

National Geographic World *published these true stories of young lifesavers.*

1 What kind of action does the situation require? (Sample answer: Someone needs to stop or steer the bus.)

2 Do you think Cindy did the right thing? Why or why not? (Yes, because the bus might have crashed; no, she might have caused further injury to herself or the driver.)

Steering to Safety

As Cindy Volpe of Vineland, New Jersey, rode to school with five other students, the bus suddenly swerved into oncoming traffic. The driver, Phil Leone, had passed out and was slumped over the steering wheel.

"I grabbed the steering wheel," Cindy **1** recalls. Though Cindy had never driven before, she managed to steer across three lanes onto the curb, just missing a telephone pole. The bus stopped but began rolling backward. Cindy opened the bus door and shouted to her schoolmates to get off. The bus seemed empty. But then Cindy realized that a five-year-old boy was still inside! "I jumped back on to get him," she says. Luckily the driver of a bus following Cindy's realized they were in trouble, stopped, and ran aboard to pull the emergency brake. No one was hurt, and Leone later recovered.

2 Cindy says she's not in a hurry to get her driver's license. "I'll stick to riding my bike for now," says the eighth-grader, "but I learned not to be scared in a difficult situation. If you have to do something that's right, just do it."

Super Strength

A family outing to a local swimming pond turned out to be no picnic for Erick Hill of Bucksport, Maine. To reach the pond, Erick's brother-in-law, Robert Field, drove Erick and two other relatives about two miles through the woods on an all-terrain vehicle (ATV).

Along the way the group had to cross a bridge over a small stream. Field worried that the old bridge wouldn't support the ATV so he decided to drive through the stream while the kids watched him. The far bank was steep and rocky. As Field tried to drive up the bank, the ATV flipped over backward into the stream, pinning him underwater.

"I knew Robert would drown if I didn't do something," remembers Erick, who waded into the water. Somehow Erick lifted the 900-pound ATV just enough so Field could slide out. He escaped with scrapes and bruises. "When I was lifting, I just kept saying to myself, 'I can do this, I can do this,' and I did," Erick says. For his heroic act, Erick was named the 1998 Youth Good Samaritan by his local American Red Cross.

3 Do you think Erick responded appropriately to the situation? Could he have responded differently?

(Sample answer: Yes, because he saved Robert's life; no, because he might have hurt himself. Erick could have asked the other relatives for help.)

Listening Comprehension: Making Judgments

Explain to students that making judgments involves thinking about what type of response is appropriate for a given situation. It also means deciding whether or not a character's actions are appropriate for the situation.

Use the questions in the margin to help assess students' understanding as you read. The questions can be used as places to stop and reread for clarification if necessary.

Teacher's Note

Tip for Read Alouds Review the story before reading to students. Look for places where you can use your voice to convey the danger and excitement of the events.

English Language Learners

Recall *brave* from *Finding the Titanic* to make sure students understand the meaning. English language learners may be unfamiliar with the following terms: *lifesaver, grabbed, recalls, waded, pinned, bank,* the acronyms *ATV* and *CPR,* and the idiomatic expression *to be no picnic.*

Reading

Twins Take Charge

First aid and emergency-rescue training helped Priscilla and Jeanette Adriano save a life. Both girls are members of Explorer Post 682 with the Gustine Police Department. They were on the way to a doctor's appointment near their home in Gustine, California, when they noticed an overturned truck in a canal. Their mother quickly pulled off the highway. The twins found the truck's driver, Jose Faria, pinned under the truck in the water. While nearby farmworkers lifted the truck with a tractor, Jeanette helped Faria's son Manuel, who had been in another truck, pull the injured man out of the water. "We could tell he wasn't breathing and was in shock," remembers Priscilla.

Teacher's Note

Vocabulary Point out to students that CPR (cardiopulmonary resuscitation) can help restore breathing and blood circulation after a person's heart has stopped beating. CPR involves giving mouth-to-mouth resuscitation and applying rhythmic pressure to the chest to get a heartbeat. First aid is any emergency treatment given to an ill or injured person before full medical care can be obtained.

4 Still chest-deep in the water, the twins leaned Faria against the bank and started CPR, or cardiopulmonary resuscitation. After a few breaths, Faria coughed and began breathing on his own. The girls stayed with him until paramedics arrived. Jeanette claims they "just happened to be in the right place at the right time." Both encourage other teens to take a first aid class. "You never know when you'll need it," says Jeanette.

4 What type of action would be appropriate in this situation?

(Sample answer: Call an ambulance, give first aid, and begin CPR.)

▶ **Discussion**

Summarize After reading, discuss the parts of the story that students found most interesting or exciting. Then, ask them to summarize the selection.

Listening Comprehension:
✓ **Making Judgments** Ask students to discuss the judgments that Cindy Volpe, Erick Hill, and the Adriano twins had to make in order to respond to the situations they found themselves in.

Personal Response Ask students to evaluate the personal characteristics of Cindy Volpe, Erick Hill, or the Adriano twins.

★ **Connecting/Comparing** Have students compare the actions of the people in this selection with the actions of someone like Dr. Martin Luther King, Jr. Ask them how both types of actions fit with the theme Heroes.

Reading

Anthology

REAL-LIFE READER BIOGRAPHY

GLORIA ESTEFAN

Grammy Award-Winning Recording Artist

Technology

Get Set for Reading CD-ROM

Gloria Estefan

Provides background building, vocabulary support, and selection summaries in English and Spanish.

Preparing to Read

▶ Using *Get Set* for Background and Vocabulary

Connecting to the Theme Remind students that the selections in this theme all deal with heroes. In the last selection, students read about Martin Luther King, Jr., a civil rights leader. Now they will read about Gloria Estefan, a famous singer whose acts of kindness have made her a hero to many people.

Discuss with students what it takes for someone become a world-famous performer. Use the Get Set to Read on pages 558–559 to give students some understanding about the path to fame.

- Have two students each read aloud one half of "Success in the Music Business."

- Ask students to examine the photographs and tell how each relates to the information in the text.

- Ask students to explain the meaning of the boldfaced Key Vocabulary words: *worldwide, tireless, career, eventually, demonstrated, contract,* and *specializes.* Have students use each word as they talk about the music business.

Get Set to Read

Gloria Estefan

Success in the Music Business

Have you ever wondered how your favorite music star achieved worldwide fame? Chances are the answer involves talent — and tireless, hard work. Many young musicians dream of a successful music career, but few actually reach that goal.

For many musicians, fame is earned slowly, one step at a time. Playing in a band might begin as only a hobby. Eventually, after much practice, the band might perform in front of audiences, slowly winning fans.

Singers rehearsing

A band performing in a concert

If a band has demonstrated enough determination and talent, it might earn a contract from a major recording company and make a CD. If enough people like a song from the recording, the song is a hit! The result could even be a gold record — and musical fame.

Now meet Gloria Estefan, a successful Cuban-American singer who specializes in blending different kinds of popular music into a style all her own.

Recording a song

The control room of a recording studio

558   559

English Language Learners

Have volunteers share what they know about Gloria Estefan. Ask students to assist by explaining *talent, ballads, pop songs, CD, hit, gold record.*

Key Concept
a career in music

Key Vocabulary
career: what someone does as a job

contract: a written agreement

demonstrated: showed clearly

eventually: at the end; finally

specializes: to be involved in a particular activity

tireless: able to work a long time without getting tired

worldwide: all over the world

See Vocabulary notes on pages 562, 564, 566, 570, and 574 for additional words to preview.

▶ Developing Key Vocabulary

Use **Transparency 5–9** to introduce Key Vocabulary from *Gloria Estefan*.

- Model how to use context clues in the sentence to figure out that *career* completes the first sentence.

- For each remaining blank have students look for clues to which Key Vocabulary word belongs there.

Remind students that it's helpful to use the Phonics/Decoding strategy when they read. For students who need more help with decoding, use the review below.

Practice/Homework Practice Book page 309.

STRATEGY REVIEW
Phonics/Decoding

Modeling Write this sentence from *Gloria Estefan* on the board, and point to *permanently*.

> *A few weeks after that, Emilio asked Gloria to join the band <u>permanently</u>.*

Think Aloud

The beginning of this word reminds me of the word person. It might sound like /pur/. Next I recognize the shorter word man. I think e-n-t might sound like /ehnt/ as in the word enter. And of course I know the -ly ending. If I blend all the sounds together, I'll say /pur•man•ehnt•lee/. Oh. It's /PUR•muh•nuhnt•lee/. That means forever. It makes sense that Emilio could have wanted Gloria to become a permanent member of the band.

 • Decoding Longer Words, pp. 607E–607F

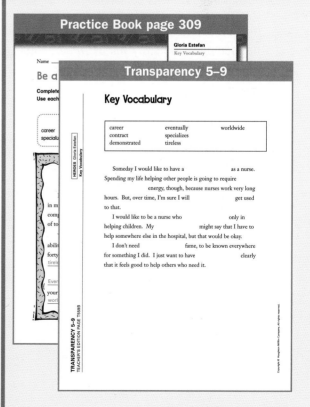

Practice Book page 309 / Transparency 5–9

Strategy/Skill Preview

▶ **Strategy Focus:**
Monitor/Clarify

Strategy Focus

As you read about Gloria Estefan's rise to musical fame, **monitor** your reading to make sure you follow the order of events. **Clarify** anything you don't understand.

Teacher's Note

Strategy/Skill Connection For a better understanding of *Gloria Estefan,* students can use the

- Monitor/Clarify Strategy
- Making Judgments Comprehension Skill

Making sure they are clear about what's happening in the story will allow students the ability to form thoughtful opinions about the selection.

As students complete their *Gloria Estefan* Judgments Chart (**Practice Book** page 310 and **Transparency 5–10**), they can test their answers to make a judgment about who heroes are.

Have students turn to page 560 and follow along as you read aloud the title and author of the story. Ask a student to read aloud the Strategy Focus. Then have students silently read the first paragraph of the story on page 561, telling them to pay attention to what they don't understand. Then model the strategy.

Teacher Modeling Tell students that to monitor, or check, their understanding of events or information, they can ask themselves questions as they read. Remind students that they can clarify any misunderstandings by rereading or reading ahead. Use the Think Aloud to show students what you mean.

Think Aloud

Wow, the first paragraph of the story gives a lot of information! I understood the first time I read it that Gloria was born in 1957 and has a younger sister. But if I reread I also learn that her sister's name is Becky, her mother was a kindergarten teacher, and her father was an officer in the army. By rereading I understand more about her family and the story takes on a deeper meaning.

Ask students to write in their journals information from this paragraph that they think they'll need to remember later in the story. Tell students that paying attention to details will help them monitor and clarify their understanding of the story as they read. Remind students to use these and their other reading strategies.

Comprehension Skill Focus:
Making Judgments

Judgments Chart Explain that as students read the selection they will focus on making judgments. That is, they will use facts presented in *Gloria Estefan* combined with personal knowledge to decide if Gloria is indeed a hero. To develop and practice the skill, students will complete a Judgments Chart. Display **Transparency 5–10** and demonstrate how to use this graphic organizer.

- Begin by having a student read aloud the third paragraph on page 562.

- Have another student read aloud the heading of the chart and offer the information from that paragraph that helps answer the question. (quickly learns English; is always at the head of her class)

- Model how to record this information in the chart and have students copy it onto **Practice Book** page 310.

- Tell students that they are to complete the chart as they read with the events that some people might use as examples of Gloria's being a hero. Tell students that their opportunity to judge whether they think famous people are heroes will come at the end of the story.

- Monitor their progress as they read, or have students check each other's charts.

Graphic Organizer: Judgments Chart

Why Might Someone Call Gloria Estefan a Hero?

Chapter One: Escaping with Music

(She quickly learns English.)

(She is allways at the head of her class.)

(She takes care of the family at the age eleven.)

(She teaches herself how to play an instrument.)

Chapter Two: Making Music with Emilio and Chapter Three: Changes

(She puts school first when offered a singing job.)

(She promises to finish college.)

(Her band becomes one of the most popular groups in Latin America.)

(Her band starts becoming popular all over the world.)

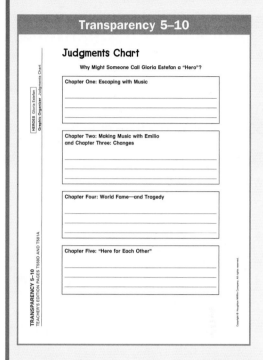

Transparency 5–10

Judgments Chart

Why Might Someone Call Gloria Estefan a "Hero"?

Chapter One: Escaping with Music

Chapter Two: Making Music with Emilio and Chapter Three: Changes

Chapter Four: World Fame—and Tragedy

Chapter Five: "Here for Each Other"

Practice Book page 310

Gloria Estefan
Graphic Organizer
Judgments Chart

Name _____

Judgments Chart

Why Might Someone Call Gloria Estefan a "Hero"?

Chapter One: Escaping with Music

She quickly learns English, and is always at the head of her class.
She takes care of the family at age eleven.
She teaches herself how to play an instrument. **(4 points)**

Chapter Two: Making Music with Emilio and Chapter Three: Changes

She puts school first when offered a singing job.
Her band becomes one of the most popular groups in Latin America.
Her band starts becoming popular all over the world. **(4)**

Chapter Four: World Fame—and Tragedy

The band sells millions of records.
She is honored by President Bush for her drug prevention work.
She recovers from a terrible bus accident. **(4)**

Chapter Five: "Here for Each Other"

She is given a Congressional Medal of Honor.
She helps hurricane victims and abused children.
She declines movie offers to be with her family. **(4)**

310   Theme 5: **Heroes**
Assessment Tip: Total 16 Points

Beginning of Segment 1: *pages 560–566*

Selection 2

Options for Reading

▶ **Reading in Segments** Students can read *Gloria Estefan* in two segments (pages 560–566 and 567–576) or in its entirety.

▶ **Deciding About Support** Students will enjoy this lively story about a talented, courageous, and interesting music star.

■ Because of the familiar genre (biography) and chronological organization, most students should be able to follow On Level reading instruction.

■ Students who have difficulty assimilating factual details may need Extra Support.

■ Significantly below-level readers can listen to the Audiotape and read the Selection Summary for *Gloria Estefan* and then read "Duke Ellington: A Life in Music" in the **Reader's Library.**

▶ **Meeting Individual Needs** Use the notes at the bottom of the pages.

REAL-LIFE READER BIOGRAPHY

GLORIA ESTEFAN

Grammy Award–Winning Recording Artist

Strategy Focus

As you read about Gloria Estefan's rise to musical fame, **monitor** your reading to make sure you follow the order of events. **Clarify** anything you don't understand.

560

Classroom Management

On Level
Reading Card 4

While Reading: Judgments Chart (**Practice Book** page 310); Literature Discussion (p. 564, Reading Card 4); generate questions

After Reading: Literature Discussion (page 576); Wrapping Up Segment 1 (page 565) and Segment 2 (page 577)

Challenge
Reading Cards 4–6

While Reading: Judgments Chart (**Practice Book** p. 310); Literature Discussion (p. 564, Card 4); Point of View (p. 571, Card 5); Multiple Meanings (p. 575, Card 6)

After Reading: Literature Discussion (p. 576); Wrapping Up Segment 1 (p. 565) and Segment 2 (p. 577)

English Language Learners

Intermediate and Advanced Fluency Have students read with an English-speaking partner who can assist with cultural references and idiomatic expressions. For English language learners at other proficiency levels, see **Language Development Resources.**

Reading Segment 1

pages 560–565

Purpose Setting As students read have them monitor their understanding of the events in Gloria Estefan's life. If necessary they should reread portions of the selection to clarify any confusion.

Journal Writing Students can use their journal to record any information, facts, and dates that help in understanding the selection.

Reinforcing Comprehension and Strategies

■ Remind students to use Monitor/Clarify and other strategies as they read and to add to their Judgments Charts (**Practice Book** page 310).

■ Use the Strategy Focus notes on pages 564 and 568 to reinforce the Monitor/Clarify strategy.

■ Use Supporting Comprehension questions beginning on page 562 to help students develop higher-level understanding of the text.

CHAPTER 1
Escaping with Music

Gloria Estefan was born Gloria Maria Fajardo [fa-HAR-doe] on September 1, 1957. She was the first child born to Gloria and José [hoe-SAY] Manuel Fajardo. She has a younger sister, Rebecca (Becky). For about the first year and a half of her life, Gloria lived with her family in Havana, Cuba. Her mother taught kindergarten there. Her father was an officer in the Cuban army.

In 1959, however, a war began in Cuba, and many Cubans fled to the United States for safety. These people were called refugees. The Fajardos were among the refugees. By the time Gloria was two years old, José Fajardo had settled the family in Miami, Florida. He then went back to Cuba to fight against Fidel Castro, who had taken control of the government.

561

Extra Support: Previewing the Text

Before each segment, preview the text, using the notes below and on page 566. **While** reading, model strategies (pp. 563 and 569). **After** reading, review each segment (pp. 564 and 575) before students join the Wrapping Up discussion.

page 561 As a child, Gloria Estefan and her family moved from Cuba to the United States. How do you think they felt leaving their homeland?

pages 562–563 Gloria's family settles in Miami, Florida. How can you tell that Miami might be a good place for newcomers from Cuba?

pages 564–566 An important turning point in Gloria's life occurs—she joins Emilio Estefan's band.

Reading

► Supporting Comprehension

1 Why does the author give so much information about José Fajardo and his illness in this biography of his daughter, Gloria Estefan? (to show the great responsibilities she had at a young age and how they might have played a role in the adult she became)

2 What does Gloria mean when she says that her father's mind "went before his body"? (Mr. Fajardo lost his awareness of the people and world around him, yet he could still do physical things such as eat and drink.)

3 How did music help Gloria when her father was ill? (Music was a way to briefly escape from the reality of her father's illness and her heavy responsibilities at home.)

Vocabulary (pages 562–563)

duty: serving in the Army, for example

nerves: parts of the body that control your muscles

ballads: songs about love

A street scene (left) and a festival (above) in a Cuban American neighborhood in Miami

Other Cuban men in Florida had also gone back to Cuba to fight. Many, including José, were captured and kept in a Cuban prison for nearly two years. Gloria and her mother were alone in the United States. The U.S. government tried to help get the prisoners back to the United States. Finally, just a few days before Christmas in 1962, José Fajardo was freed. He returned to Miami.

Life in the United States wasn't easy for the family. The Fajardos spoke only Spanish. Many Americans didn't want Cuban refugees in the United States. They treated the refugees badly.

But Gloria was determined to succeed. At school she quickly learned English and caught up with the other children. She was always at the head of her class, even when her home life became very difficult.

When Gloria's father came back from Cuba, he joined the U.S. Army. In 1966, when war began between the United States and Vietnam, José Fajardo volunteered for duty. He served in Vietnam for two years.

562

 English Language Learners

As you read, pause and use a map to help students locate all of the places mentioned in the selection: Havana, Cuba; Miami, Florida; Vietnam; Syracuse, New York; Scranton, Pennsylvania; and New York City.

Gloria was ten when her father came home. The girls and their mother knew something was wrong with him. Even though he had not been hurt in the fighting, Gloria says, "He'd fall for no reason."

Her father was told he had multiple sclerosis. This disease can cause many kinds of problems because it attacks the nerves. In just a few months, her father could not walk. Mrs. Fajardo went back to work to support the family. She also went back to college and got an American teaching degree. Then she taught public school in Miami.

Gloria helped out at home as much as she could. She became a little mother to her family. From the age of 11 until she was 16, Gloria took care of her sister, Becky, and her father. **1**

José Fajardo needed constant care. "It was around the clock," says Gloria. "It wasn't easy. His mind went before his body. There were times when he wasn't aware of who I was, or who any of us were. It was very hard." **2**

During those years, music became very important to Gloria. She remembers, "When my father was ill, music was my escape. I'd lock myself up in my room with my guitar."

In her room, Gloria would listen to music for hours and hours. She loved to sing along with the ballads and pop songs. She learned to play the guitar. Soon she could play along with her favorite songs. **3**

Gloria and her mother in a recent photograph

563

Extra Support

Strategy Modeling

Monitor/Clarify Use this example to model the strategy.

When I first read page 562, I thought that Gloria's father returned to Cuba a second time to fight. It doesn't make sense to me that Mr. Fajardo would return to fight in Cuba, having been imprisoned there for nearly two years. To check my understanding, I reread the page slowly and carefully. This time I see that in 1966 Mr. Fajardo fought not in Cuba but in Vietnam.

Revisiting the Text

Review/Maintain

Comprehension Skill Lesson
Text Organization

OBJECTIVES

Students

- identify how the text is organized
- identify the purpose of various features

Survey with students the selection title, chapter titles, photos, captions, and the key (underlined) words. Ask students to think about what purpose each feature serves.

Point out that the title of the first chapter is "Escaping with Music." This chapter introduces one of the selection's main ideas—that music has given Gloria not only a profession but also a source of personal strength. The word *escaping* in the chapter title helps the reader predict that the chapter will discuss unpleasant experiences from which Gloria needed to escape.

Help students identify examples of text features and their purpose as they complete the chart.

Feature	Example	Purpose
Selection Title		
Chapter Titles	"Escaping with music"	predicts what she escapes from
Quotations		
Photos		
Captions		
Key Words		

Skill Finder

- **Instruction,** Theme 1, pp. 107A–107B
- **Reteaching,** Theme 1, p. R14

▶ ## Strategy Focus: Monitor/Clarify

Teacher/Student Modeling Remind students to use Monitor/Clarify while they read.

▶ ## Supporting Comprehension

4 What pros and cons probably occurred to Gloria about whether to join Emilio's band? (Pros: make money; become famous. Cons: might not finish college; might not fit in with the band.)

5 How did the role of music in Gloria's life change after she joined Emilio's band? (Before, Gloria sang mostly for fun; after, Gloria earned money and realized that music was her life's calling.)

Vocabulary (pages 564–565)

rehearsals: times to practice

scholarship: money given to a student to attend college

career: what someone does as a job

calling: the work someone was meant to do

CHAPTER 2
Making Music with Emilio

Music became more and more important to Gloria as she went through her teen years. During her senior year in high school, she and some friends put together a band to play for a party.

The father of another band member knew Emilio Estefan, a popular band leader in Miami. The father invited Emilio to one of the girls' rehearsals, to give the girls a few tips.

Gloria met Emilio again three months after the first meeting. She says, "My mother dragged me to this wedding that I really didn't want to go to, and Emilio's band was playing. Emilio remembered me and asked me to sing a song with the band." A few weeks after that, Emilio asked Gloria to join the band permanently.

At first, Gloria said no. She had just begun classes at the University of Miami. Because her high school grades were so good — she made honor roll every semester — Gloria had received a scholarship.

564

Extra Support

Segment 1: Review

Before students join the whole class for Wrapping Up on page 565, have them

- review their purpose

- take turns modeling Monitor/Clarify and other strategies they used

- help you add to **Transparency 5–10,** check and revise their Judgments Chart on **Practice Book** page 310, and use it to summarize

On Level   Challenge

Reading Card 4

Literature Discussion

In mixed-ability groups of five or six, students can discuss their own questions and the discussion prompts on Reading Card 4.

- What were some challenges that Gloria's parents faced when Gloria was a child? What were some challenges that Gloria faced growing up in her family?

- Do you think that Gloria enjoyed middle school and high school? Why or why not?

She had never thought about joining a band or following a full-time musical career. Of course, she loved music and liked to sing, but mostly for fun. She worried that if she joined Emilio's band, she would not have enough time for her studies. Gloria's mother worried, too.

But Emilio promised Gloria that she would perform only on weekends and vacations. Her mother agreed that Gloria could sing, but only if Gloria agreed to finish college. Gloria promised, then accepted Emilio's offer. "I loved music so much that I couldn't let a great opportunity like this pass me by," she says.

4

With Gloria as lead singer, the band had a better, different, very special sound. Soon, Emilio changed the band's name from the Miami Latin Boys to Miami Sound Machine. "All of a sudden," Gloria says, "I was going to parties every weekend, singing with the whole band behind me." She loved to perform and came to realize that music was her calling.

5

Gloria performing with the band

End of Segment 1:
pages 560–565

Wrapping Up Segment 1

pages 560–565

First, provide Extra Support for students who need it (page 564). Then bring all students together.

- **Review Predictions/Purpose** Discuss ways students monitored their reading and clarified confusing parts.

- **Model Strategies** Refer students to the **Strategies Poster** and have them take turns modeling Monitor/Clarify and other strategies they used as they read. Provide models if needed (p. 563).

- **Share Group Discussions** Have students share their questions and literature discussions.

- **Summarize** Help students use the transparency and their Judgments Chart to summarize what has happened in Gloria's life so far.

Comprehension/Critical Thinking

1 Why did Gloria's family leave Cuba and settle in the United States? (They did not want to be a part of a government run by Fidel Castro, who had taken over the country.) **Drawing Conclusions**

2 Based on Gloria's experience, how do you think it feels to have an escape, such as music, when life is filled with challenges? (It is important to have a way to escape and refresh yourself when life gets tough at times.) **Making Generalizations**

English Language Learners

English language learners may identify closely with the difficulties Gloria and her family faced when they first moved to Miami. Use Gloria's success as an example of the potential of a non-native English speaker's ability to accomplish great things in the United States. Have a class discussion on the idea, and encourage all students to give their opinions and observations.

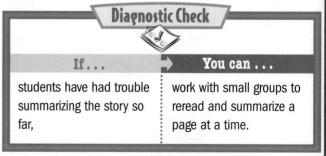

Diagnostic Check

If . . .	You can . . .
students have had trouble summarizing the story so far,	work with small groups to reread and summarize a page at a time.

Reading Segment 2

pages 566–576

Purpose Setting Have students summarize the biography so far and continue to monitor and clarify their reading during Segment 2.

 Journal Writing Students can record any important events or turning points that aid in their understanding of the biography.

> ### Vocabulary *(pages 566–567)*
> **director:** person in charge of
>
> **marketing:** part of a company that deals with selling and advertising
>
> **veteran:** someone who served in the Army, for example

Through their music, Gloria and Emilio got to know each other. Like the Fajardos, Emilio and his family had come from Cuba. Like many Cuban refugees, they had settled in Miami. They were very poor when they arrived in the United States, so Emilio worked at many jobs to help support the family. By the time he met Gloria, Emilio was the director of marketing at a Miami company.

But Emilio's real passion was music, and his part-time band was one of the most popular dance bands in Miami. By the time Gloria joined the band, Emilio had long been thinking about quitting his job and working with his band full time.

Gloria sang with the band for a year and a half before Emilio asked her out. They fell in love, dating steadily during Gloria's last two years at the university. In May 1978, Gloria graduated from college. Three months later, on September 1, 1978, she married Emilio.

Gloria and Emilio Estefan

566

 Extra Support: Previewing the Text

Before reading Segment 2, preview the text, using the notes below. **While** reading, model strategies (p. 569). **After** reading, review the segment (p. 575) before students join the Wrapping Up discussion.

pages 567–569 Changes occur in Gloria's life both personally and professionally. What do you think they might be?

pages 570–573 Who is the man pictured with Gloria, Emilio, and Nayib on page 571? How do you think the Estefan family happened to meet this man?

pages 574–576 Read the title to chapter 5 and look at the photos on pages 574–576. What do you think the title means in Gloria's life?

Gloria Estefan

CHAPTER 3
Changes

After their marriage, Gloria and Emilio began a long, hard job — getting the band known all over the world. The Miami Sound Machine's first album, *Renacer* (1978), was a collection of disco, pop, and original ballads sung in Spanish. During the next two years, the band released two more albums. All the albums sold well in Miami, but they didn't get much attention anywhere else.

In 1980, two changes took place in Gloria's family. Her father died after twelve years of crippling illness. He had been in a Veteran's Administration Hospital since 1975. His long illness had brought the family much grief. Gloria says, "It just gets to the point where you pray that the suffering will end, because you can't imagine why anyone has to go through something like that."

That same year, though, Gloria and Emilio's first child was born, bringing much joy and happiness to the family. The couple named the boy Nayib. They decided at once that their son was the most important thing in their lives.

567

MEETING INDIVIDUAL NEEDS
English Language Learners

Summarizing

Have students pause at the end of page 566 and summarize what has happened so far. Guide the discussion with questions such as: *Where was Gloria's family from? Why did they leave Cuba? Where did they move to in the United States? What happened to Gloria's father? When did Gloria start singing?*

Comprehension Skill Lesson
Compare and Contrast

OBJECTIVES

Students compare and contrast the two main characters in the selection.

Explain to students that when they think about how two or more things are alike, they are comparing them. Contrasting is thinking of how things are different. Explain that identifying similarities and differences helps readers

■ understand the characters and events in a story

■ become more involved in a story

■ relate a story to their own lives

Point out that page 566 outlines similar and different experiences that Gloria and Emilio had. Draw two intersecting circles (a Venn diagram) on the board. Write *Gloria* over the left circle and *Emilio* over the right one. Have students list differences between Gloria and Emilio, at the time when they met, in the outside parts of the circles. Have students list in the center of the diagram similarities between Gloria and Emilio.

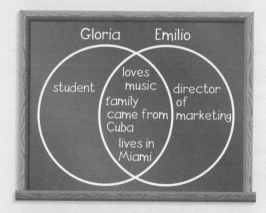

Skill Finder

• **Instruction,** Theme 3, pp. 357A–357B

• **Reteaching,** Theme 3, p. R10

• **Review,** Th. 2, p. 193; Th. 3, p. 369; Th. 4, p. 495

▶ Strategy Focus: Monitor/Clarify

Student Modeling Ask students to clarify the significance of Gloria and the Miami Sound Machine's growing popularity among English-speaking listeners. If necessary, use the following prompt:

Why, in their contract with CBS, did the band keep the right to record in English?

▶ Supporting Comprehension

6 Why do you think the author includes so many of Gloria's own words in the biography?
(to make the biography more interesting; to show that a reliable source of the selection's information is Gloria Estefan herself)

7 What are some important decisions and events that led to Gloria and the Miami Sound Machine's achieving worldwide fame?
(the band's keeping the right to record in English; recording some very popular albums and songs in English)

Vocabulary *(page 568)*

contract: a written agreement

specializes: to be involved in a particular activity

eventually: at the end; finally

worldwide: all over the world

Not long after Nayib was born, Emilio quit his full-time job. He wanted to give all of his attention to making a success of Gloria and the Miami Sound Machine.

Soon the group signed a contract with Discos CBS International, the Miami-based Hispanic division of CBS Records. Discos CBS International specializes in Latin music. Company officials decided that the Miami Sound Machine should release albums only in Spanish. The band's recordings would be sold in the Latin American countries, where the people speak mostly Spanish.

6 Gloria explains, "CBS thought we would sell better in Latin America if we sang in Spanish. But we kept the right to record in English, because eventually we wanted to try for the States."

During the next several years, Miami Sound Machine recorded four Spanish-language albums. From those albums came a dozen songs that became worldwide hits. By 1984, Miami Sound Machine was one of the most popular recording groups in Latin America. And — even better — Gloria Estefan and the Miami Sound Machine were becoming popular all over the world.

The Miami Sound Machine in concert

568

 Extra Support

Strategy Modeling

Monitor/Clarify Use this example to model the strategy.

When I first read the paragraph about "Dr. Beat," I didn't see why the author made such a big deal about the song. Then I reread and noticed that "Dr. Beat" was the band's first hit in English. Rereading helps me understand why the author gives so much space on a page to one song. Scoring a hit in English-speaking America was a big break for the Miami Sound Machine.

CHAPTER 4
World Fame and Tragedy

Throughout the rest of the 1980s, Gloria and the Miami Sound Machine recorded song after song. Each was a bigger success than the one before. During those years, too, the group began to record English-language songs.

The string of hits began with "Dr. Beat" (1984), a Latin-style dance song that the group recorded in English. "Dr. Beat" was on the record's B side, the side that usually gets no air time on the radio. But it wasn't long before "Dr. Beat" could be heard on many Miami radio stations, both Spanish- and English-language. When CBS released it nationally as a dance single, it zoomed to number ten on the dance charts.

In 1984 the group also recorded the album *Eyes of Innocence*; *Primitive Love* came out the next year. These two albums made Gloria and the Miami Sound Machine a success all over English-speaking America. In fact, "Conga," a single from *Primitive Love*,

7

569

English Language Learners

English language learners will need explanation of the many entertainment-industry terms used throughout the selection. Allow English-speaking students the opportunity to describe such terms as often as possible. Examples include: *dance charts* (page 569), *American pop charts* and *Billboard magazine* (page 570), *American Music Awards* and *Grammy Awards* (page 571).

Revisiting the Text

Writer's Craft Lesson
Sequence Words and Phrases
OBJECTIVES

Students

- identify words and phrases that signal the order in which events happen
- describe sequences of events signaled by these words and phrases

Explain that writers use signal words, such as *now* and *at the same time,* to describe two or more events that happen simultaneously. Writers use other signal words, such as *before* and *after,* to tell when one event occurs in relation to another. Writers also use dates to order events in a story.

Model by reading aloud the following from page 568: *Not long after Nayib was born, Emilio quit his full-time job. He wanted to give all of his attention to making a success of Gloria and the Miami Sound Machine.*

Point out that the phrase *not long after* help readers order two events: Nayib's birth and Emilio's devoting himself full-time to the band. Then have students identify additional words and phrases on pages 568 and 569 that help them determine the order in which events occurred. (*eventually, By 1984, Throughout the rest of the 1980s, During those years*)

Ask students to find additional examples on previous pages of words and phrases that signal the order of events. Have students describe the order of events that these signal words or phrases clarify.

Reading

▶ Supporting Comprehension

8 How has the author prepared you to understand the Cuban government's protest over the performance by Gloria and the Miami Sound Machine at the Pan American games? (The author explains earlier that Gloria's and Emilio's families left Cuba to escape from the government.)

9 Why do you think the author interweaves three stories—that of Gloria, her family, and the band? (because they are three main parts of Gloria's life)

10 How do you think Nayib felt when he visited the White House? (excited; nervous; very proud of his parents)

Vocabulary (pages 570–571)

demonstrated: showed clearly

prevention: stopping someone from doing something

tragedy: disaster

---

went to number two on the American pop charts. The song also made *Billboard*'s dance, Latin, and Black charts — the first song in American music history to appear on four charts at the same time.

Let It Loose (1987) stayed on the pop charts for more than two years. The album sold three million copies in the United States alone, and it produced four top ten hits. The group performed at the closing of the 1987 Pan American games — even though the Cuban government protested because it wanted a Latin-American band to play. And, in 1989, *Cuts Both Ways* demonstrated Gloria's talent as a songwriter. The album contained ten of the many songs she had written during a 20-month tour.

8

Gloria receiving flowers from a fan

570

MEETING INDIVIDUAL NEEDS

Challenge

Reading Card 5

Point of View

The story is told from the third-person point of view. A narrator outside the action describes the important events and people in Gloria's life. Have students discuss how the story might be different if it were told from the first-person point of view. If Gloria herself described all the important events and people in her life,

- Would the reader feel closer or farther away from events in the story?

- Would the reader trust the information in the story more or less?

The Estefan family meeting with President George Bush at the White House

The early months of 1990 carried on the streak of success. Gloria and the band performed at the American Music Awards and the Grammy Awards ceremonies. From CBS, they received the Crystal Globe award, a prize that goes to performers who sell more than 5 million records outside their own country. Gloria met President George Bush at the White House, where he honored her for her drug prevention work with teenagers. Life shined brightly for Gloria, her family, and the band.

9

10

But on March 20 — the day after she visited the White House — tragedy struck.

571

Reading Fluency

- **Rereading for Fluency:** Have students choose a favorite part of the story to reread to a partner, or suggest that they read page 571 through the last complete paragraph. Encourage students to read with feeling and expression.

- **Assessing Fluency:** See guidelines in the Theme Assessment Wrap-Up, pages 608–609A.

▶ Supporting Comprehension

11 What does Gloria mean when she says *I was forced to really keep a lot of control because I didn't want him* [Nayib] *to feel that we had lost that grip for him, so he helped me hang on?* (Her love for Nayib and desire to protect him made Gloria not tell how much pain she was in.)

12 What does the author mean when she makes a contrast between a completely successful operation and a complete recovery? (The success of the operation was quickly achieved, but recovery from the accident, and the surgery, took a long time.)

13 How does the author show that Gloria's fans not only liked her music but also cared about her? (by the thousands of cards that they sent, which brought good wishes and support to Gloria)

Vocabulary *(pages 572–573)*

tractor trailer: a big truck

jackknifed: folded in two

collarbone: a bone in your shoulder

paralyzed: not able to walk

therapy: working with a doctor to get well

Headed for their next concert in Syracuse, New York, Gloria, Emilio, and Nayib were traveling through a snowstorm. Near the Pennsylvania-New York state line, a tractor trailer had jackknifed across the road and was blocking traffic. As Gloria's tour bus came to a stop, it was hit from behind. The tour bus was pushed into a truck that was stopped ahead of it on the road. The front of the bus caved in, and all three family members were thrown to the bus floor.

Emilio was not seriously hurt. He found Nayib lying under a mountain of purses, books, and bags with a broken collarbone.

Gloria was relieved that her husband and son were alive. But she was in terrible pain. She had been thrown from the couch on which she had been lying, and she could not move. For more than an hour, Gloria sat waiting for a police helicopter. She didn't want Nayib to know how much pain she was in. "I was forced to really keep a lot of control," Gloria remembers, "because I didn't want him to feel that we had lost that grip for him, so he helped me hang on."

11

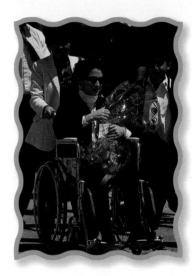

On the road to recovery

572

Gloria's first performance after the bus accident

When Gloria finally arrived at the hospital in Scranton, the doctors told her what she had suspected: her back was broken. Gloria thought her career as a performer was over.

Flown to the Hospital for Joint Diseases in New York City, she underwent a new and very risky kind of surgery on March 23. If the operation failed, she would be paralyzed forever.

The operation was a complete success. However, complete recovery was another matter. It took many months of rest and therapy. **12**

Thousands of cards and letters from fans all over the country brought good wishes and support to Gloria. That support helped her through the long months of recovery. By January 1991, Gloria was performing again. **13**

573

Revisiting the Text

Visual Literacy Lesson
Photography

OBJECTIVES

Students compare the impact on the reader of a photograph and of the corresponding text.

Remind students that photographs can

- give information

- show what the writer tells

- make a selection easier to understand

Point out that the photograph on page 572 helps the reader pause and take in the impact of Gloria's accident on her life. The photo of Gloria using a wheelchair helps readers understand the writer's observation on page 573 that complete recovery would take months.

Ask students to discuss the impact of the photograph on page 572 compared to the words. (The photograph makes the accident real and makes the reader feel sad, while the words describe the accident but allow the reader to keep it at a distance.)

In contrast ask students to discuss the impact of the photo on page 573 showing Gloria performing again.

MEETING INDIVIDUAL NEEDS

Extra Support

Strategy Modeling

Phonics/Decoding Use this example to model the strategy.

When I look carefully at the word recovery, *I see the prefix* re-, *the shorter word* cover, *and the* y *ending which probably makes the* /ee/ *sound like in the word* happy. /ree•cuhv•ur•ee/ *I've heard the word before. I think if someone recovers from being sick it means they get better. It makes sense that it could take months for Gloria to get completely better.*

▶ Supporting Comprehension

14 Why do you think that Gloria is most proud of her Ellis Island Congressional Medal of Honor? (because it means so much to her to be an American, and to represent all Americans when she travels)

15 Do you think that people in Miami are correct that Gloria is a *star with a heart*? (Yes, because Gloria uses her recording celebrity to help the less fortunate.)

16 What is the author's attitude toward people giving something back to their communities? How can you tell? (The author admires them. It's apparent in the author's description of the many ways Gloria helps others.)

Vocabulary *(pages 574–575)*

Congressional: having to do with the U.S. Congress, a part of the government

passionate: eager

tireless: able to work a long time without stopping

CHAPTER 5
"Here for Each Other"

Since the accident, Gloria has had many more successes. She and the Miami Sound Machine keep turning out hit albums. They perform for world leaders and at important events. And Gloria keeps piling up honors and awards. She is most proud of her Ellis Island **14** Congressional Medal of Honor. The medal makes her a representative for all Americans when she travels. She also represents the millions of Hispanics who, like her family, make their homes in the United States.

In 1994, there was more good news for Gloria and Emilio. They became parents again when Emily Marie Estefan Fajardo was born on December 5. Emily was a dream come true for the Estefans. Before the bus accident, they had talked about another baby. But,

574

Cross-Curricular Connection

Social Studies Ellis Island was the first taste of America for approximately 13 million immigrants who entered the United States from the 1890s to the mid 1950s. It is located in New York Harbor and was a symbol of hope for immigrants from around the world. Many immigrants spent their life savings to get to Ellis Island and they often arrived with everything they owned. Today over 100 million living Americans can trace their roots back to a relative who came through Ellis Island.

 English Language Learners

Have students describe orally the many ways Gloria has helped people throughout her life. List these examples on the board. Then ask volunteers to describe why Gloria Estefan is considered a hero.

Damage caused by Hurricane Andrew (above). Gloria viewing the damage with the National Guard (right).

after the accident, no one was sure that Gloria would be able to have another child.

Gloria is also a passionate, tireless worker for those with troubles. People throughout Miami call her "a star with a heart." When Hurricane Andrew roared through Miami, she wrote and recorded the song "Always Tomorrow." The song brought nearly $3 million to Gloria and Emilio — all of which they gave to the people who lost their homes and loved ones to Hurricane Andrew.

For many years, Gloria has also worked hard to help battered and abused children in Miami. "I've seen things that have ruined the lives of children," she says.

15

16

575

Challenge

Reading Card 6

Multiple Meanings

Over time, many words acquire more than one meaning. Readers can be delighted—or confused—by multiple-meaning words. For example:

- On page 574, Gloria is pictured near one star shape on the ground and another star shape on a plaque that she is holding.

- On page 575, Gloria is described as a *"star [celebrity] with a heart."*

Have students find other multiple meaning words from the story. Have them list and write two definitions for each word.

• SELECTION •

Gloria Estefan

Revisiting the Text

Tested Skill

Comprehension Skill Lesson
Making Judgments

OBJECTIVES

Students make judgments about the author's viewpoint.

Explain to students that they can form opinions about an author's viewpoint by looking at specific details and using their own knowledge as they read. Have students reread pages 574 and 575 to decide what the author's viewpoint is toward how Gloria has spent her time since the accident. Make a list on the board.

Information Author Gives
- made hit albums
- performed for world leaders
- performed at important events
- gave birth to a daughter
- gave money from song to hurricane victims
- worked to help battered and abused children

■ Have students discuss the author's point of view toward the information that she gives. Elicit that the author, like the people of Miami, sees Gloria Estefan as a *star with a heart*.

■ Through class discussion, lead students to make a judgment about the author's viewpoint. Do they think that the author sees Gloria Estefan clearly? Does she present both Gloria's strengths and weaknesses?

■ Have students give evidence from the selection to support their opinions.

• **Instruction,** page 581

• **Reteaching,** page R10

• **Review,** Th. 2, p. 173; Th. 4, p. 497; Th. 5, p. 593

Reading the Selection 575

▶ Supporting Comprehension

17 Does the world need more Gloria Estefans, as Laurie Kay suggests? Why or why not? (Yes, because Gloria is so generous, and there are so many people in need; no, because each person has his or her own gift to give the world.)

18 What evidence does the author give to show that Gloria really believes *We're here for each other*? (The author describes many ways in which Gloria has used her fame to help others.)

19 Has the author told the story of Gloria Estefan's life in an interesting way? What, if any, suggestions would you give the author for a revision? (Answers will vary.)

---

17 "The children in our care are fortunate that Gloria and Emilio have both given so much of themselves," says Dr. Mary Louise Cole of the Children's Home Society of Florida. Laurie Kay, the Society's Director of Development, gives Gloria credit for the very existence of Children's Home Society. "Gloria and her husband have done wonders for us," she says. "I wish there were more Gloria Estefans."

To be with her own children, Gloria has turned down several offers for movie roles. "Right now, I just want to concentrate on my children and watch them grow up into happy, healthy adults," she states. She tries to see to it that their home on one of Miami Beach's islands is always filled with fun and friends.

18 Gloria is ever thankful she was able to recover from her accident and return to the performing she loves. "I was always a thankful person," she says, "because I did go through some difficult things, but you tend to forget and get caught up in petty stuff. The bottom line is that we're here for each other."

19

A benefit concert for the American Cancer Society (right)

The Estefan family "here for each other" (left)

576

Extra Support

Segment 2 Review

Before students join in Wrapping Up on page 557, have them

- review their purpose
- take turns modeling the reading strategies they used
- help you complete **Transparency 5–10**
- summarize the whole story

On Level   Challenge

Literature Discussion

Have small groups of students discuss the story, using their own questions, the questions in Think About the Selection on page 578, or the discussion prompts on Reading Card 4.

MEET THE AUTHOR

Sue Boulais says that it is her curiosity that has kept her writing for twenty-five years. "I want to know why and what kind and how much and who," she says. "Writing gives me an opportunity and a direction in which to explore a subject. . . . Writing also lets me share what I learn with others."

Boulais's first writing job was for the *Weekly Reader* school newspaper. Since then, she has published many books, articles, puzzles, and games. She says she was very pleased to have a chance to write about Gloria Estefan.

"The more I read and learned about her, the more I respected her," says Boulais. "She uses her talent well; she works very hard to be a great singer. I especially respected her determination to get well after her accident. She didn't cry or feel sorry for herself or make a lot of excuses — she used all her energy to do what she had to do to get her body well."

Other books: *Famous Astronauts* and *Hispanic American Achievers*

Internet

To learn more about Sue Boulais, log on to Education Place. **www.eduplace.com/kids**

End of Segment 2:
pages 567–576

Wrapping Up Segment 2
pages 567–576

First, provide Extra Support for students who need it (p. 576). Then bring all students together.

- **Review Predictions/Purpose** Discuss ways students monitored their reading and clarified confusing parts.

- **Model Strategies** Have students tell how they used the Monitor/Clarify strategy, and then have them take turns modeling it. Ask what other strategies they found helpful while reading.

- **Share Group Discussions** Have students share their reactions to how Gloria has handled opportunities and challenges in her life.

- **Summarize** Help students use their Judgments Chart to recall important parts of Gloria's life and what judgments they made about them.

Comprehension/Critical Thinking

1. Does the author give facts, opinions, or both facts and opinions about Gloria Estefan? Give examples to support your answer. (Both. That Gloria's son, Nayib, was born in 1980 is a fact. That *life shined brightly for Gloria and her band* is an opinion.) **Fact and Opinion**

2. How do you think Gloria Estefan feels about her life? (pleased and grateful) **Making Inferences**

Diagnostic Check

If . . .	You can . . .
students express enjoyment of the genre,	refer them to biographies of other women and men who might be considered heroes.

Responding

....

▶ Think About the Selection

Discuss or Write Have students discuss or write their answers. Sample answers are provided; accept reasonable responses that are supported with evidence from the story.

1 **Making Inferences** Music was her escape from the sadness of her father's illness and she loves to sing.

2 **Making Judgments** Possible answer: Yes, because Gloria is a great singer and she adds a special sound and style to the band. Emilio writes and arranges great songs for the band.

3 **Drawing Conclusions** It had never been done before and each chart appeals to a different group of people.

4 **Making Inferences** She is strong-willed, determined, and a positive thinker.

5 **Making Judgments** Answers will vary.

6 **Connecting/Comparing** Making Generalizations
Gloria Estefan is a hero to her family because she always puts them first even since she was young. She is a hero to the public because she raises money for worthy causes and is a positive role model.

Responding

Think About the Selection

1. Why do you think Gloria Estefan enjoyed music so much while she was growing up?

2. Do you think Gloria and Emilio Estefan make a good musical team? Explain.

3. Why was it such a great achievement for Gloria Estefan's song "Conga" to appear on four different music charts at the same time?

4. What do you learn about Gloria Estefan's personality from the way she recovered from her accident?

5. Would you enjoy having the kind of fame that Gloria Estefan has achieved? Why or why not?

6. **Connecting/Comparing** What qualities and accomplishments make Gloria Estefan a hero?

Write a Book Jacket Summary

Many book jackets present highlights of the story to tempt people to buy and read the book. Write a summary of Sue Boulais's book *Gloria Estefan* that could be printed on its jacket. Tell the most important events.

Tips
- Look at book jackets for models of story summaries.
- To get started, list the main events. Then circle the most important and interesting ones.
- Follow the sequence of events in the book.

578

 English Language Learners

Beginning/Preproduction Help students create a word web of words to describe Gloria and her life.

Early Production and Speech Emergence Ask students to give examples of the ways music has always been a part of Gloria's life.

Intermediate and Advanced Fluency Ask partners to find examples of the ways Gloria Estefan combines her music career with her family.

Personal Response

Invite volunteers to share their personal responses to *Gloria Estefan*. As an alternative, ask students to write in their journals about another well-known person who serves as a role model.

 ## Comprehension Check

Assign **Practice Book** page 311 to assess students' understanding of the selection.

Practice Book page 311

Gloria Estefan
Comprehension Check

Name _____

Music World

Help the reporter from *Music World* write an article on Gloria Estefan by answering his questions about the star. Use complete sentences.

I hear you have read a lot about Gloria Fajardo Estefan. Tell me something about her childhood, up to age 16. She was born in Cuba but came with her family to the U.S. in 1959. She had a lot of family responsibilities. Music was Gloria's escape. She learned to sing and play the guitar. **(2 points)**

Tell me the story of how Gloria became a member of Emilio Estefan's band—and how they fell in love. Estefan gave advice to a band Gloria sang with. Later he asked Gloria to join his band. Gloria and Emilio had a lot in common and they fell in love. **(2)**

In your opinion, what were Gloria's most important achievements before her accident in 1990? What are the most important things she has done since then?

Before the accident: Gloria recorded a string of worldwide hits with the Miami Sound Machine. She received many musical honors—as well as recognition for her drug prevention work with teens. **(2)**

Since the accident: Gloria made a complete recovery through bravery, hard work, and determination. She continued to produce hit albums with the Miami Sound Machine. **(2)**

What can a young person learn from Gloria Estefan? Answers will vary. Possible answers: Hard work pays off. Happiness comes from helping others in whatever way you can. **(2)**

Theme 5: **Heroes** 311
Assessment Tip: Total **10** Points

Gloria Estefan

Social Studies

Create a Time Line

Make a time line showing the most important events in Gloria Estefan's life. Draw a straight line across a sheet of paper. Mark off every ten years: 1950, 1960, and so on. Put the events and their dates on the appropriate places on the time line.

Bonus Using the same time line, add at least three historical events that occurred during this time period.

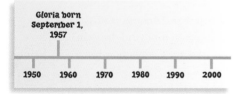

Gloria born
September 1,
1957

| 1950 | 1960 | 1970 | 1980 | 1990 | 2000 |

Listening and Speaking

Present a Song

Listen to recordings of some popular songs. Then meet with a group to brainstorm a creative way to present one song to the class. A volunteer from your group might introduce the song the way a radio disc jockey would. Other ideas include dancing or lip-synching to the recording.

Internet

Take an Online Poll

What is *your* favorite kind of music? Tell the world and learn what other students think about music by taking the Education Place online poll.

www.eduplace.com/kids

579

English Language Learners

Show students examples of book jacket summary notes. Point out some of the language used to tempt the reader. Then have students work in small groups to brainstorm a list of the most important events in Gloria Estefan's biography. Allow students to refer to this list when writing.

 ### End-of-Selection Assessment

Selection Test Use the test in the **Teacher's Resource Blackline Masters** to assess selection comprehension and vocabulary.

Student Self-Assessment Have students assess their reading with additional questions such as

- What parts of this selection were difficult for me? Why?

- What strategies helped me understand the selection?

- Would I recommend this biography to my friends? Why?

Health Link

pages 580–581

▶ Skill: How to Follow a Recipe

Read aloud the title and subtitle. Have students read the first paragraph silently. Then call on a volunteer to tell what the title *¡Sabroso!* means. Have students look at the recipe on page 581. Tell them that by carefully reading and preparing the recipe they will not only get practice in reading and following directions but they will also get to eat something *sabroso.*

Before You Read Have students read each step in the first box in the left column on page 580.

Ask students to relate Step 2 in How to Follow a Recipe to the type of link it is (health). (Staying safe is part of being healthy. Following the directions in Step 2 will help students stay safe.)

While You Read Have students take notes on what they learn about Gloria Estefan and the meanings of the Spanish words they find in the link. If your class includes Spanish language speakers, ask them to demonstrate the correct pronunciation of *sabroso, ropa vieja,* and *ensalada de fruta tropical.*

Health Link

¡Sabroso!

A Recipe from Gloria Estefan's Restaurant

Skill: How to Follow a Recipe

1 **Read** the entire recipe carefully.

2 **Ask** an adult to help if you have to use knives or the stove or oven.

3 **Gather together** all the ingredients and kitchen tools.

4 When you are preparing the food, **reread** each step of the recipe before you follow it.

5 **Follow** the steps in the correct order.

If you like the Cuban flavor of Gloria Estefan's music, you should try the food at one of her restaurants. It's *sabroso* — delicious!

Gloria Estefan owns Larios on the Beach in Miami Beach, Florida, with her husband and the Larios family. Larios on the Beach serves typical Cuban food. One of their popular dishes is a beef stew called *ropa vieja* [ROH-pah BYEH-hah], which means "old clothes." Another is *ensalada de fruta tropical,* a tropical fruit salad that combines many fruits from the Caribbean, where Cuba is located.

Gloria Estefan and her mother stir it up in her restaurant kitchen.

Classroom Management

All Students

Reading the Link This link provides an opportunity for kinesthetic learners to work collaboratively with visual learners. If time and resources allow, assist two or three volunteers in preparing *ensalada de fruta tropical.*

- Peel and cut the fruit before class.

- Assemble utensils and prepared ingredients in plain view.

- Have students who are observing read the steps in the recipe aloud as the student "chefs" follow the directions.

Ensalada de fruta tropical

This salad can be served with a meal or by itself. It serves about four people — depending on how much people eat!

Ingredients

$\frac{3}{4}$ cup pineapple
$\frac{1}{2}$ cup cantaloupe
$\frac{1}{2}$ cup honeydew melon
$\frac{1}{2}$ cup watermelon
$\frac{1}{2}$ cup papaya
$\frac{1}{2}$ cup mango
$\frac{1}{2}$ cup grapes
$\frac{1}{2}$ kiwi
$\frac{1}{3}$ cup shredded coconut
lettuce leaves
fresh mint leaves

Steps

1. Ask an adult to help you peel and cut the fruit (except for the grapes) into one-inch cubes. Combine the fruit in a large bowl.

2. Clean and dry the lettuce leaves and put them in four plates or bowls.

3. Put about one cup of the fruit mixture on the lettuce in each plate or bowl.

4. Sprinkle shredded coconut and a few mint leaves on top.

5. Serve and enjoy.

581

English Language Learners

Find out about students' experience with recipes and cooking. Ask: *Do you ever cook? If so, with whom? What do you like to cook? Who cooks dinner in your house? Does he/she cook from a written recipe or from memory? Have you ever used a recipe? What dish would you like to learn how to cook?* Explain that the recipe on page 581 is in typical recipe format; point out the words *ingredients* and *steps*, the fractions, and the sequence of steps.

▶ Comprehension Check

Have students refer to their notes to discuss what new information they learned about Gloria Estefan and to tell what Spanish words they learned by reading the link. Record students' responses in a chart like this:

Gloria Estefan	Spanish Words and Meanings
Owns a Cuban restaurant in Miami Beach	sabroso= delicious
Has partners in restaurant business: Emilio Estefan and Larios family.	ropa vieja= old clothes
	ensalada de fruta tropical= tropical fruit salad

Comprehension/Critical Thinking

1. Why do you think Gloria Estefan wanted to own a restaurant? (as a business investment; to share her enjoyment of Cuban food) **Drawing Conclusions**

2. Which of the two dishes described, *ropa vieja* or *ensalada de fruta tropical,* would you most like to try? Why? (Answers will vary.) **Making Judgments**

3. Why is the number of servings that the recipe makes an estimate? (The number of servings will vary depending on how much each person eats.) **Cause and Effect**

4. **Connecting/Comparing** How are Gloria's restaurant and her music alike? (Both have a Cuban "flavor," that is, they are extensions of Cuban traditions.) **Compare and Contrast**

Practice Book page 310

Gloria Estefan
Graphic Organizer
Judgments Chart

Name

Transparency 5–10

Judgments Chart

Why Might Someone Call Gloria Estefan a "Hero"?

Chapter One: Escaping with Music

Chapter Two: Making Music with Emilio and Chapter Three: Changes

Chapter Four: World Fame—and Tragedy

Chapter Five: "Here for Each Other"

TRANSPARENCY 5–10
TEACHER'S EDITION PAGES T580 AND T581A

Comprehension Skills

Making Judgments

▶ Teach

Using **Transparency 5–10,** teach students how to make judgments by discussing

- the events in Gloria Estefan's life that could be considered heroic

- if her actions make her a hero

- how inferences are needed to make judgments

- how it's important to consider all sides of an issue before forming an opinion

Students can refer to the selection and to **Practice Book** page 310.

Chapter Four: World Fame—and Tragedy
(The band sells millions of records.)
(She is honored by President Bush for her drug prevention work with teenagers.)
(She recovers from a terrible bus accident.)

Chapter Five: "Here for Each Other"
(She is given a Congressional Medal of Honor.)
(She helps hurricane victims.)
(She helps abused children.)
(She declines movie offers to be with her family.)

Modeling Tell students that when they read something, it's often a good idea to ask themselves, "Do I agree with this? Is this right or fair?" This is called making a judgment. Have students think about this as you read aloud from the final paragraph on page 569, beginning with *In 1984 the group …,* through the first paragraph on page 571, ending with *Life shined brightly for Gloria and the band.* Use the Think Aloud below to make your point.

> **Think Aloud**
>
> *In this section the author lists many of the band's awards and tells how many records they sold. The author calls this a success. I don't agree. I don't think how many awards you have and how much money you're making makes you a success. I think being a success has to do more with how you feel about yourself. Rather than calling the band a success, the author should've used the word* popular.

Tell students that when making judgments there is never only one correct answer because judgments are actually opinions.

....

▶ Practice

Have pairs of students make judgments about stars being heroes. Choose two popular, public figures from today and have students create a chart to determine if these people are heroes. Label the chart "Is _____ a Hero?" Label column 1 "Yes, because ...." Label column 2 "No, because ...." Challenge students not to make up their minds until they have filled both columns with as many reasons as they can. Be sure to save enough time for the class to discuss their thoughts.

....

▶ Apply

Use **Practice Book** pages 312–313 to diagnose whether students need Reteaching. Students who do not need Reteaching may work on Challenge/Extension Activities, page R11. Students who need extra support may apply the skill to an easier text using the **Reader's Library** selection "Duke Ellington: A Life in Music" and its Responding activity.

Skill Finder	Revisiting, page 575	Review, Th 2, p. 173; Th 4, p. 497; Th 5, p. 593	Reteaching, page R10

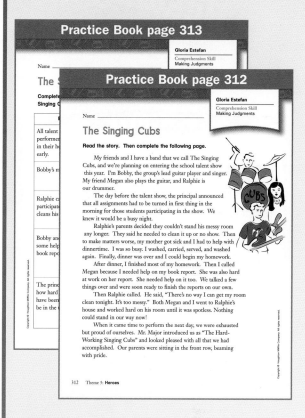

Practice Book page 313

Gloria Estefan
Comprehension Skill
Making Judgments

Name _____

The S...

Complete
Singing C...

All talent performer... in their h... early.	
Bobby's m...	
Ralphie c... participate cleans his...	
Bobby an... some help... book repo...	
The princ... how hard... have been... be in the...	

Practice Book page 312

Gloria Estefan
Comprehension Skill
Making Judgments

Name _____

The Singing Cubs

Read the story. Then complete the following page.

My friends and I have a band that we call The Singing Cubs, and we're planning on entering the school talent show this year. I'm Bobby, the group's lead guitar player and singer. My friend Megan also plays the guitar, and Ralphie is our drummer.

The day before the talent show, the principal announced that all assignments had to be turned in first thing in the morning for those students participating in the show. We knew it would be a busy night.

Ralphie's parents decided they couldn't stand his messy room any longer. They said he needed to clean it up or no show. Then to make matters worse, my mother got sick and I had to help with dinnertime. I was so busy. I washed, carried, served, and washed again. Finally, dinner was over and I could begin my homework.

After dinner, I finished most of my homework. Then I called Megan because I needed help on my book report. She was also hard at work on her report. She needed help on it too. We talked a few things over and were soon ready to finish the reports on our own.

Then Ralphie called. He said, "There's no way I can get my room clean tonight. It's too messy." Both Megan and I went to Ralphie's house and worked hard on his room until it was spotless. Nothing could stand in our way now!

When it came time to perform the next day, we were exhausted but proud of ourselves. Mr. Major introduced us as "The Hard-Working Singing Cubs" and looked pleased with all that we had accomplished. Our parents were sitting in the front row, beaming with pride.

312   Theme 5: **Heroes**

Extra Support

MEETING INDIVIDUAL NEEDS

- Reteaching, page R10

- **Reader's Library:** *Heroes*
  Selection 2, "Duke Ellington: A Life in Music"

Diagnostic Check

If ...	You can ...
students need extra help to make judgments,	use the Reteaching Lesson on page R10.
students have successfully met the lesson objectives,	Assign the Challenge/Extension Activities on page R11.

Comprehension Skills   581B

Information & Study Skills
Conduct an Interview

Tell students that one way to get the information you are looking for is by interviewing someone. Explain that an interview is when one person (the interviewer) asks another person (the interviewee) a series of questions and listens to the interviewee's answers. When the interviewer plans to use information gathered from the interview, he or she will also record the interview in some form. Interviews may be conducted for personal use, printed in magazines, broadcast on the radio, or shown on television.

▶ **Teach**

Tell students that it is very important to prepare for an interview. Point out that there are things they can do to make sure that they ask all the questions they need to ask and that they get all the information they want. For example:

■ Find and read articles that provide background information on the topic you will ask about.

■ Write down the questions you want to ask beforehand.

■ Use a tape recorder to record the interview.

Modeling Use the following situation to model some of those techniques: Students will conduct an interview with the director of the local hospital that wants to build a new building next to the school. The director only has forty-five minutes in which to answer questions.

Think Aloud

I know that the director's time is limited, so before I go I will write down all the questions I want her to answer. I also remember that there was an article about the hospital's plans in last week's paper. I can read that article to get some information ahead of time. That way, I won't have to ask the director as many questions. I'll use the school's tape recorder so that I don't have to write everything down. Also, by recording the interview, I'll be sure not to misquote the director. Afterward, I can listen to the recording and write down the information I need for my article.

Using a Tape Recorder You may want to have students practice using a tape recorder in class before they conduct their interviews. Remind them to first check that the batteries (if there are any) are working and the tape recorder is recording. Have them practice recording someone and then playing the recording back to see how close they should place the microphone to the person they are recording kand to determine the proper volume setting.

▶ Practice

Have students suggest questions they would ask the director. Encourage them to ask questions that will get answers to these questions: *Who? What? When? Where? Why?* and *How?* Explain that the answers to these questions are an important part of any news article.

▶ Apply

Have students work in small groups to plan an interview with Gloria Estefan. Suggest that they reread *Gloria Estefan* for background information and for topics they would like to know more about. Have each group come up with a list of questions they would like to ask Gloria Estefan. Invite the groups to share their questions with the class.

Word Work

	Word Work Instructions
DAY 1	• Spelling Pretest • Spelling Instruction
DAY 2	• Structural Analysis Instruction • Spelling Practice
DAY 3	• Phonics Instruction • Spelling Practice
DAY 4	• Structural Analysis Reteaching • Vocabulary Skill Instruction • Spelling Game
DAY 5	• Expanding Your Vocabulary • Spelling Test

OBJECTIVES

Students

- read words in which final *y* has been changed to *i*

- read words and syllables that have the two sounds of *g*

- Use the Phonics/Decoding strategy to decode longer words

Decoding Longer Words

✅ Structural Analysis: Changing Final y to i Spelling Connection

▶ Teach

Write this sentence on the chalkboard: *Gloria and the band performed at the American Music Awards and the Grammy Awards <u>ceremonies</u>.*

Point to the word *ceremonies.* Remind students that this is the plural form of the base word *ceremony.* Write ceremony on the board, and ask students how the spelling of the word changed when -*es* was added. (The *y* changed to *i*.) Write *easier, cried,* and *luckiest* on the board. Ask students to name the base word of each word. (easy, cry, lucky) Elicit that when -*es*, -*er*, -*ed*, or -*est* is added to a base word that ends in *y*, the *y* is changed to *i*.

Modeling Display the following sentence and model how to decode *carried: The early months of 1990 <u>carried</u> on the streak of success.*

> **Think Aloud**
>
> *When I look at this word, I recognize the shorter word carry, except there is an i where the y should be. However, I know that when a base word ends with y (write carry on the board and circle the y ending) the y is changed to an i before adding -ed. That's probably what happened here. Then the word would be pronounced /KAR•eed/. I know what that means and it makes sense here.*

▶ Practice

Display these sentences and have students copy the underlined words: *Three months later, Gloria <u>married</u> Emilio. It was one of the <u>happiest</u> days of her life. The album sold three million <u>copies</u>.* Have students work in pairs to decode the words and give their meanings. Call on individuals to model the Phonics/Decoding strategy at the board.

▶ Apply

Have students complete **Practice Book** page 314.

Skill Finder	• Strategy Review: Phonics/ Decoding, p. 559B	• Reteaching, p. R16

Phonics: Two Sounds of g

▶ Teach

Tell students that understanding the two sounds of the letter *g* can help them use the Phonics/Decoding strategy to decode unfamiliar words. Explain that

- the letter *g* usually has the / g / sound

- the spelling patterns *ge*, *gi*, and *gy* can have the / j / sound

Modeling Display this sentence and model how to decode *surgery: She underwent a new and very risky kind of surgery on March 23.*

Think Aloud

When I look at this word, I see a VCCV pattern, u-r-g-e. I'll split the word between the consonants r and g. The first part probably sounds like / sur /. I know the letter g usually has the / g / sound as in girl, but here I see the ge spelling pattern. I know that pattern can have the / j / sound, so this next part might sound like / jur /. Finally, I see the y ending which usually sounds like / ee /. When I put it all together I say / sur•jur•ee /. Oh, it's / SUR•juh•ree /. That means an operation. That makes sense.

▶ Practice

Write these sentences on the board and have students copy the underlined words: *Her mother taught <u>kindergarten</u>. Gloria <u>graduated</u> from <u>college</u>. You can't imagine why anyone has to go through <u>something</u> like that.* Tell students to circle the / g / and / j / spellings and decode each word. Call on individuals to model the Phonics/Decoding strategy.

▶ Apply

Ask students to decode the following words from *Gloria Estefan* and discuss their meanings: *refugees*, page 561; *government*, page 562; *changed*, page 565; *original*, page 567; *recording groups*, page 568; *English-language*, page 569; *teenagers*, page 571.

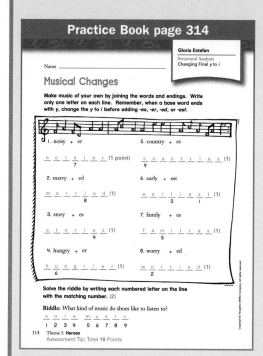

Practice Book page 314

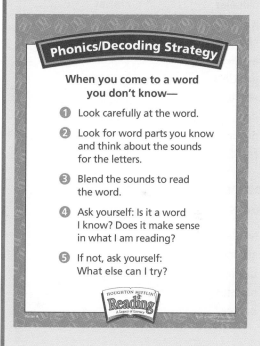

Phonics/Decoding Strategy

When you come to a word you don't know—

1. Look carefully at the word.

2. Look for word parts you know and think about the sounds for the letters.

3. Blend the sounds to read the word.

4. Ask yourself: Is it a word I know? Does it make sense in what I am reading?

5. If not, ask yourself: What else can I try?

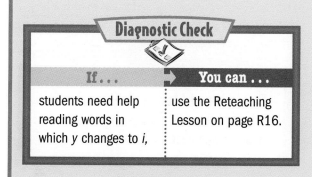

Diagnostic Check

If...	You can...
students need help reading words in which *y* changes to *i*,	use the Reteaching Lesson on page R16.

Word Work

OBJECTIVES

Students write spelling words formed by adding -es, -ed, -er, or -est to base words that end with a consonant and y.

Spelling Words

Basic Words

sunnier	ferries
cloudier	crazier
windier	funnier
cities*	earlier*
heaviest	copied*
prettiest	hobbies
studied*	angriest
easier*	emptied
noisier	worried*
families*	happiest*

Review Words

hurried
stories
carried*
pennies
babies*

Challenge Words

iciest
hazier
breezier
companies*
qualities

Forms of these words appear in the literature.

Extra Support

Basic Word List You may want to use only the left column of Basic Words with students who need extra support.

Spelling
✔ Changing Final y to i

Day 1 — Teaching the Principle

Pretest Use the Day 5 Test Sentences. Say each underlined word, read the sentence, and then repeat the word. Have students write only the underlined word.

Teach Write these word equations on the board:

city + es = cities	study + ed = studied
sunny + er = sunnier	heavy + est = heaviest

Point to and say each base word and its inflected form, and have students repeat the words. Point out that each base word ends in a consonant and *y*. Then ask the class to tell what happened to the *y* in each base word when the ending or suffix was added. (It was changed to i.) Explain that when *-es, -ed, -er,* or *-est* is added to a base word that ends with a consonant and *y*, the *y* is changed to *i*. Write the remaining Basic Words on the board. Select students to spell each word's base word.

Practice/Homework Assign **Practice Book** page 425. Tell students to use this Take-Home Word List to study the words they missed on the Pretest.

Day 2 — Reviewing the Principle

Practice/Homework Review the spelling principle and assign **Practice Book** page 315.

Day 3 — Vocabulary

Riddle Clues Write the Basic Words on the board. Then dictate each clue below. Ask students to write the Basic Word that best fits each clue.

What did the students do to get ready for a test? (studied)

If a boy arrives before a girl, what is he? (earlier)

What are groups of relatives called? (families)

If a flower is the best looking one in a bunch, what is it? (prettiest)

Next, have students use each Basic Word from the board orally in a sentence. (Sentences will vary.)

Day 3 *continued....*

Practice/Homework For spelling practice, assign **Practice Book** page 316.

Day 4 — Ending Bingo

Ask students to work in groups of three or more, including an announcer. Supply the announcer with a list of Basic and Review Words, and give the players a supply of bingo-type markers. Have each student divide a sheet of paper into nine squares, and then write one of these endings in a corner of each square: *-es, -ed, -er, -est.*

To play, the announcer reads a list word. (The announcer cannot use a word more than once during the game.) Players write the word in a square that has that ending and place a marker on the square. Play continues until one player has markers on three correct spellings across, down, or at an angle.

Practice/Homework For proofreading and writing practice, assign **Practice Book** page 317.

Day 5 — Spelling Assessment

Test Say each underlined word, read the sentence, and then repeat the word. Have students write only the underlined word.

Basic Words

1. It will be <u>sunnier</u> after the clouds pass.
2. It will rain if the sky grows <u>cloudier</u>.
3. You need a much <u>windier</u> day to fly a kite.
4. Are <u>cities</u> larger than towns?
5. This box is the <u>heaviest</u> one to lift.
6. Roses are the <u>prettiest</u> flowers of all.
7. We read and <u>studied</u> all about foods.
8. Work is <u>easier</u> if you ask for help.
9. Barking dogs are <u>noisier</u> than cats.
10. Each of the <u>families</u> has one child.
11. People cross the river on <u>ferries</u>.
12. Monkeys act <u>crazier</u> than a clown.
13. Is my joke <u>funnier</u> than yours?
14. I leave five minutes <u>earlier</u> than you.
15. She <u>copied</u> every word by hand.
16. One of his <u>hobbies</u> is fishing.
17. The <u>angriest</u> workers quit their jobs.
18. A dump truck <u>emptied</u> the dirt here.
19. The storm <u>worried</u> my father.
20. The <u>happiest</u> child laughs and plays.

Challenge Words

21. This is the <u>iciest</u> winter day we have had.
22. The afternoon is becoming <u>hazier</u>.
23. The weather is <u>breezier</u> now.
24. He has worked for both <u>companies</u>.
25. She has many fine <u>qualities</u>.

Spelling Spree!™

Students may use the **Spelling Spree!™** for extra practice with the spelling principles taught in this lesson.

Practice Book page 425
Take-Home Word List   Take-Home Word List   Take-Home Word List

Practice Book page 317
Gloria Estefan

Practice Book page 316
Gloria Estefan

Practice Book page 315

Gloria Estefan
Spelling Changing Final *y* to *i*

Name _____

Changing Final *y* to *i*

If a word ends with a consonant and *y*, change the *y* to *i* when adding *-es, -ed, -er,* or *-est.*
city + es = cities   study + ed = studied
sunny + er = sunnier   heavy + est = heaviest

Write each Spelling Word under its ending.
Order of answers for each category may vary.

Spelling Words
1. sunnier
2. cloudier
3. windier
4. cities
5. heaviest
6. prettiest
7. studied
8. easier
9. noisier
10. families
11. ferries
12. crazier
13. funnier
14. earlier
15. copied
16. hobbies
17. angriest
18. emptied
19. worried
20. happiest

-es or -ed
cities (1 point)
studied (1)
families (1)
ferries (1)
copied (1)
hobbies (1)
emptied (1)
worried (1)

-er or -est
sunnier (1)
cloudier (1)
windier (1)
heaviest (1)
prettiest (1)
easier (1)
noisier (1)
crazier (1)
funnier (1)
earlier (1)
angriest (1)
happiest (1)

Theme 5: Heroes   315
Assessment Tip: Total 20 Points

••• **Houghton Mifflin Spelling and Vocabulary** •••
Correlated instruction and practice

Challenge

Challenge Word Practice Students can use the Challenge Words to write a weather report for a radio or TV broadcast.

Vocabulary Skills

 **Homophones**

▶ Teach

Display **Transparency 5–11,** blocking out all but the definition of *homophone.* Read the definition aloud. Explain that homophones are words that not only have different spellings and meanings but different word histories as well. Next uncover sentences 1 through 4. Point to the homophones at the end of the first sentence and tell students that these homophones sound the same, but only one of them makes sense in the sentence. Read each sentence out loud and spell out the correct word that belongs in the sentence. Repeat the procedure with sentences 2 through 4.

Modeling Uncover numbers 5 through 10 on the transparency, showing four pairs of homophones. Model how to decide which word to choose.

Think Aloud

In sentence 5, the person needs two cups of either f-l-o-u-r or f-l-o-w-e-r for a recipe. Both words sound alike but are spelled differently, and they mean two different things. Flour is a ground grain used to make breads and cakes, and a flower is a plant. Looking at this pair, I recognize that the spelling I need is f-l-o-u-r. Knowing the meaning of both words helped me to pick the right answer. If I come across words and don't know what they mean, I can always look the words up in a dictionary to be sure.

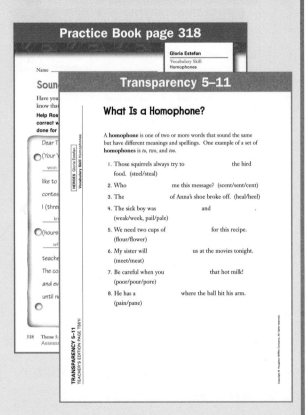

Practice Book page 318

Transparency 5–11

What Is a Homophone?

A **homophone** is one of two or more words that sound the same but have different meanings and spellings. One example of a set of **homophones** is *to, two,* and *too.*

1. Those squirrels always try to _____ the bird food. (steel/steal)
2. Who _____ me this message? (scent/sent/cent)
3. The _____ of Anna's shoe broke off. (heal/heel)
4. The sick boy was _____ and _____. (weak/week, pail/pale)
5. We need two cups of _____ for this recipe. (flour/flower)
6. My sister will _____ us at the movies tonight. (meet/meat)
7. Be careful when you _____ that hot milk! (poor/pour/pore)
8. He has a _____ where the ball hit his arm. (pain/pane)

Practice

Have students match each word in the remaining pairs of homophones with its meaning by inviting volunteers to use each word in a sentence that shows they understand what it means.

▶ **Apply**

Have students complete **Practice Book** page 318.

Expanding Your Vocabulary
Musical Instruments

Invite students to name instruments they might hear in a band. Explain that in large bands and orchestras, instruments are grouped by type. Write the following words on the board: *strings, percussion, brass, woodwinds.* Begin a word web for string instruments.

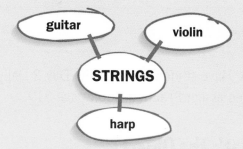

Ask students to work with partners to find additional names of string instruments to add to the web. Have other pairs of partners create word webs for percussion, brass, and woodwinds.

 • Challenge/Extension Activities, p. R17

···· **Houghton Mifflin Spelling and Vocabulary** ····
Correlated instruction and practice

 English Language Learners

Most English language learners will already be aware that many words in English sound alike but are spelled differently. Write an example that students know such as *to, two,* and *too.* Ask a volunteer to read each word aloud. Continue with another familiar example such as *for* and *four.* Then proceed with the activity.

Writing and Language Instruction

DAY 1	• Daily Language Practice • Grammar Instruction • Journal Writing
DAY 2	• Daily Language Practice • Writing a Problem/Solution Paragraph • Journal Writing • Grammar Practice
DAY 3	• Daily Language Practice • Grammar Instruction • Write a Book Jacket Summary
DAY 4	• Daily Language Practice • Listening/Speaking/Viewing • Writing: Improving Your Writing • Grammar Practice
DAY 5	• Daily Language Practice • Grammar: Improving Your Writing

OBJECTIVES

Students

- identify object pronouns
- use object pronouns correctly
- use *I* and *me* correctly
- proofread and correct sentences with grammar and spelling errors
- use subject and object pronouns correctly to improve writing

Wacky Web Tales

Students may use the **Wacky Web Tales** floppy disk to create humorous stories and review parts of speech.

Grammar Skills

Object Pronouns

Day 1

Display the chart at the top of **Transparency 5–12** and go over the examples of object pronouns and the use of *I* and *me.* Then display the sentences at the bottom of the transparency. Have students read the sentences, and ask volunteers to choose the correct subject or object pronoun to replace the underlined words in each sentence. Write the pronoun on the line provided. Then go over the following rules and definitions:

- *Me, you, him, her, it, us,* and *them* are object pronouns.

- Use object pronouns after action verbs and words such as *to, with, for,* and *at.*

- Use the pronoun *I* as the subject of a sentence.

- Use the pronoun *me* as an object pronoun.

- When speaking of another person and you, name yourself last.

Have students look at *Gloria Estefan* to find examples of object pronouns and *I* and *me.* Ask students to share the examples they find. Then have them correct the Day 1 Daily Language Practice sentences on **Transparency 5–14**.

Day 2

Practice/Homework Have students correct the Day 2 Daily Language Practice sentences. Then assign **Practice Book** page 319.

Day 3   What's the Object?

Divide the class into groups of four or five students. Ask each group to write down four sentences with nouns used as objects. Remind students that the objects may consist of more than one word. Then have groups exchange sentences. Ask one group to read the sentences they have been given, one by one. Then have members of the group go to the board and rewrite their sentences, replacing the noun objects with object pronouns. Repeat the exercise for each of the other groups. Then have students correct the Day 3 Daily Language Practice sentences.

Day 4

Practice/Homework Have students correct the Day 4 Daily Language Practice sentences. Assign **Practice Book** page 320.

Day 5 | Improving Your Writing

Using the Correct Pronouns Point out that good writers are careful to use correct subject and object pronouns in their sentences. Have students read the sentences on **Transparency 5–13.**

Ask students to choose the correct pronoun for each sentence from those given in parentheses and underline it. Then have students review a piece of their own writing to see if they can improve it by using subject and object pronouns correctly.

Practice/Homework Have students correct the Day 5 Daily Language Practice sentences. Then assign **Practice Book** page 321.

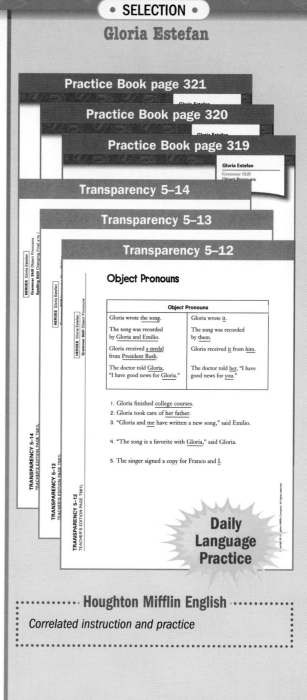

Practice Book page 321

Practice Book page 320

Practice Book page 319

Transparency 5–14

Transparency 5–13

Transparency 5–12

Object Pronouns

Object Pronouns	
Gloria wrote the song.	Gloria wrote it.
The song was recorded by Gloria and Emilio.	The song was recorded by them.
Gloria received a medal from President Bush.	Gloria received it from him.
The doctor told Gloria, "I have good news for Gloria."	The doctor told her, "I have good news for you."

1. Gloria finished college courses.
2. Gloria took care of her father.
3. "Gloria and me have written a new song," said Emilio.
4. "The song is a favorite with Gloria," said Gloria.
5. The singer signed a copy for Franco and I.

Daily Language Practice

·········· **Houghton Mifflin English** ··········
Correlated instruction and practice

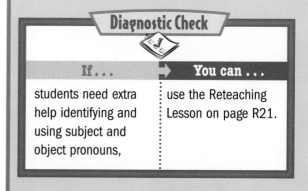

Diagnostic Check

If . . .	You can . . .
students need extra help identifying and using subject and object pronouns,	use the Reteaching Lesson on page R21.

OBJECTIVES

Students

- identify the characteristics of a problem/solution paragraph
- write a problem/solution paragraph
- combine sentences with pronouns to improve their writing

Transparency 5–16

Sentence Combining with Pronouns

Transparency 5–15

A Problem/Solution Paragraph

To Dance or Not to Dance?

Should I take dance classes after school or take a part-time job? Studying dance is one solution. Mom and Dad want me to study. They say I can get a job later. Besides, if I don't study now, I may never have the training I need to dance later. The downside is that I won't be making any money. I'd like to feel independent. The other choice is to work after school. One advantage is, I'll have money to pay for my lessons. The downside is that I will not be able to learn to dance well. My parents will also be disappointed. I think the best thing is to take dance lessons and get a job later.

Writing Skills
Writing a Problem/Solution Paragraph

▶ Teach

Tell students that a problem/solution paragraph presents a problem to be solved and then possible solutions to consider. For any solution there are pros, reasons for choosing that solution, and cons, reasons against choosing that solution. The topic sentence states the problem. The body of the paragraph examines solutions. The concluding sentence states the solution the writer chose.

▶ Practice

Display **Transparency 5–15.** Have students read the problem/solution paragraph. Ask:

- **What is the problem?** (whether she should take dance classes or work after school)

- **What are the pros for the first possible solution?** (parents want her to; if she doesn't get training now, she won't be able to dance later)

- **What are the cons for the first possible solution?** (won't be making any money, won't be independent)

- **What are the pros of the second possible solution?** (pay for her lessons herself)

- **What are the cons of the second possible solution?** (won't be able to learn to dance well; parents will be disappointed)

- **What is Gloria's solution?** (to take dance classes and get a job later)

Discuss with students the guidelines for writing a problem/solution paragraph.

Guidelines for
Writing a Problem/Solution Paragraph

- Begin with a topic sentence that clearly states the problem.
- Consider a possible solution.
- Write about the pros and cons for that solution.
- Consider a second possible solution.
- Write about the pros and cons for that solution.
- Conclude with a statement stating the solution you chose.

► Apply

Students can use **Practice Book** page 322 to help them plan and organize their writing. Have them use the graphic organizer to help them plan a problem/solution paragraph. Ask them to write about a current problem at school or home. Post final paragraphs as part of a Problem Solvers display.

Improving Your Writing
Sentence Combining with Pronouns

Teach Remind students that a pronoun takes the place of a noun. Tell them that they can use pronouns to avoid repeating the same noun again and again. Combining sentences using pronouns also helps to vary sentence length in your writing.

Practice To model combining sentences using pronouns, display **Transparency 5–16.** Have students read the examples at the top of the page. Have them note how pronouns have been used to replace nouns. Point out that sometimes words have to be added or changed when the sentences are combined. Then have students use pronouns to combine the sentences on the transparency.

Apply Assign **Practice Book** page 323. Then have students review their problem/solution paragraphs to see if there are sentences that can be combined, using pronouns.

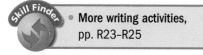
Skill Finder • More writing activities, pp. R23–R25

Gloria Estefan

Technology

The Writer's Resource Library

Students may use this set of reference tools as they work on their own writing.

©Sunburst Technology Corporation, a Houghton Mifflin Company. All Rights Reserved.

Type to Learn™

Students may use **Type to Learn™** to learn proper keyboarding technique.

©Sunburst Technology Corporation, a Houghton Mifflin Company. All Rights Reserved.

···· **Houghton Mifflin English** ····
Correlated instruction and practice

Portfolio Opportunity

Save students' problem/solution paragraphs as samples of their writing development.

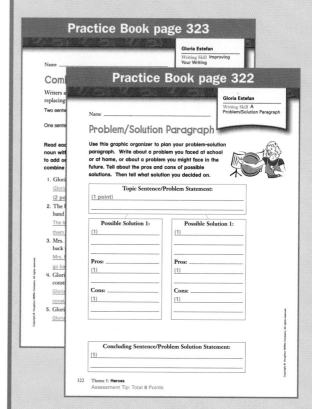

Practice Book page 323

Gloria Estefan
Writing Skill Improving
Your Writing

Name ____

Com...

Writers a...
replacing...

Two sente...

One sente...

Read eac...
noun wit...
to add o...
combine...

Practice Book page 322

Gloria Estefan
Writing Skill A
Problem/Solution Paragraph

Name ____

Problem/Solution Paragraph

Use this graphic organizer to plan your problem-solution paragraph. Write about a problem you faced at school or at home, or about a problem you might face in the future. Tell about the pros and cons of possible solutions. Then tell what solution you decided on.

| Topic Sentence/Problem Statement: |
| (1 point) |

| Possible Solution 1: | Possible Solution 1: |
| (1) | (1) |

| Pros: | Pros: |
| (1) | (1) |

| Cons: | Cons: |
| (1) | (1) |

| Concluding Sentence/Problem Solution Statement: |
| (1) |

322 Theme 5: **Heroes**
Assessment Tip: Total 8 Points

Listening/Speaking/Viewing
Listen for Different Purposes

▶ Teach

Explain to students that listening can serve different purposes at different times. For example, at the moment they are listening so that they can understand the lesson. Have students suggest other purposes for listening. Write their ideas on the board, guiding them to include the following:

> - For learning, as with a school lesson
> - For getting information, as with a weather bulletin
> - For communication, as in a conversation
> - For enjoyment, as with music

Explain to students that how people listen often depends on the purpose for listening. For example, people might even listen to the same piece of music in different ways because they have different purposes in doing so. Help students brainstorm other purposes for listening to music besides pure enjoyment. (Someone might be trying to learn the music so that he or she can later play or sing it. A conductor or music producer may be listening to music performers and directing them or giving them tips for improvement. Someone may be studying the piece in a music class. Someone may want to perform—for example, dance or ice skate—to the music and need to feel its rhythm. The listener might be a music critic, teacher, or talent scout who is judging the players and singers.)

English Language Learners

Talk about where, when, and how students listen to music. Suggest possibilities such as when riding in a car, while relaxing, with a radio or a Walkman, and so on. List students' responses on the board. Ask students to explain how the music they listen to makes them feel. As needed, brainstorm a list of descriptive words such as *energized, relaxed, happy.*

Practice

Play a short piece of music of your choosing and ask students to listen just for enjoyment. Invite them to describe how they felt as they listened, asking such questions as these: Was your body tense or relaxed? Did you feel yourself moving with the music? What were you thinking about?

 Apply

Ask a pair of volunteers to act out how they would listen to piece of music. Assign each student a role, such as a musician trying to learn the piece. Play the piece again, then ask the role-players to tell how their purpose for listening affected the way they listened. How was it different from just listening for enjoyment? Repeat the activity, having students listen for different purposes.

Improving Listening Skills

- Remind students that being aware of their purpose in listening can help them listen more effectively and increase their enjoyment.

- Suggest that even when they do have other purposes for listening, such as learning music, they first do so strictly for enjoyment so that they can get a feel for the whole piece.

- Point out that when they are enjoying music—for example, playing it on a stereo system or on headphones—they should keep in mind other people's comfort, as well as their own hearing. They can do so by keeping the volume at a reasonable level, even checking with others to make sure they are comfortable with the volume. Not having to argue over loudness makes listening more enjoyable.

Lou Gehrig: The Luckiest Man

Different texts for different purposes

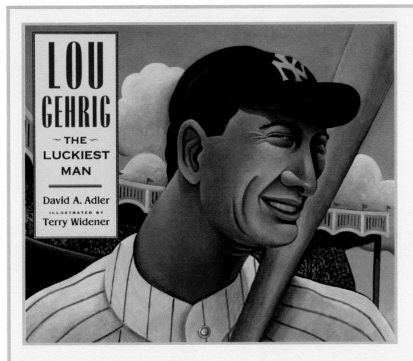

LOU GEHRIG
~ THE ~
LUCKIEST MAN

David A. Adler
ILLUSTRATED BY
Terry Widener

Anthology: Main Selection

Purposes

- strategy focus: evaluate
- comprehension skill: fact and opinion
- vocabulary development
- critical thinking, discussion

Genre: Biography

A true story of the life of a real person.

Awards

- ★ ALA Notable
- ★ *Bulletin* Blue Ribbon
- ★ CCBC Choices
- ★ *New York Times* Best Book of the Year

Selection Summary

A son of poor immigrants, Gehrig became one of the greatest Yankees ever. He held the record for most consecutive games. When ALS struck, Gehrig left the team and faced his illness with dignity and courage.

Teacher's Edition: Read Aloud

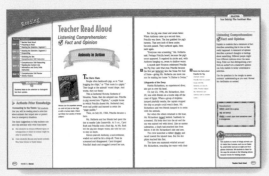

Purposes

- listening comprehension: fact and opinion
- vocabulary development
- critical thinking, discussion

Anthology: Get Set to Read

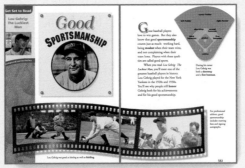

Purposes

- background building: good sportsmanship
- developing key vocabulary

Anthology: Content Link

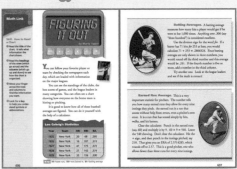

Purposes

- content reading: math
- skill: how to read a chart
- critical thinking, discussion

Leveled Books and Resources

See Cumulative Listing of Leveled Books.

Reader's Library

Very Easy

Mark McGwire: Home Run Hero
by Richard Merchant

(Also available on blackline masters)

Purposes

- fluency practice in below-level text
- alternate reading for students reading significantly below grade level
- strategy application: evaluate
- comprehension skill application: fact and opinion
- below-level independent reading

Lesson Support

- Guided Reading lesson, page R6
- Alternate application for Comprehension Skill lesson on fact and opinion, page 607A
- Reteaching for Comprehension Skill: fact and opinion, page R12

Selection Summary Masters

Lou Gehrig: The Luckiest Man
Teacher's Resource Blackline Masters

Audiotape

**Lou Gehrig:
The Luckiest Man**
Audiotape for
Heroes

Inclusion Strategy

Significantly Below-level Readers

Students reading so far below level that they cannot read *Lou Gehrig: The Luckiest Man* even with the suggested Extra Support should still participate with the class whenever possible.

- Include them in the Teacher Read Aloud (p. 582E) and Preparing to Read (pp. 583A–583D).

- Have them listen to *Lou Gehrig: The Luckiest Man* on the audiotape for *Heroes* and read the Selection Summary while others read Segment 1 of the selection.

- Have them read "Mark McGwire: Home Run Hero" in the Reader's Library collection for *Heroes* while others read Segment 2 of *Lou Gehrig: The Luckiest Man*.

- Have all students participate in Wrapping Up Segment 2 (p. 603) and Responding (p. 604).

Theme Paperbacks

Easy

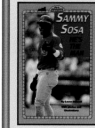

Sammy Sosa: He's the Man
by Laura Driscoll

Lesson, TE page 557I

On Level

Mrs. Mack
by Patricia Polacco

Lesson, TE page 557K

Challenge

The Wreck of the Ethie
by Hilary Hyland

Lesson, TE page 557M

Technology

Get Set for Reading CD-ROM
Lou Gehrig: The Luckiest Man
Provides background building, vocabulary support, and selection summaries in English and Spanish.

Education Place
www.eduplace.com

Log on to Education Place for more activities relating to *Lou Gehrig: The Luckiest Man.*

Book Adventure
www.bookadventure.org

This Internet reading incentive program provides thousands of titles for students.

Suggested Daily Routines

Instructional Goals	Day 1	Day 2

Reading
 ✓ *Strategy Focus:* Evaluate
 ✓ *Comprehension Skill:* Fact and Opinion
 Comprehension Skill Review: Making Judgments; Author's Viewpoint
 ✓ *Information and Study Skills:* Collecting Data (Tables and Charts)
	Teacher Read Aloud
	 Animals in Action, 582E
	 Preparing to Read *Lou Gehrig: The Luckiest Man*
	 • Get Set: Background and Vocabulary, *583A*
	 • Key Vocabulary, *583B*
	   Selection Vocabulary, *Practice Book,* 324
	 • Strategy/Skill Preview, *583C*
	   Fact and Opinion Chart, *Practice Book,* 325
	 Reading Segment 1
	 Lou Gehrig: The Luckiest Man, 584–591
	 • Supporting Comprehension
	 • Strategy Focus, *590*
	 Wrapping Up Segment 1, *591*
		Reading Segment 2
		 Lou Gehrig: The Luckiest Man, 592–602
		 • Supporting Comprehension
		 • Strategy Focus, *594*
		 Wrapping Up Segment 2, *603*
		 Responding
		 • Comprehension Questions: Think About the Selection, *604*
		 • Comprehension Check, *Practice Book,* 326
		 Revisiting the Text
		 • Comprehension: Fact and Opinion, *589*

Word Work ✓ *Spelling:* VCV Pattern *Decoding Longer Words:* ✓ *Structural Analysis:* VCV Pattern *Phonics:* Two Sounds of c ✓ *Vocabulary:* Dictionary: Word Histories	**Spelling** • Pretest, *607G* • Instruction: VCV Pattern, *607G* • Take-Home Word List, *Practice Book: Handbook*	**Decoding Longer Words Instruction** • Structural Analysis: VCV Pattern, *607E* • *Practice Book,* 329 **Spelling** • *Practice Book,* 330

Writing & Language
 ✓ *Grammar:* Singular and Plural Possessive Pronouns
 ✓ *Writing:* Writing a Magazine Article; Combining Sentences with Possessive Pronouns
 Listening/Speaking/Viewing: Present an Oral Book Report
	Daily Language Practice, *607L*
	 Grammar Instruction
	 • Singular and Plural Possessive Pronouns, *607K*
	  Writing
	 • Journal Writing, *585*
		Daily Language Practice, *607L*
		 Grammar Instruction
		 • Singular and Plural Possessive Pronouns, *Practice Book,* 334
		  Writing Instruction
		 • Writing a Magazine Article, *607M*
		 • Journal Writing, *592*

✓ = tested skills

 Leveled Books   *See Cumulative Listing of Leveled Books.*

Reader's Library
• **Very Easy** *Mark McGwire: Home Run Hero,* Lesson, *R6*
Book Links: Anthology, *530*
Bibliography: Teacher's Edition, *526C*
Houghton Mifflin Classroom Bookshelf, Level 4

Theme Paperbacks, Lessons, *557H–557N*
• **Easy** *Sammy Sosa: He's the Man*
• **On Level** *Mrs. Mack*
• **Challenge** *The Wreck of the Ethie*

Allow time every day for students to read independently from self-selected books.

Technology

Lesson Planner CD-ROM:
Customize your planning for *Lou Gehrig: The Luckiest Man* with the Lesson Planner.

Day 3

Revisiting the Text
- Visual Literacy: Perspective, *595*

Comprehension Skill Instruction
- Fact and Opinion, *607A*
- *Practice Book, 327*

Phonics Instruction
- Two Sounds of *c*, *607F*

Spelling
- *Practice Book, 331*

Daily Language Practice, *607L*

Grammar Instruction
- Whose Is It?, *607K*

 Writing
- Responding: Write a Persuasive Paragraph, *604*

Day 4

Comprehension Skill Instruction
- Reteaching Fact and Opinion with Reader's Library, *R12*
- Independent Application, *Practice Book, 328*

Reading the Math Link
- "Figuring It Out," *606–607*

Information and Study Skills Instruction
- Collecting Data (Tables and Charts), *607C*

Decoding Longer Words
- Reteaching Structural Analysis: VCV Pattern, *R18*
- Challenge/Extension Activities, *R19*

Spelling
- *Practice Book, 332*

Vocabulary Skill Instruction
- Dictionary: Word Histories, *607I*
- *Practice Book, 333*

Daily Language Practice, *607L*

Grammar
- Reteaching, *R22*
- Whose Is It?, *Practice Book, 335*

 Writing
- Combining Sentences with Possessive Pronouns, *607N*

Listening/Speaking/Viewing
- Present an Oral Book Report, *607O*

Day 5

Revisiting the Text: Comprehension Review Skill Instruction
- Making Judgments, *593*
- Author's Viewpoint, *597*

Rereading for Fluency
Lou Gehrig: The Luckiest Man, 584–603

Activity Choices
- Responding Activities, *605*
- Challenge/Extension Activities, *R13*
- Cross-Curricular Activities, *R26*

Vocabulary Expansion
- Sports Terminology, *607J*

Spelling
- Posttest, *607H*

Daily Language Practice, *607L*

Grammar
- Proofreading for its and it's, *607L*
- *Practice Book, 336*

 Writing
- Proofreading for its and it's, *607L*
- Writing Activities, *R23*
- Sharing Students' Writing: Author's Chair

Reading-Writing Workshop: Personal Essay

Based on the **Student Writing Model** in the Anthology, this workshop guides students through the writing process and includes skill lessons on—

- Main Idea and Details   See Teacher's Edition, *pages 556–557G.*
- Introductions and Conclusions
- Pronoun Reference

Allow time every day for students to write independently on self-selected topics.

Reading Instruction

DAY 1	• Teacher Read Aloud • Preparing to Read • Reading the Selection, Segment 1
DAY 2	• Reading the Selection, Segment 2 • Responding
DAY 3	• Revisiting the Text • Comprehension Skill Instruction
DAY 4	• Comprehension Skill Reteaching • Reading the Content Link • Information and Study Skills Instruction
DAY 5	• Comprehension Skill Review • Activity Choices

OBJECTIVES

Students listen to the selection to distinguish fact from opinion.

▶ **Activate Prior Knowledge**

Connecting to the Theme Tell students that you will be reading aloud a selection about animals that helped save or protect lives in emergency situations.

Use these suggestions to help students connect the selection with what they know:

■ Ask students to discuss different types of emergencies in which an animal might be able to provide help.

■ Have students discuss any heroic animals they have known or heard about.

Teacher Read Aloud

Listening Comprehension:
✓ Fact and Opinion

Animals in Action

Heroes can be anywhere among us—and not just on two legs or with a human brain. Check out these true stories of heroic critters!

The Hero Ham

People often badmouth pigs, as in "Quit hogging the chips," or "That room is a pigsty." They laugh at the animals' round shape. And worse, they eat them!

This so bothered Victoria Herberta of Houston, Texas, that she adopted one. Priscilla (a pig) moved into "Pigdom," a purple house in which Priscilla shared Ms. Herberta's bed, wore nail polish and learned to swim the "piggy paddle."

Then, on July 29, 1984, Priscilla became a hero.

Ms. Herberta and her friends had spent the day at nearby Lake Somerville. At 5 P.M., Carol Burk and Priscilla took a final dip. As Ms. Burk led the pig into deeper water, she told her son to stay on shore.

Eleven-year-old Anthony, a non-swimmer, waded out until he hit a drop-off. Then he screamed and disappeared. Carol dropped Priscilla's leash and struggled toward her son.

But the pig was closer and swam faster. When Anthony came up a second time, Priscilla was there. The boy grabbed the pig's harness. That sent both of them under. Seconds passed. They surfaced again, then sank again.

"Everyone was screaming," Ms. Herberta said. Perhaps Priscilla heard, because the pig's snout appeared. It regained its stroke and, with Anthony hanging on, swam to shallow water.

1 A month later Houston celebrated Priscilla the Pig Day. Later that year, Priscilla became the first pet inducted into the Texas Pet Hall of Fame—giving Ms. Herberta one more reason for making her home "A Shrine to Swine."

Lifeguards of the Deep

Martin Richardson, an experienced diver, also got in over his head.

On July 23, 1996, Mr. Richardson, then 29, was with friends on a tourist ship off the coast of Egypt. When a group of dolphins jumped playfully nearby, the captain stopped the ship so people could watch them. Mr. Richardson and two friends jumped in to swim with the animals.

But when the others returned to the boat, Mr. Richardson lagged behind. Suddenly he screamed. His body shot into the air and the sea was stained red with blood. Like an enemy submarine, a shark had attacked him from below. It bit Mr. Richardson's side and arm.

The crew launched a rubber dinghy and raced toward the injured man. But the dolphins reached him first.

The three sea mammals whirled around Mr. Richardson, smacking the water with their

---

1 Name two facts about Priscilla the Pig.
(Sample answer: Priscilla lived in a purple house with Ms. Herberta; on July 29, 1984, Priscilla helped Ms. Herberta's son Anthony swim to shallow water.)

Listening Comprehension: ✓ Fact and Opinion

Explain to students that a statement of fact describes something that is true or that really happened. A statement of opinion describes a person's thoughts or feelings about something. Different people might have different opinions about the same thing. Point out that distinguishing a fact from an author's or a character's opinion can help readers to better understand a selection.

Use the questions in the margin to assess students' understanding as you read. Reread for clarification as needed.

Vocabulary
induct: admit into a group

lag: fall behind

dinghy: a small, open boat sometimes used in emergencies

 English Language Learners

Ask students to name of things animals can do better than humans, such as run faster, fly, smell better and see at night and from greater distances. Tell students to listen for the ways the animals in the following articles became heroes for helping people.

(Teacher Read Aloud, *continued***)**

2 What is your opinion of Mr. Richardson and the dolphins? (Sample answer: Mr. Richardson should have checked the water before jumping in; he was unlucky to be bitten but lucky to have encountered the dolphins; the dolphins were smart and brave.)

2 tails and whipping it into a frothy shield. They protected him as they would a dolphin calf.

Mr. Richardson recovered, his life saved by friendly strangers that risked themselves to rescue him.

A Hare-Raising Tale

Fuzzy little house rabbits aren't known for protecting people. Yet that's what Francesca, an eight-pound brown rabbit, did one April night in 1987 in Bloomington, Indiana.

College student Kate Stanley was sleeping soundly when Francesca thumped her hind feet. Exhausted from studying, Ms. Stanley ignored the noise.

Then the bunny climbed a bedside stool and bounded on top of her. The rabbit tugged at the covers with its teeth. Ms. Stanley woke up.

That's when she noticed another noise—one coming from her bedroom window. Was someone breaking in? Ms. Stanley flipped on the lights and went to the kitchen. Francesca followed. Still groggy, Ms. Stanley reached for the backdoor knob. But Francesca bit her ankle and Ms. Stanley stopped.

"That brought me to my senses," Ms. Stanley says. She stood still and listened. Silence. Deciding she must have had a bad dream, Ms. Stanley returned to bed. Still, she couldn't sleep.

3 "I turned on the television," Ms. Stanley says. "Francesca stayed on the bed with me. She wouldn't leave."

The next day, Ms. Stanley told her story to a policeman. The officer found marks on Ms. Stanley's window where someone had removed the screen. He said Ms. Stanley was lucky. That same night an intruder had broken in across the street.

If not for the bunny bite, Ms. Stanley might have come face to face with the intruder.

3 Give one fact about the rabbit. Then give an opinion about the rabbit. (Sample answer: Fact: The rabbit in this selection woke Ms. Stanley up. Opinion: The rabbit in this selection is a real hero.)

▶ **Discussion**

Summarize After reading, discuss parts of the selection that students found most interesting. Then ask them to summarize the selection.

Listening Comprehension:
✓ **Fact and Opinion** Write the following chart headings on the board: *Fact, Opinion.* Have students write statements based on the selection under the appropriate headings.

Personal Response Have students tell whether or not they were surprised by the animals' behavior in this selection, and why.

★ **Connecting/Comparing** Ask students to compare the events in this selection to the events in other selections in the theme *Heroes.*

Reading

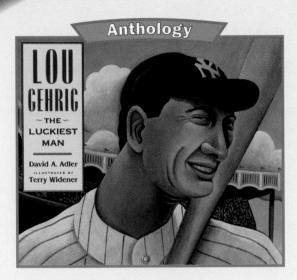

Anthology

LOU GEHRIG
~ THE ~
LUCKIEST MAN

David A. Adler

ILLUSTRATED BY
Terry Widener

Technology

Get Set for Reading CD-ROM

Lou Gehrig: The Luckiest Man
Provides background building, vocabulary support, and selection summaries in English and Spanish.

Preparing to Read

▶ Using *Get Set* for Background and Vocabulary

Connecting to the Theme Remind students that in this theme they are reading about heroes. They have read about Dr. Martin Luther King, Jr., and Gloria Estefan. Now students will read *Lou Gehrig: The Luckiest Man,* a biography about the Hall of Fame New York Yankees baseball player.

Discuss with students what they believe makes a sports star great. Then use the Get Set to Read on pages 582–583 to explain about sportsmanship and Lou Gehrig.

- Have a volunteer read aloud "Good Sportsmanship."

- Ask a student to read aloud the captions and use the photographs to discuss the differences between baseball today and in the 1930s. Mention how Yankee Stadium, where Lou Gehrig played, is still used today.

- Ask students to define the boldfaced Key Vocabulary words: *sportsmanship, modest, honor, shortstop, first baseman,* and *fielding.* Have students use each word as they talk about baseball.

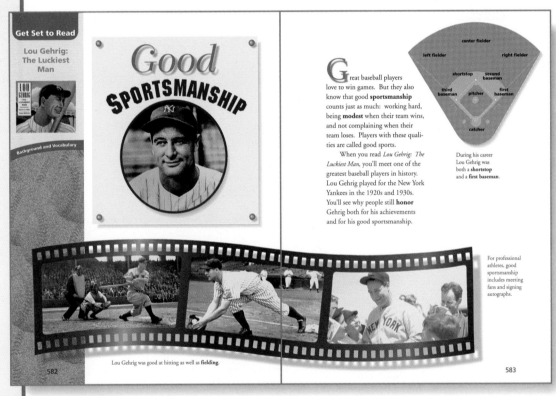

Get Set to Read

Lou Gehrig: The Luckiest Man

Background and Vocabulary

Good SPORTSMANSHIP

Great baseball players love to win games. But they also know that good **sportsmanship** counts just as much: working hard, being **modest** when their team wins, and not complaining when their team loses. Players with these qualities are called good sports.

When you read *Lou Gehrig: The Luckiest Man,* you'll meet one of the greatest baseball players in history. Lou Gehrig played for the New York Yankees in the 1920s and 1930s. You'll see why people still **honor** Gehrig both for his achievements and for his good sportsmanship.

center fielder
left fielder   right fielder
shortstop   second baseman
third baseman   pitcher   first baseman
catcher

During his career Lou Gehrig was both a **shortstop** and a **first baseman**.

For professional athletes, good sportsmanship includes meeting fans and signing autographs.

Lou Gehrig was good at hitting as well as **fielding**.

582   583

English Language Learners

Ask students familiar with baseball to share their knowledge. Explain fans and the traditions of autographs and baseball cards. List key vocabulary.

▶ Developing Key Vocabulary

Use **Transparency 5–17** to introduce Key Vocabulary from *Lou Gehrig: The Luckiest Man.*

■ Model how to figure out from context clues that *first baseman* belongs in the first blank.

■ For each remaining blank, ask students to use context clues to determine which Key Vocabulary word belongs in what blank. Ask students to share their reasoning.

Remind students that it's helpful to use the Phonics/Decoding Strategy when they read. For students who need more help with decoding, use the review below.

Practice/Homework Practice Book page 324.

Strategy Review
Phonics/Decoding

Modeling Write this sentence from *Lou Gehrig: The Luckiest Man* on the board, and point to *tremendous.*

> *The stadium let out a <u>tremendous</u> roar.*

Think Aloud

As I read the letters from left to right, I notice the shorter word men. The part before it probably says / tree /. The last part includes the o-u spelling pattern, which usually has the / ow / sound as in out. When I blend it with the letters around it, I say / dows /. / tree•mehn•dows / That's close to a word I know, / trih•MEHN•duhs /. It means really big. That makes sense because a loud cheer from a crowd could be described as a tremendous roar.

Decoding Longer Words, pages 607E–607F

Key Concept
sportsmanship

Key Vocabulary

consecutive: following one right after the other

fielding: in baseball, picking up the ball and throwing it to the correct player

first baseman: the baseball player who guards the area around first base

(to) honor: to show special respect for

modest: having a quiet, humble view of oneself

shortstop: the baseball player who guards the area between second base and third base

sportsmanship: the quality someone has when acting with dignity in difficult situations

See Vocabulary notes on pages 586, 588, 590, 592, 594, 596, 598, and 600 for additional words to preview.

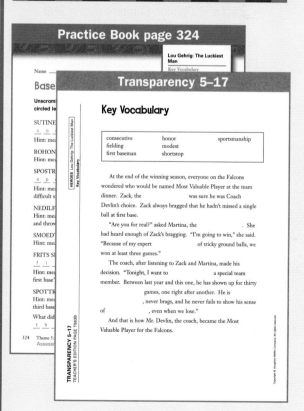

Practice Book page 324

Transparency 5–17

Reading

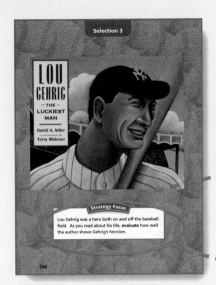

Teacher's Note

Strategy/Skill Connection For a better understanding of *Lou Gehrig: The Luckiest Man*, students can use the

- Evaluate Strategy
- Fact and Opinion Comprehension Skill

Telling apart facts and opinions allows students to see which statements show Lou Gehrig as heroic. Analyzing those statements, students can then evaluate how well the author shows him as a hero.

As students complete their Lou Gehrig Fact and Opinion Chart (**Practice Book** page 325 and **Transparency 5–18**), they can use their entries to explain the differences between facts and opinions.

(Preparing to Read, *continued*)

Strategy/Skill Preview

✓ Strategy Focus:
Evaluate

Strategy Focus

Lou Gehrig was a hero both on and off the baseball field. As you read about his life, **evaluate** how well the author shows Gehrig's heroism.

Have students turn to page 584 as you read aloud the selection's title and author. Have someone read the Strategy Focus. Give students a chance to read page 585, telling them to think about the Strategy Focus prompt. Discuss with students if they can evaluate how well the author shows Lou Gehrig as a hero. Then model the strategy.

Teacher Modeling Tell students that to evaluate is to make a judgment. And any good judgment is supported by details from the text. Tell students that to evaluate is to form an opinion based on evidence. Use the Think Aloud to model this idea based on the text on page 585.

Think Aloud

There isn't much that clearly shows Lou Gehrig as a hero on this page, but the author does give a hint. He begins by saying 1903 was a year of great beginnings. He then says that Mr. Gehrig's life began in that year. The author is connecting Mr. Gehrig with the word great. Wow, that wasn't obvious, but it was good. I got the idea that the author thinks Mr. Gehrig is a hero because he calls him great. I'll be sure to read closely to see how else the author tells us that Mr. Gehrig was heroic.

Tell students that asking themselves questions about what the author has to say will help them evaluate. Remind students to use their other reading strategies as they read.

✓ **Comprehension Skill Focus:**
Fact and Opinion

Fact and Opinion Chart Explain that as students read *Lou Gehrig: The Luckiest Man,* they will focus on the differences between facts and opinions. They will be looking for statements that can or cannot be proven.

To develop and practice the skill, students will complete the Fact and Opinion Chart on **Practice Book** page 325. Display **Transparency 5–18** and demonstrate how to use the graphic organizer.

■ Return to page 385 and ask a student to read it aloud.

■ Have another student read the first entry in the chart's middle column and ask someone to offer a fact from that page.

■ Model how to write this in the left column of the chart.

■ Ask a student to explain why that statement is a fact, asking where he or she can find proof. Write this explanation in the right column.

■ Have students copy these answers onto **Practice Book** page 325.

■ Explain to students that the statements they choose may be different than their classmates'. Be sure students also know to explain how they can tell if the statement is a fact or opinion, by saying where they can check the facts, for instance.

■ Monitor students' progress as they read.

Graphic Organizer: Fact and Opinion Chart

Statement (Answers *may vary*. Samples provided)	Fact or Opinion	How Can You Tell? Explain.
page 585 (The first World Series was played in 1903.)	**Fact**	(I can look this up in an encyclopedia.)
page 586 (Through eight years of school Lou didn't miss a single day.)	**Fact**	(I can check the school's records.)
page 589 (Those were the first two games in what would become an amazing record.)	**Opinion**	(No one can prove what is "amazing.")

Transparency 5–18

Fact and Opinion Chart

Statement	Fact or Opinion	How Can You Tell? Explain.
page 585	Fact	
page 586	Fact	
page 589	Opinion	
page 590	Fact	
page 594	Opinion	
page 597	Opinion	
page 598	Fact	

TRANSPARENCY 5–18
TEACHER'S EDITION PAGES 583D AND T607A

Practice Book page 325

Name _____

Lou Gehrig: The Luckiest Man
Graphic Organizer Fact and Opinion Chart

Fact and Opinion Chart

Statement Sample answers provided.	Fact or Opinion	How Can You Tell? Explain. Sample answers provided.
page 585 The first World Series was played in 1903. **(1 point)**	Fact	I can look this up in an encyclopedia. **(1)**
page 586 Through eight years of school Lou didn't miss a single day. **(1)**	Fact	I can check the school's records. **(1)**
page 589 Those were the first two games in what would become an amazing record. **(1)**	Opinion	No one can prove what is "amazing." **(1)**
page 590 He was selected again as the league's MVP in 1936. **(1)**	Fact	I can check this in a baseball record book. **(1)**
page 594 The 1927 Yankees were perhaps the best team ever. **(1)**	Opinion	What is "best" can't be proven. **(1)**
page 597 It was a courageous speech. **(1)**	Opinion	What is "courageous" can be different from person to person. **(1)**
page 598 The more than sixty thousand fans in Yankee Stadium stood to honor Lou Gehrig. **(1)**	Fact	I can talk to someone who was there and check the team records. **(1)**

Theme 5: **Heroes** 325
Assessment Tip: Total 14 Points

Reading

Selection 3

Options for Reading

▶ **Reading in Segments** Students can read *Lou Gehrig: The Luckiest Man* in two segments (pages 584–591 and 592–602) or in its entirety.

▶ **Deciding About Support** This picture biography of a great baseball legend and American hero is accessible even to students with little interest in or knowledge of baseball.

■ Straightforward narration and engaging illustrations will enable most students to follow On Level reading instruction.

■ Students who are unfamiliar with the baseball terminology used will benefit from Extra Support.

■ Significantly below-level readers can listen to the Audiotape and read the Selection Summary for *Lou Gehrig: The Luckiest Man*, and then read "Mark McGwire: Home Run Hero" in the **Reader's Library**.

▶ **Meeting Individual Needs** Use the notes at the bottom of the pages.

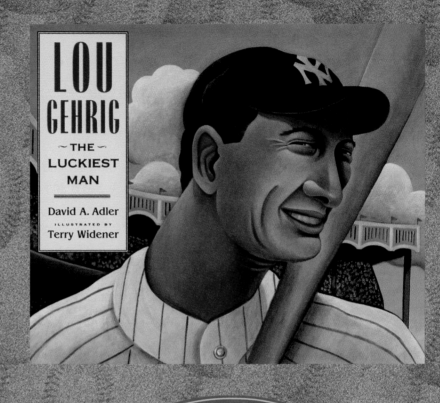

LOU GEHRIG
~ THE ~
LUCKIEST MAN

David A. Adler

ILLUSTRATED BY
Terry Widener

Strategy Focus

Lou Gehrig was a hero both on and off the baseball field. As you read about his life, **evaluate** how well the author shows Gehrig's heroism.

584

Classroom Management

On Level
Reading Cards 8, 10

While Reading: Fact and Opinion Chart (**Practice Book** page 325); Literature Discussion (p. 590, Reading Card 8); Developing Details (p. 598, Reading Card 10); generate questions

After Reading: Literature Discussion (page 602); Wrapping Up Segment 1 (page 591) and Segment 2 (page 603)

Challenge
Reading Cards 7–10

While Reading: Fact and Opinion Chart (**Practice Book** page 325); Specialized Language (p. 588, Reading Card 7); Quotations and Invented Dialogue (page 596)

After Reading: Literature Discussion (page 602); Wrapping Up Segment 1 (page 591) and Segment 2 (page 603)

English Language Learners

Intermediate and Advanced Fluency Begin a time line at 1903 on the board. As you read in a group, pause frequently to fill in the time line with events in Lou Gehrig's life and to work on vocabulary.

For English language learners at other proficiency levels, see **Language Development Resources**.

Lou Gehrig: The Luckiest Man

Reading Segment 1
pages 584–591

Purpose Setting Have students read the title of the selection and look at the illustrations. Ask them to evaluate how Lou Gehrig might be feeling and why. While reading, notice details the author includes to make the selection moving.

 Journal Writing Students can use their journal to record details that make Lou Gehrig special and the selection so moving.

Reinforcing Comprehension and Strategies

- Remind students to use Evaluate and other strategies as they read and to add to their Fact and Opinion Chart (**Practice Book** page 325).

- Use the Strategy Focus notes on pages 590 and 594 to reinforce the Evaluate strategy.

- Use Supporting Comprehension questions beginning on page 586 to help students develop higher-level understanding of the text.

1903 was a year of great beginnings. Henry Ford sold his first automobile and the Wright Brothers made the first successful flight in an airplane. In baseball, the first World Series was played. The team later known as the Yankees moved from Baltimore to New York. And on June 19, 1903, Henry Louis Gehrig was born. He would become one of the greatest players in baseball history.

Lou Gehrig was born in the Yorkville section of New York City. It was an area populated with poor immigrants like his parents, Heinrich and Christina Gehrig, who had come to the United States from Germany.

585

Extra Support: Previewing the Text

Before each segment, preview the text, using the notes below and on page 592. **While** reading, model strategies (pages 589 and 597). **After** reading, review each segment (pages 590 and 602) before students join the Wrapping Up discussion.

page 585 Lou Gehrig was born in New York City in 1903. From the illustration, can you tell some ways life was different then?

pages 586–587 It was important to Lou Gehrig's mother that he get a good education

but Gehrig loved sports. He managed to do both things.

pages 588–589 Lou Gehrig went to college and played baseball there.

pages 590–591 Lou Gehrig was a great player for the New York Yankees for many years, but then he had trouble playing. How do you think he felt?

▶ Supporting Comprehension

1 Why do you think Christina Gehrig wanted her son to go to college? (The Gehrigs were poor immigrants and Mrs. Gehrig wanted her son to have the education and skills to make a good life for himself.)

2 What can you infer about Lou Gehrig never missing a day of grade school? (He respected his mother's opinion and honored her wishes that he get an education.)

3 How did Gehrig balance his respect for his mother's opinion about sports with his love of sports? (He played before school and also participated in sports at school.)

Vocabulary *(pages 585–586)*

immigrants: people who leave their homeland and come to a new country to live

accountant: a person whose job is to help people or companies handle their money

engineer: person whose job is to use scientific knowledge to build or design things

---

1   Christina Gehrig had great hopes for her son Lou. She dreamed that he would attend college and become an accountant or an engineer. She insisted that he study hard. Through eight years of grade school,

2 Lou didn't miss a single day.

    Lou's mother thought games and sports were a waste of time. But Lou loved sports. He got up early to play the games he loved — baseball, soccer, and football. He played until it was time to go to school.

3 In high school Lou was a star on his school's baseball team.

586

Extra Support

Strategy Modeling

Phonics/Decoding Use this example to model the strategy.

When I look at the word e-n-g-i-n-e-e-r, I recognize /ehn/ from the word enter. Next I see the g-i spelling pattern which makes the /j/ sound followed by a vowel-consonant-e pattern, so maybe it says /jyn/. I know the -er ending. It's /ehn•jyn•ur/. That's not a word I recognize. Maybe the middle part is /jihn/, and the last part sounds like /eer/. It's /ehn•juh•NEER/!

Lou Gehrig: The Luckiest Man

587

English Language Learners

Building Vocabulary English language learners may be unfamiliar with baseball terms, including scout (page 588), American League and MVP (page 590), and lineup and benching (page 592). Encourage students knowledgeable about baseball to explain these terms as you read.

Reading

▶ Supporting Comprehension

4 What might Gehrig have said to his mother to calm her down after he quit college to join the Yankees? (Answers will vary. Possible answer: We really need the money, and I can return to college if my baseball career doesn't work out.)

5 Why do you think the Yankee manager sent Gehrig to bat for the shortstop? (probably because the shortstop was not hitting the ball or he got injured)

6 Although the author does not state it directly, what can you infer about the position Gehrig played throughout his career? (His position appears to be first base, since that is the last position mentioned in the biography that Gehrig played.)

Vocabulary *(pages 588–589)*

scout: a person hired by a team to search for talented athletes to sign up

salary: the money paid for work done

shortstop: the baseball player who guards the area between second base and third base

first baseman: the baseball player who guards the area around first base

consecutive: one following right after the other

Cross-Curricular Connection

Social Studies During the decade in which Lou Gehrig was born, nearly 9 million immigrants came to the United States—the most of any decade in history. Immigration came to a halt during World War I (1914–1918) but then picked up again until 1921, when laws began to limit the number of people who could enter the country.

After high school Lou Gehrig went to Columbia University. He was on the baseball team there, too, and on April 26, 1923, a scout for the New York Yankees watched him play. Lou hit two long home runs in that game. Soon after that he was signed to play for the Yankees.

The Yankees offered Lou a $1,500 bonus to sign plus a good salary. His family needed the money. Lou quit college and joined the Yankees. Lou's mother was furious. She was convinced that he was ruining his life.

4

588

 Challenge

Reading Card 7

Specialized Language

Almost every kind of pastime—from stamp collecting to white-water rafting—has its own special terms to describe equipment and activities. Baseball is no exception. Besides the "official" terms, there is usually a fair amount of slang that grows up around a sport or a hobby. How many of these baseball words do you recognize?

| balk | designated hitter | slider |
| change-up | relief pitcher | two-bagger |

On June 1, 1925, the Yankee manager sent Lou to bat for the shortstop. The next day Lou played in place of first baseman Wally Pipp. Those were the first two games in what would become an amazing record: For the next fourteen years Lou Gehrig played in 2,130 consecutive Yankee games. The boy who never missed a day of grade school became a man who never missed a game.

5

6

589

Revisiting the Text

Tested Skill

Comprehension Skill Lesson
Fact and Opinion

OBJECTIVES

Students identify facts and opinions in the selection.

Explain the differences between facts and opinions:

■ A fact is a statement that can be proved true or false. It can usually be supported with evidence from a reference source.

■ An opinion is what someone thinks, feels, or believes. You can agree or disagree with an opinion, but you cannot prove it true or false.

Write this sentence from page 588: *She was convinced he was ruining his life.* This is Gehrig's mother's opinion when Gehrig signs with the Yankees. Point out that opinions in the book can be important to the understanding of nonfiction. Now write the following from page 589: *Those were the first two games in what would become an amazing record.* The *amazing record* is an opinion held by the author. Have students record facts and opinions on a chart like this.

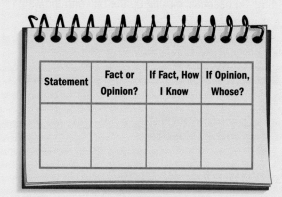

Statement	Fact or Opinion?	If Fact, How I Know	If Opinion, Whose?

Skill Finder

• Instruction, pages 607A–607B

• Reteaching, page R12

• Review, Theme 6, p. 665

Extra Support

Strategy Modeling

Evaluate Use this example to model the strategy.

The author has done a good job making me realize just how special Lou Gehrig was as a person and a baseball player. His parents never had much since they immigrated to the United States. And through his abllity at baseball he was able to take care of them. It's hard to believe he played baseball for fourteen years and never missed a game!

Reading

Lou Gehrig played despite stomachaches, fevers, a sore arm, back pains, and broken fingers. Lou's constant play earned him the nickname Iron Horse. All he would say about his amazing record was, "That's the way I am."

Lou was shy and modest, but people who watched him knew just how good he was. In 1927 Lou's teammate Babe Ruth hit sixty home runs, the most hit up to that time in one season. But it was Lou Gehrig who was selected that year by the baseball writers as the American League's Most Valuable Player.

7 He was selected again as the league's MVP in 1936.

590

▶ Strategy Focus: Evaluate

Teacher/Student Modeling Have students list criteria by which they can evaluate the author's success in showing Lou Gehrig to be a hero.

▶ Supporting Comprehension

7 What is the point the author is trying to make about Gehrig's being named MVP in 1927 even though Babe Ruth hit a record number of home runs? (There is more to being named MVP than just a player's home run record.)

8 How does the author show that Gehrig's problem wasn't just poor play on the field? (He mentions that Gehrig fell down in the clubhouse while getting dressed.)

> ### Vocabulary (pages 590–591)
> **modest:** having a quiet, humble view of oneself
>
> **apparent:** easily seen or understood
>
> **fielding:** in baseball, picking up the ball and throwing it to the correct player
>
> **clubhouse:** locker rooms used by a sports team

 Extra Support

Segment 1: Review

Before students join the whole class for Wrapping Up on page 591, have them

- check their predictions
- take turns modeling the Evaluate strategy and any other strategies they used
- check and revise their Fact and Opinion Chart on **Practice Book** page 325, and use it to summarize

 On Level   Challenge

Reading Card 8

Literature Discussion

In mixed-ability groups of five or six, students can discuss their own questions and the discussion prompts on Reading Card 8.

- How do you think reading this selection without the illustrations would be? How do you think it would be different with photographs?
- How does the author make you care about what is happening to Gehrig?

Then, during the 1938 baseball season — and for no apparent reason — Lou Gehrig stopped hitting. One newspaper reported that Lou was swinging as hard as he could, but when he hit the ball it didn't go anywhere.

Lou exercised. He took extra batting practice. He even tried changing the way he stood and held his bat. He worked hard during the winter of 1938 and watched his diet.

But the following spring Lou's playing was worse. Time after time he swung at the ball and missed. He had trouble fielding. And he even had problems off the field. In the clubhouse he fell down while he was getting dressed.

8

End of
Segment 1:
pages 584–591

English Language Learners

Review the steps Lou Gehrig took to improve his game after the 1938 season (page 591). Ask a volunteer to read the second paragraph aloud. Ask students to describe Lou Gehrig's character.

Wrapping Up Segment 1
pages 584–591

First, provide Extra Support for students who need it (p. 590). Then bring all students together.

- **Review Predictions/Purpose** Discuss the details the author includes to make Lou Gehrig special and heroic.

- **Model Strategies** Refer students to the **Strategies Poster** and have them take turns modeling Evaluate and other strategies they used as they read. Provide models if needed (page 589).

- **Share Group Discussions** Have students share their questions and literature discussions.

- **Summarize** Have students use the transparency and their Fact and Opinion Chart to summarize the events in the story so far.

Comprehension/Critical Thinking

1. Why do you think Gehrig didn't go to see a doctor as soon as he started having problems hitting the ball? (Because he had no idea that he had a medical problem. He has always accomplished things by working hard—and harder.) **Making Inferences**

2. In what other order could the author have presented the story of Lou Gehrig? How would the author have had to change his narrative? (Starting from a memorable moment; starting at the end of his life. In each case there would have needed to be flashbacks instead of simple chronological order.) **Sequence of Events**

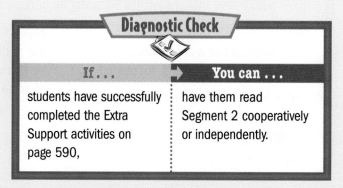

Diagnostic Check

If...	You can...
students have successfully completed the Extra Support activities on page 590,	have them read Segment 2 cooperatively or independently.

Reading Segment 2

pages 592–602

Purpose Setting Have students summarize the story so far and evaluate their feelings for Gehrig as a person, baseball player, and hero. Then have students read pages 592–602.

Journal Writing Students can record their feelings about Lou Gehrig and compare and contrast their feelings with the author's.

Vocabulary *(pages 592–593)*

lineup: players in a baseball game; the order in which players bat

specialists: doctors who focus on one area of the body

central nervous system: brain and spinal cord

umpire: baseball official who rules on plays

Some people said Yankee manager Joe McCarthy should take Lou out of the lineup. But McCarthy refused. He had great respect for Lou and said, "Gehrig plays as long as he wants to play." But Lou wasn't selfish. On May 2, 1939, he told Joe McCarthy, "I'm benching myself . . . for the good of the team."

When reporters asked why he took himself out, Lou didn't say he felt weak or how hard it was for him to run. Lou made no excuses. He just said that he couldn't hit and he couldn't field.

On June 13, 1939, Lou went to the Mayo Clinic in Rochester, Minnesota, to be examined by specialists. On June 19, his thirty-sixth birthday, they told Lou's wife, Eleanor, what was wrong. He was suffering

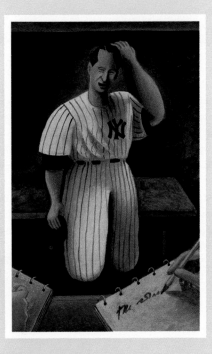

592

Extra Support: Previewing the Text

Before reading Segment 2, preview the text, using the notes below. **While** reading, model strategies (page 594). **After** reading, review the segment (page 602) before students join the Wrapping Up discussion.

pages 592–593 Gehrig went to a hospital and learned he had a deadly disease. He stayed with the team but did not play anymore.

pages 594–599 Lou Gehrig Appreciation Day was held at Yankee Stadium. How do you think Gehrig felt? How did the fans feel?

pages 600–601 Eventually Gehrig had to stay at the hospital. He tried not to speak of his illness or dying to visitors. Why do you think he acted that way?

page 602 Lou Gehrig died at the age of thirty-seven. Were you surprised at his death, or had the author prepared you for it?

from amyotrophic lateral sclerosis, a deadly disease that affects the central nervous system.

Lou stayed with the team, but he didn't play. He was losing weight. His hair was turning gray. He didn't have to be told he was dying. He knew it. "I don't have long to go," he told a teammate.

Lou loved going to the games, being in the clubhouse, and sitting with his teammates. Before each game Lou brought the Yankee lineup card to the umpire at home plate. A teammate or coach walked with him, to make sure he didn't fall. Whenever Lou came onto the field the fans stood up and cheered for brave Lou Gehrig.

593

MEETING INDIVIDUAL NEEDS

English Language Learners

After reading page 593, discuss Gehrig's statement, *I'm benching myself ... for the good of the team,* on page 592 and what had happened. Ask volunteers to explain how benching himself was an example of good sportsmanship.

Revisiting the Text

Review/Maintain

Comprehension Skill Lesson
Making Judgments

OBJECTIVES

Students make judgments about an element of a biography.

Remind students to look at specific details and use their own knowledge and values to form opinions about characters, situations, and the author's viewpoint.

Ask students what they think about Gehrig's decision to attend games even though he didn't play. Was it a good one, based on his personality and health? Have students cite evidence from the story and their own experience in analyzing Gehrig's decision. They can organize their responses in a chart like the one below.

Reasons to Go to the Stadium PROS (+)	**Reasons Not to Go to the Stadium** CONS (–)
For the team	Bad for his health
To feel useful	He could fall
To keep trying	He might miss playing
It made him happy	

Point out that although the fans cheered for "the brave Lou Gehrig," it was not a reason to go to the stadium. Nor was the possibility that he wanted people to feel sorry for him. Have students look at their chart. Then decide and explain if they think Gehrig made a good decision to go to the stadium. What would they have done in his place?

Skill Finder

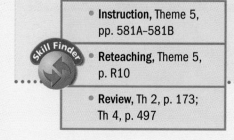

- **Instruction,** Theme 5, pp. 581A–581B
- **Reteaching,** Theme 5, p. R10
- **Review,** Th 2, p. 173; Th 4, p. 497

Strategy/Focus: Evaluate

Student Modeling Ask students to model their evaluations of how successful the author is in showing Lou Gehrig's heroism. If necessary use the following prompts:

Are there more places in Segment 2 than in Segment 1 where the author has opportunities to show Gehrig's heroism? Does he make the best use of them?

 Supporting Comprehension

9 How could you decide if the author's opinion that the 1927 Yankees was *perhaps the best baseball team ever* is something you might agree or disagree with? (If the author means just based on statistics, you could look them up and compare it with the statistics for other teams in baseball history.)

10 Why do you think the illustrator chose the view he did to illustrate these two pages? (because he wanted to show the huge numbers of fans compared to Gehrig down by himself on the field)

Vocabulary *(pages 594–595)*

(to) honor: to show special respect for

prototype: an original example

sportsmanship: acting with dignity in difficult situations

But Yankee fans and the team wanted to do more. They wanted Lou to know how deeply they felt about him. So they made July 4, 1939, Lou Gehrig Appreciation Day at Yankee Stadium.

Many of the players from the 1927 Yankees — perhaps the best baseball team ever — came to honor their former teammate. There was a marching **9** band and gifts. Many people spoke, too. Fiorello La Guardia, the mayor of

594

 Cross-Curricular Connection

Science There are about 5,000 new cases of ALS each year in the United States. Certain nerve cells in the brain and the spinal cord —the central nervous system, which controls voluntary movement— slowly wear out. Muscles that they control weaken and waste away, until a person cannot move. The course of the disease depends on which muscles weaken first. Men are more likely to get ALS than women by about one and a half times. There is no cure nor proven treatment yet to prevent or stop the course of the disease.

New York City, told Lou, "You are the greatest prototype of good sportsmanship and citizenship."

When the time came for Lou to thank everyone, he was too moved to speak. But the fans wanted to hear him and chanted, "We want Gehrig! We want Gehrig!"

10

595

Visual Literacy Lesson
Perspective

OBJECTIVES

Students identify different perspectives in illustrations.

Explain that the artist has used different perspectives—points of view—to illustrate the selection. In addition to providing visual variety, it complements what is going on in the text.

For example, point out how on pages 594–595 the fans seem to overwhelm the tiny Lou Gehrig on the field. The close-up on three of those fans shows how enthusiastic the crowd was. This reinforces the text: *When the time came for Gehrig to thank everyone, he was too moved to speak. But the fans wanted to hear him and chanted, "We want Gehrig! We want Gehrig!"*

Ask students to say what they think the purpose is of shifting to a close-up of Gehrig on the next spread of the selection.

Have the students start at the beginning of the selection and go look at each illustration. Ask them to make notes on what, if anything, they think the artist does by way of perspective (such as, close-up, distance scene, looking up from ground, looking down) to enhance the text. Have them comment on the strong and weak points of specific illustrations.

Reading

▶ Supporting Comprehension

11 Do you think Gehrig was sincere by saying that he was *the luckiest man on the face of the earth*? (Based on what we know up to now about him, it's quite possible he really meant it.)

12 How much do you think of what happened to Gehrig in his career and personal life was lucky? (Answers will vary.)

13 If you had been in the stands on Appreciation Day or listened to Gehrig over the radio, what might you have felt at that moment? (Answers will vary. Possible answers: proud, sympathetic, sad, inspired.)

Vocabulary *(page 596)*
array: a group arranged in an order

596

 **Challenge**

Reading Card 9

Quotations and Invented Dialogue

To add drama to the narrative of a biography, some authors add quotations by and about the subject. If the author cannot find any, sometimes he or she makes them up. This *invented dialogue* often is used in biographies aimed at young readers. Sometimes, it became so connected to a historical figure that everyone thinks it was an actual quote. Today, however, authors are usually more careful at getting "real" quotes, although sometimes an author uses invented dialogue for a certain purpose. In this selection, does the author seem to use invented or real dialogue? Explain.

Dressed in his Yankee uniform, Lou Gehrig walked slowly to the array of microphones. He wiped his eyes, and with his baseball cap in his hands, his head down, he slowly spoke.

"Fans," he said, "for the past two weeks you have been reading about a bad break I got. Yet today I consider myself the luckiest man on the face of the earth."

It was a courageous speech. Lou didn't complain about his terrible illness. Instead he spoke of his many blessings and of the future. "Sure, I'm lucky," he said when he spoke of his years in baseball. "Sure, I'm lucky," he said again when he spoke of his fans and family.

Lou spoke about how good people had been to him. He praised his teammates. He thanked his parents and his wife, whom he called a tower of strength.

11

12

13

597

Revisiting the Text

Review/Maintain

Comprehension Skill Lesson
Author's Viewpoint

OBJECTIVES

Students infer the author's viewpoint to understand his overall message.

Remind students that an author's viewpoint reflects his or her attitude, values, and unstated beliefs. Readers usually have to infer an author's viewpoint from evidence in the selection. It is helpful to pay attention to the author's opinions and efforts to influence the reader's thinking with tone or mood.

Tell students that in a biography, as in other nonfiction, they can use a word web with the person or subject of discussion in the center and words used to describe the person or subject radiating from it. Model using the description of Gehrig on page 590.

Based on the web have students describe the author's opinion of Gehrig. Have them go through the rest of the selection and make similar word webs to back up their assessments.

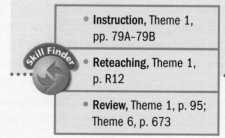

* **Instruction**, Theme 1, pp. 79A–79B
* **Reteaching**, Theme 1, p. R12
* **Review**, Theme 1, p. 95; Theme 6, p. 673

Skill Finder

Extra Support

MEETING INDIVIDUAL NEEDS

Strategy Modeling

Phonics/Decoding Use this example to model the strategy.

The author is successful in showing Gehrig's heroism on page 597 through quotes and reporting on his speech at Appreciation Day. He said "Sure, I'm lucky" twice—once about baseball and the other about his fans and family. He spoke about how good people had been to him, praising his teammates and thanking his parents and his wife.

▶ Supporting Comprehension

14 Why do you think the author spends so much of the selection writing about Appreciation Day compared with other things? (because nothing else shows Gehrig's personality so clearly, supporting the author's viewpoint)

15 If you have some idea as to the outcome of Gehrig's illness, what do you make of his statement, *I'm going to remember this day for a long time*? (It's ironic in a sad way; he'd remember the day for the rest of his life, which was a short time.)

16 Even before Gehrig took the job with the Parole Commission, do you think he did more for the city than the city had done for him? (Answers will vary.)

Vocabulary *(page 599)*

parole: releasing a prisoner who has not yet completed his prison sentence

---

The more than sixty thousand fans in Yankee Stadium stood to honor Lou Gehrig. His last words to them — and to the many thousands more sitting by their radios and listening — were, "So I close in saying that I might have had a bad break, but I have an awful lot to live for. Thank you."

Lou stepped back from the microphones and wiped his eyes. The stadium crowd let out a tremendous roar, and Babe Ruth did what many people must have wanted to do that day. He threw his arms around Lou Gehrig and gave him a great warm hug.

The band played the song "I Love You Truly," and the fans chanted, "We love you, Lou."

14
15

When Lou Gehrig left the stadium later that afternoon, he told a teammate, "I'm going to remember this day for a long time."

598

On Level   Challenge

Reading Card 10

Developing Details

What makes one writer's work seem so vivid, while another's is just ho-hum? Aside from an exciting story (whether fiction or nonfiction), memorable characters, and an engaging style, an author's best friend may be details. They can give a work of fiction the texture of real life and help to re-create scenes from real life for the reader's delight. Dialogue or quotes are one kind of detail the author uses. Here are some others the author uses on pages 598–599: the name of the song the band plays, retiring the uniform, telling which city agency Gehrig goes to work for and why.

English Language Learners

After reading page 597, ask a volunteer to act out Gehrig's trip to the microphones and to read his lines aloud. Then discuss why Gehrig felt he was the luckiest man despite his illness. Also discuss the idiom *bad break* and the metaphor *tower of strength* used to describe Gehrig's parents and wife.

In December 1939 Lou Gehrig was voted into the Baseball Hall of Fame. And the Yankees retired his uniform. No one else on the team would ever wear the number four. It was the first time a major-league baseball team did that to honor one of its players.

Mayor Fiorello La Guardia thought Lou's courage might inspire some of the city's troubled youths to be courageous, too. He offered Lou a job working with former prisoners as a member of the New York City Parole Commission. Lou had many opportunities to earn more money, but he believed this job would enable him to do something for the city that had given him so much. **16**

Within little more than a year, Lou had to leave his job. He was too weak to keep working. He stayed at home, unable to do the simplest task.

599

English Language Learners

Remind students that Lou Gehrig's career preceded television. Refer to the illustrations on pages 591–592 and 598, and explain that unless you attended a game, newspapers and radio were the only ways to keep up with baseball. Also, discuss the illustration headline "Gehrig Slumps" and the illustration of writing pads and Gehrig scratching his head.

Reading Fluency

- **Rereading for Fluency:** After finishing the story, have students choose a passage from either Segment 1 or Segment 2 to reread to a partner, or have them reread page 598. Encourage students to read with feeling and expression.

- **Assessing Fluency:** See the guidelines in the Theme Assessment Wrap-Up, pages 608–609A.

Reading

▶ Supporting Comprehension

17 Why would Gehrig tell people that he was going to get better even though he knew he wouldn't? (He was trying to make them feel less sad over his illness even though he was actually very sick.)

18 What do you think Gehrig meant by *We have much to be thankful for*? (Gehrig was probably talking about friends and family.)

19 The illustration on this spread shows the outside of Yankee Stadium on the day of Lou Gehrig's funeral. Do you think it is a fitting subject for the illustration on this page? (Answers will vary. Probably it is fitting because Yankee Stadium was the place where Gehrig gained his fame and spent many happy years.)

Vocabulary *(page 600)*
visibly: in a way that can be seen

17

18

Lou had many visitors. He didn't speak to them of his illness or of dying. When he saw one friend visibly upset by the way he looked, Lou told him not to worry. "I'll gradually get better," he said. In cards to his friends Lou wrote, "We have much to be thankful for."

600

By the middle of May 1941, Lou hardly left his bed. Then on Monday, June 2, 1941, just after ten o'clock at night, Lou Gehrig died. He was thirty-seven years old.

On June 4 the Yankee game was canceled because of rain. Some people thought it was fitting that the Yankees did not play; this was the day of Lou Gehrig's funeral.

19

601

▶ Supporting Comprehension

20 How does the ending of the book mirror the end of Gehrig's life? (Just as there were no speeches at Gehrig's funeral, the author ends quietly, without going over Gehrig's achievements or adding words of praise.)

21 Why do you think the illustrator made this illustration to end Lou Gehrig's biography? (Answers will vary.)

20 At the funeral the minister announced that there would be no speeches. "We need none," he said, "because you all knew him." That seemed fitting, too, for modest Lou Gehrig.

21

602

Segment 2 Review

Before students join in Wrapping Up on page 603, have them

- review their purpose
- take turns modeling the reading strategies they used
- help you complete **Transparency 5–18** and their Fact and Opinion Charts
- summarize the whole story

Literature Discussion

Have small groups of students discuss the story, using their own questions or the questions in Think About the Selection on page 604.

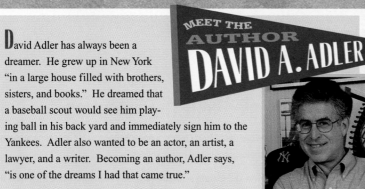

David Adler has always been a dreamer. He grew up in New York "in a large house filled with brothers, sisters, and books." He dreamed that a baseball scout would see him playing ball in his back yard and immediately sign him to the Yankees. Adler also wanted to be an actor, an artist, a lawyer, and a writer. Becoming an author, Adler says, "is one of the dreams I had that came true."

Adler loves his work because he can still follow his many interests. He has published more than one hundred books on topics such as math, science, and history. He's also written puzzle books, biographies, mysteries, and adventures.

Other books: the *Cam Jansen* mystery series, *A Picture Book of Helen Keller, Fraction Fun*

Whenever Terry Widener illustrates a book, he tries to make the author's words come alive through his pictures. He hopes that his illustrations are exciting and entertaining, especially to young readers.

Widener's advice to young artists is to be patient to achieve their dreams. "It's very hard to wait," he says, "but I have found that if you work towards your goal, things seem to happen." When he's not illustrating, Widener likes to coach soccer and travel.

Internet

To find out more about David Adler and Terry Widener, visit Education Place.
www.eduplace.com/kids

End of Segment 2:
pages 592–602

Wrapping Up Segment 2
pages 592–602

First, provide Extra Support for students who need it (page 602). Then bring all students together.

- **Review Predictions/Purpose** Have students evaluate Lou Gehrig as a hero and the details the author included to show him as a hero.

- **Model Strategies** Have students tell how they used the Evaluate strategy, and then have them take turns modeling it. Ask what other strategies they found helpful while reading.

- **Share Group Discussion** Have students discuss how they feel about the story as a whole, now that they have finished reading it.

- **Summarize** Have students use their Fact and Opinion charts to summarize the story. Ask them how the charts helped them with their reading.

Comprehension/Critical Thinking

1 What do you think Lou Gehrig might have accomplished in his career if he had not gotten sick? (Answers will vary.) **Predicting Outcomes**

2 What do you think Lou Gehrig's career might have been like if he had been born in 1973 instead of 1903? (Answers will vary. He would have been known by more people because of TV; he would have made more money.) **Compare and Contrast**

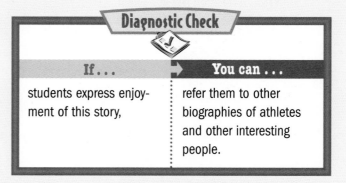

Diagnostic Check

If . . .	You can . . .
students express enjoyment of this story,	refer them to other biographies of athletes and other interesting people.

Responding

▶ Think About the Selection

Discuss or Write Have students discuss or write their answers. Sample answers are provided; accept reasonable responses that are supported with evidence from the story.

1 **Fact and Opinion** He was a great ballplayer because he was an excellent fielder and hitter who practiced hard when he thought he needed to. When he realized that he couldn't play well anymore, he stopped playing for the good of the team.

2 **Making Inferences** He never missed school and studied hard to get into college. He got up early so that he could play sports so it didn't keep him from school or homework. When he joined the Yankees, he played in 2,130 consecutive games.

3 **Making Generalizations** Gehrig played hard and played his best every day, but he didn't brag. He gave the fans his all and didn't expect or want hero worship.

4 **Making Inferences** The fans probably felt very sad and very proud of Gehrig; answers will vary.

5 **Drawing Conclusions** Gehrig said he was lucky because he had been able to play baseball on a terrific team and because he had great fans, parents, and a wife.

⭐ Connecting/Comparing Making Judgments Both Lou Gehrig and Gloria Estefan served as role models for their fans through their own good behavior and clean living. Both gave of their time to work with young people.

Responding

Think About the Selection

1. What made Lou Gehrig a great ballplayer? Give facts about both his achievements and his character.

2. How did Gehrig's childhood habits help him when he joined the Yankees?

3. What does Gehrig's life teach you about good sportsmanship?

4. How do you think the fans felt when they heard Gehrig's speech at Yankee Stadium? Would you have felt the same?

5. Why did Lou Gehrig call himself "the luckiest man on the face of the earth"? Do you agree?

6. ⭐ **Connecting/Comparing** Lou Gehrig and Gloria Estefan are not only stars but also good citizens. Explain.

Write a Persuasive Paragraph

There are many great baseball players, but Lou Gehrig's story has a special meaning in baseball history. Write a paragraph to persuade a reader that Lou Gehrig was one of the country's greatest baseball heroes. Go back to the story for details.

Tips

- To help you get started, write out the goal of your paragraph.
- Be sure to support your statements with facts and examples.

604

🔖 MEETING INDIVIDUAL NEEDS English Language Learners

Beginning/Preproduction Help students describe Lou Gehrig as a baseball player and as a person.

Early Production and Speech Emergence Ask partners to describe good sportsmanship. Then have students describe the way Gehrig was a good sportsman.

Intermediate and Advanced Fluency Have partners review the selection to create a list of possible reasons Lou Gehrig called himself the luckiest man.

Personal Response

Invite volunteers to share their personal responses to *Lou Gehrig: The Luckiest Man.* As an alternative, ask students to write in their journals about something in their lives that makes them feel lucky.

Comprehension Check

Assign **Practice Book** page 326 to assess students' understanding of the selection.

Practice Book page 326

Name _____

Lou Gehrig: The Luckiest Man
Comprehension Check

Lou Hits a Home Run

Start at home plate and round the bases. Add words to complete each sentence that tells about an important event in Lou Gehrig's life.

3. Lou played 2,130 consecutive games for the New York Yankees (1 point)

4. Lou had to stop playing baseball because he suffered from a serious disease that affects the central nervous system (1)

2. He was a star on his high school's baseball team (1)

1. Lou Gehrig was born on June 19, 1903 (1)

5. Lou was inducted into the Baseball Hall of Fame (1) in December 1939 and is remembered for his courage, modesty and good sportsmanship (1)

326   Theme 5: **Heroes**
Assessment Tip: Total **6** Points

Math

Find the Difference

Lou Gehrig's record for consecutive games was broken in 1995 by Cal Ripken, Jr., of the Baltimore Orioles. The new record is 2,632 consecutive games. Figure out how many more consecutive games Cal Ripken played than Lou Gehrig. Go back to the story for clues.

Bonus Lou Gehrig played an average of 152 games a year for 14 years. Estimate how many more years Lou Gehrig would have had to play to reach the current record of 2,632 games.

Viewing

Compare Baseball Then and Now

Work with a partner. Go back to the story and look at the illustrations of baseball uniforms, baseball stadiums, and the fans. Then compare those with modern pictures from magazines or television. How are the styles different? How are they similar?

Internet

Go on a Web Field Trip

Connect to Education Place to explore Yankee Stadium, the National Baseball Hall of Fame, and other fun sports sites.
www.eduplace.com/kids

605

English Language Learners

Explain that the purpose of a persuasive paragraph is to make the reader agree with what you write. Work with students to brainstorm a list of examples from the story that demonstrate Gehrig's greatness as a baseball player. Allow students to draw from this list when writing.

End-of-Selection Assessment

Selection Test Use the test in the **Teacher's Resource Blackline Masters** to assess selection comprehension and vocabulary.

Student Self-Assessment Have students assess their reading with additional questions such as

- What parts of this selection were difficult for me? Why?

- What strategies helped me understand the story?

- Would I recommend this story to my friends? Why or why not?

Math Link

pages 606–607

▶ ## Skill: How to Read a Chart

Read aloud the title of the link. Point out that a chart is a great way to place a lot of information in a small area—and make it easy to read as well.

Before You Read Have students read the numbered steps in the left column on page 606.

While You Read Have students read the chart with Lou Gehrig's statistics.

Vocabulary *(pages 606–607)*

standings: wins and losses

statistics: information given in numbers

calculate: figure out

innings: parts of a baseball game that each last until both teams make three outs; there are usually nine innings in a game

errors: pitching or fielding mistakes that allow a player to get to a base or score a run

walks: times a batter reaches a base when the pitcher throws four balls that don't go over the home plate in the correct place

---

Math Link

Skill: How to Read a Chart

❶ Read the **title** of the chart. It tells what information the chart shows.

❷ Read the **headings** of the **rows** (which go across) and the **columns** (which go up and down) to see how the chart is organized.

❸ Move your finger across the rows and columns to find the information you want.

❹ Look for a **key** to help you understand symbols or abbreviations.

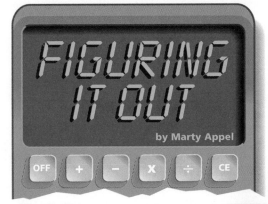

FIGURING IT OUT

by Marty Appel

You can follow your favorite player or team by checking the newspapers each day, which are loaded with information on the major leagues.

You can see the standings of the clubs, the box scores of games, and the league leaders in many categories. You can often see a chart showing how everyone on the home team is hitting or pitching.

It is good to know how all of these baseball averages are figured. You can do it yourself with the help of a calculator.

Lou Gehrig's Statistics

Year	Team	HR	RBI	BA
1925	New York	20	68	.295
1926	New York	16	107	.313
1927	New York	47	175	.373
1928	New York	27	142	.374
1929	New York	35	126	.300

Key: **HR**–home runs; **RBI**–runs batted in; **BA**–batting average

606

Classroom Management

All Students

Reading the Article "Figuring It Out" should be within the reach of your On Level readers. For students who have difficulty with math concepts, you may need to explain several times the way the statistics in the chart are derived. You may have to encourage them to move their fingers along rows and columns as they read the information. You can familiarize students further with numerical charts by having them make their own, collecting their data from easily observable events. You can also provide them with additional baseball statistics for further practice.

Batting Averages. A batting average measures how many hits a player would get if he were to bat 1,000 times. Anything over .300 (say "three hundred") is considered excellent.

Use the division sign for the word *for*. If a batter has 71 hits *for* 253 at bats, you would calculate 71 ÷ 253 = .2806324. Since batting averages are only shown in three numbers, you would round off the third number and this average would be .281. If the fourth number is five or more, add a number in the third column.

Try another one. Look at the league leaders and see if the math is correct!

Earned Run Average. This is a very important statistic for pitchers. The number tells you how many earned runs they allow for every nine innings they pitch. An earned run is a run that scores without help from errors, even a pitcher's own error. It is a run that has scored simply by hits, walks, and hit batters.

Clear the calculator. Punch in the earned runs (say, 60) and multiply it by 9. 60 × 9 = 540. Leave the 540 showing. Don't clear the calculator. Hit the ÷ sign, and then punch in the innings pitched, say 210. That gives you an ERA of 2.5714285, which rounds off to 2.57. This is a good pitcher, one who allows fewer than three runs for every nine innings.

607

▶ **Activating Prior Knowledge**

Invite students to discuss numerical charts they have looked at in other contexts. These may include charts from different sections of the newspaper, from cereal boxes, or on the back of trading cards. They may also be familiar with mileage charts in atlases and charts of comparative temperatures.

Purpose Setting Have students read "Figuring It Out" so they will have the knowledge necessary to fully understand the chart.

▶ **Comprehension Check**

Comprehension/Critical Thinking

1 In which year, from 1925 to 1929, did Lou Gehrig hit the most home runs as well as have the most runs batted in (RBIs)? (1927) **Compare and Contrast**

2 What would the chart look like if you reorganized the data according to batting average, from lowest to highest? (The BA column would be on the far left of the chart, and the rows would be rearranged according to the order of batting averages.) **Categorize and Classify**

3 Do you think sports stars should be judged only on how well they do in a game or a match, or do you think they should be judged on their character as well? (Answers will vary.) **Making Judgments**

4 **Connecting/Comparing** Some like to imagine present-day sports stars competing against star athletes from the past. Do you think it makes sense to compare these different athletes? (Answers will vary.) **Making Judgments**

Comprehension Skills

✓ Fact and Opinion

▶ **Teach**

Review the facts and opinions in *Lou Gehrig: The Luckiest Man.* Use **Transparency 5–18** to discuss

■ how facts can be proven and opinions cannot

■ certain words that signal opinions

■ how some opinions are blended with facts

Students can refer to the selection and to **Practice Book** page 325.

page 597 (It was a courageous speech.)	**Opinion**	(What is "courageous" can be different from person to person.)
page 598 (The more than sixty thousand fans in Yankee stadium stood to honor Lou Gehrig.)	**Fact**	(I can talk to someone who was there and check the team records.)
page 601 (This was the day of Lou Gehrig's funeral.)	**Fact**	(I can check newspaper reports from that day.)

Practice Book page 325

Name _____

Fact

Lou Gehrig: The Luckiest Man

Graphic Organizer Fact and

Sam ...
page 585
The first ...
played in ...
page 586
Through ...
didn't m ...
page 589
Those w ...
what wo ...
record. ...
page 590
He was ...
league's ...
page 594
The 1927 ...
the best ...
page 597
It was a ...
page 598
The mor ...
fans in Y ...
honor L ...

Transparency 5–18

Fact and Opinion Chart

Statement	Fact or Opinion	How Can You Tell? Explain.
page 585	Fact	
page 586	Fact	
page 589	Opinion	
page 590	Fact	
page 594	Opinion	
page 597	Opinion	
page 598	Fact	

TRANSPARENCY 5–18
TEACHER'S EDITION PAGES T605D AND T607A

HEROES Lou Gehrig: The Luckiest Man
Graphic Organizer Fact and Opinion Chart

Modeling Review with students how facts can be proven by looking them up in a reference source while opinions cannot. Explain how some authors may combine facts with opinions to try to get readers to agree unknowingly with their view. Explain that even though you may agree that the author's opinion is true, you still cannot prove it. Have students follow along on page 597 as you read aloud from the beginning of the page through the first sentence of the third paragraph, ending with *It was a courageous speech.* Then use the Think Aloud below to model the idea.

> **Think Aloud**
>
> *The author is describing the beginning of Mr. Gehrig's farewell speech. He describes how Mr. Gehrig wipes his eyes and speaks slowly with his head down. It's obviously difficult for Mr. Gehrig to speak about being ill. The author then calls the speech courageous. I certainly agree that it took courage for Mr. Gehrig to speak in front of the crowd that day. I don't think I could've done it. But I still can't prove that it was courageous. What is courageous is different for every person. It's an opinion. Though I agree with the author, I cannot prove that he is correct.*

Point out to students the effectiveness of wrapping opinions around facts to get people to agree.

 Practice

Have students work in pairs to understand further the difference between facts and opinions. Ask students to take out their Fact and Opinion Charts (**Practice Book** page 325) and have them rewrite the facts as opinions and vice versa. Ask them also to indicate where they can verify the facts and what word(s) indicate(s) the opinions they create. To organize their information, students should create a chart similar to the one below. (Sample answers provided.) Have the class discuss their answers once they finish.

Original Statement	New Statement (Fact or Opinion?)	Why?
page 585 The first World Series was played in 1903.	The first World Series in 1903 was the most important. (opinion)	No one can prove what is important.
page 586 Through eight years of school Lou didn't miss a single day.	Unbelievably, Lou didn't miss a single day of school in eight years. (opinion)	What is unbelievable is different for every person.
page 589 Those were the first two games in what would become an amazing record.	Those were the first two games of the record. (fact)	I can check a baseball almanac.

Apply

Use **Practice Book** pages 327–328 to diagnose whether students need Reteaching. Students who do not need Reteaching may work on Challenge/Extension Activities, page R13. Students who need extra support may apply the skill to an easier text using the **Reader's Library** selection "Mark McGwire: Home Run Hero" and its Responding activity.

Skill Finder • Revisiting, p. 589	• Review, Theme 6, p. 665	• Reteaching, p. R12

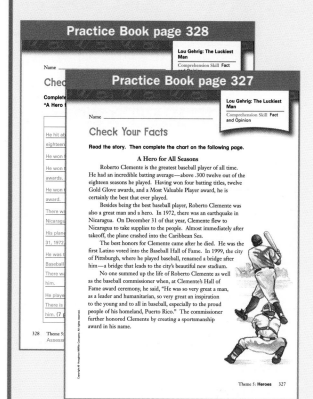

Practice Book page 328

Practice Book page 327

Lou Gehrig: The Luckiest Man
Comprehension Skill Fact and Opinion

Name _____

Check Your Facts

Read the story. Then complete the chart on the following page.

A Hero for All Seasons

Roberto Clemente is the greatest baseball player of all time. He had an incredible batting average—above .300 twelve out of the eighteen seasons he played. Having won four batting titles, twelve Gold Glove awards, and a Most Valuable Player award, he is certainly the best that ever played.

Besides being the best baseball player, Roberto Clemente was also a great man and a hero. In 1972, there was an earthquake in Nicaragua. On December 31 of that year, Clemente flew to Nicaragua to take supplies to the people. Almost immediately after takeoff, the plane crashed into the Caribbean Sea.

The best honors for Clemente came after he died. He was the first Latino voted into the Baseball Hall of Fame. In 1999, the city of Pittsburgh, where he played baseball, renamed a bridge after him—a bridge that leads to the city's beautiful new stadium.

No one summed up the life of Roberto Clemente as well as the baseball commissioner when, at Clemente's Hall of Fame award ceremony, he said, "He was so very great a man, as a leader and humanitarian, so very great an inspiration to the young and to all in baseball, especially to the proud people of his homeland, Puerto Rico." The commissioner further honored Clemente by creating a sportsmanship award in his name.

Theme 5: Heroes 327

Extra Support

- Reteaching, page R12
- **Reader's Library:** *Heroes* Selection 3, "Mark McGwire: Home Run Hero"

Diagnostic Check

If . . .	You can . . .
students need extra help to identify fact and opinion,	use the Reteaching Lesson on page R12.
students have successfully met the lesson objectives,	have them do the Challenge/Extension Activities on page R13.

Transparency 5–19

Collecting Data (Tables and Charts)

	WEEK 1	WEEK 2	WEEK 3	WEEK 4
TEAM A	Home Game	Away Game	Away Game	Home Game
TEAM B	Away Game	Home Game	Home Game	Away Game
TEAM C	Away Game	Away Game	Home Game	Home Game
TEAM D	Home Game	Home Game	Away Game	Away Game

TRANSPARENCY 5–19
TEACHER'S EDITION PAGE T607C

HEROES: Lou Gehrig: The Luckiest Man
Information and Study Skills
Collecting Data (Tables and Charts)

Information & Study Skills

 ## Collecting Data (Tables and Charts)

▶ Teach

Explain to students that sometimes it is necessary for them to collect their own information firsthand, rather than rely on printed materials such as an encyclopedia or a magazine article. Tell students that some ways of collecting raw data include

- **conducting interviews**

- **taking a poll**

- **collecting a questionnaire or survey**

Stress that it is important that, when embarking on such a research project, students think carefully about choosing the right method for collecting their data. Discuss with students the primary differences among these methods. Also, students will need to ask themselves, "What is the best source for the information I am seeking?" Ask students if they can think of some situations where collecting their own data would be required of them. Explain that these methods of data collection can be particularly useful when researching

- **a very narrow topic**

- **a local issue**

- **a personal project**

- **a topic with a shortage of published information relating to it**

Organizing the Data Explain that a chart is a general word used to refer to a way of visually organizing information. Tables, diagrams, and graphs are all kinds of charts. A table is a method of organizing information in a way so that a reader can easily see the way individual pieces of data all relate to one another by breaking it down into columns and rows.

Display the chart on **Transparency 5–19.** Begin by explaining that reading a chart is not difficult if students remember that they must look at the information in two ways. Point out that columns are vertical, or up and down. Point out that rows are horizontal, or from left to right. Explain that Coach Diamond is trying

to keep track of all the games in August. To do so, he created this chart. There are four weeks of games and the league has four teams that play teams from other nearby schools. So Coach made four rows and four columns and left space for the headings.

Modeling Use a pointer as you model how to use the chart to find out where Team C will be in Week 3.

> **Think Aloud**

I am on Team C and I need to know where my game is scheduled for week 3. Whenever I use a chart, the first thing I do is read the headings for the columns and rows. I know that I have to move my finger across the rows and columns to find the information I want. So if I want to know where Team C is playing during week 3, I find the row headed Team C, then I move my finger across until I come to the column marked Week 3. This is going to be a home game, so I won't need a ride.

▶ Practice

Have students show how they would determine the location of the following games: Team B in Week 4; Team A in Week 2; Team D in Week 1; Team C in Week 4. Then ask students how they would find out where each team is playing during Week 3.

▶ Apply

List on the board several topics that will require the collection of data among the class. (Possibilities include student birthdays, places of birth, number of siblings, or favorite hobbies.) Assign a research topic to moderate sized groups. Have each group choose a method to collect the relevant data from their peers and record the information carefully. Then, instruct students to assemble the information using a table.

If students are to poll one another about their birthdays, for example, establish in advance that they will need twelve columns, one for each month. Have them allow one row for each student in the group and label each one with a name. Suggest that each group decide how they will indicate each person's birthday. For example, they might simply mark an X, or they could enter the date.

As a follow-up, ask students how they would make one chart for the entire class or have them choose another method of presentation, such as a bar graph to further compute possible trends.

Word Work

Word Work Instructions	
DAY 1	• Spelling Pretest • Spelling Instruction
DAY 2	• Structural Analysis Instruction • Spelling Practice
DAY 3	• Phonics Instruction • Spelling Practice
DAY 4	• Structural Analysis Reteaching • Vocabulary Skill Instruction • Spelling Game
DAY 5	• Expanding Your Vocabulary • Spelling Test

OBJECTIVES

Students

- read words with the VCV pattern

- read words and syllables that have two sounds of *c*

- use the Phonics/Decoding strategy to decode longer words

Decoding Longer Words

☑ Structural Analysis: VCV Pattern *Spelling Connection*

▶ Teach

Write this sentence: *I'm going to <u>remember</u> this day for a long time.* Point out that the letters *e-m-e* follow a *VCV* (vowel-consonant-vowel) pattern. Explain that in a word with the *VCV* pattern, the word is often divided between the first vowel and the consonant, and the first vowel has a long sound. Write on the board: *r e / m e m b e r.* Pronounce the word, emphasizing the initial long vowel sound. When encountering a *VCV* pattern, students should first try breaking the word in this way. If this pronunciation doesn't make sense, however, students should try dividing the word into syllables after the consonant and use a short vowel sound. Use the words *talent, cabin,* and *cover* as examples.

Modeling Display this sentence and model how to decode *silent: The crowd grew <u>silent</u> when Lou Gehrig stepped up to the microphone.*

> **Think Aloud**
>
> *I notice that* silent *has a VCV pattern, i-l-e. First I try breaking the word between the initial vowel and the consonant, and pronouncing a long vowel sound. I'll break the word between the i and the l. /SY•luhnt/. It means quiet. It makes sense that the crowd would be quiet so that they could hear Lou Gehrig's speech.*

▶ Practice

Display these phrases and have students copy the underlined words: *great <u>beginnings</u>; the team <u>later</u> known; the <u>mayor</u> of New York City; <u>retired</u> his uniform; <u>finish</u> the game.* Tell students to work in pairs to circle the VCV pattern in each word, draw a line showing where the word should be broken into syllables, and pronounce the word.

▶ Apply

Have students complete **Practice Book** page 329.

Skill Finder	• **Strategy Review:** Phonics/ Decoding, p. 583B	• **Reteaching,** p. R18

Phonics: Two Sounds of c

▶ Teach

Tell students that understanding the two sounds of the letter *c* can help them use the Phonics/Decoding strategy to decode unfamiliar words. Explain that

- The spelling patterns *c* and *ck* can have the / k / sound.

- The spelling patterns *ci* and *ce* can have the / s / sound.

Modeling Display this sentence and model how to decode *canceled: On June 4 the Yankee game was* <u>canceled</u> *because of rain.*

Think Aloud

When I look at this word, I see the shorter word can *which has the c spelling of the / k / sound. Next I notice the c-e spelling pattern. I know this pattern usually has the / s / sound like in the word* center, *so I think the next part might be said / sehl /. When I put it together and add on the -ed ending, I say / KAN•sehld /. Oh, it's / KAN•suhld /. I know that word and it makes sense that the game would be called off if it was raining.*

▶ Practice

Write these phrases on the board and have students copy the underlined words: *first* <u>successful</u> *flight;* <u>become</u> *one of the greatest players;* <u>central</u> *nervous system; in the* <u>clubhouse</u>*;* <u>consider</u> *myself the* <u>luckiest</u> *man.* Have students work in pairs to circle the / k / and / s / spelling patterns and decode each word. Call on individuals to model at the board.

▶ Apply

Ask students to decode the following words from *Lou Gehrig: The Luckiest Man* and discuss their meanings: *college,* page 586; *convinced,* page 588; *exercised, practice,* page 591; *citizenship,* page 595; *complain,* page 597.

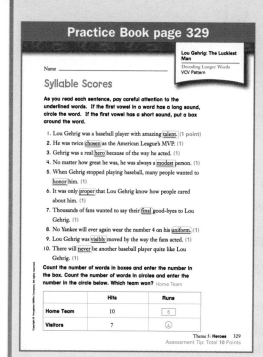

Practice Book page 329

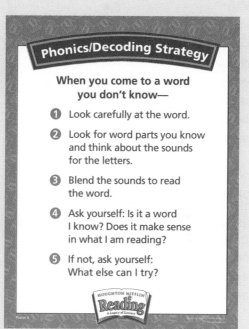

Phonics/Decoding Strategy

When you come to a word you don't know—

1. Look carefully at the word.

2. Look for word parts you know and think about the sounds for the letters.

3. Blend the sounds to read the word.

4. Ask yourself: Is it a word I know? Does it make sense in what I am reading?

5. If not, ask yourself: What else can I try?

Diagnostic Check

If . . .	You can . . .
students need help reading words with the VCV pattern,	use the Reteaching Lesson on page R18.

Word Work

Spelling Words

Basic Words

pilot	never*
depend	modern
visit*	tiny
human	tuna
seven*	event
chosen	fever*
paper*	moment
reason*	prison*
become*	basic
parent*	open

Review Words	Challenge Words
before*	alert
travel	license
orange	select*
ever*	radar
begin*	feature

Forms of these words appear in the literature.

Extra Support

Basic Word List You may want to use only the left column of Basic Words with students who need extra support.

Spelling
✓ VCV Pattern

Day 1   Teaching the Principle

Pretest Use the Day 5 Test Sentences. Say each underlined word, read the sentence, and then repeat the word. Have students write only the underlined word.

Teach Tell students that dividing a word that has the VCV pattern into syllables can help them to spell it. Then write the following on the board:

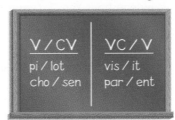

Say each word and have students repeat it. Point to the first column and ask whether the first vowel sound in each word is short or long. (long) Explain that a VCV word is divided before the consonant if its first vowel sound is long. Then point to the second column and ask whether the first vowel sound in each word is short or long. (short) Explain that a VCV word is divided after the consonant if the first vowel sound is short and followed by a consonant sound. Write the remaining Basic Words on the board, say each one, and have students repeat it. Work with students to divide the words into syllables.

Practice/Homework Assign **Practice Book** page 425. Tell students to use this Take-Home Word List to study the words they missed on the Pretest.

Day 2   Reviewing the Principle

Practice/Homework Review the spelling principle and assign **Practice Book** page 330.

Day 3   Vocabulary

Jargon Tell students that jargon is the specialized language used by people in the same trade, profession, or similar group. Then write *open* on the board and explain that in the jargon of some sports and games, an *open* is a contest for both amateurs and professionals. Ask students to brainstorm jargon terms used in a selected game or sport. (Responses will vary.) Next, list the Basic Words on the board. Have students use each word from the board orally in a sentence. (Sentences will vary.)

Practice/Homework For spelling practice, assign **Practice Book** page 331.

Day 4 Word Hunt

Ask students to search through books, magazines, and newspapers for VCV words. Allow 5–10 minutes for finding the words, and another 5–10 minutes for dividing the words. Provide the necessary print materials. Then have students form small groups and follow these steps:

- Each student hunts for and lists two-syllable VCV words.

- Each student divides his or her list words into syllables, using the principles learned in this lesson.

- When time is called, group members meet to pool and record their words.

Select one or more students to list each group's words on the board or on a chart. Give a prize to the group that has the most words, divided correctly into syllables.

Practice/Homework For proofreading and writing practice, assign **Practice Book** page 332.

Day 5 Spelling Assessment

Test Say each underlined word, read the sentence, and then repeat the word. Have students write only the underlined word.

Basic Words

1. The <u>pilot</u> landed our plane safely.
2. Farmers <u>depend</u> on a good crop.
3. Maria stopped by for a short <u>visit</u>.
4. A monkey seems <u>human</u> at times.
5. A week has <u>seven</u> days in it.
6. Has the team <u>chosen</u> its leader?
7. The copy machine has no <u>paper</u>.
8. What is your <u>reason</u> for being late?
9. The bud will <u>become</u> a flower.
10. Which <u>parent</u> found the lost child?
11. I have <u>never</u> been here in my life.
12. The cars you see today are <u>modern</u>.
13. The eye of the needle is so <u>tiny</u>.
14. They went fishing for <u>tuna</u>.
15. Are these flowers for a special <u>event</u>?
16. She is sick with a cold and a <u>fever</u>.
17. A <u>moment</u> of time is very brief.
18. He locked them inside a <u>prison</u> cell.
19. The engine is a <u>basic</u> part of a car.
20. The shop will <u>open</u> its doors at noon.

Challenge Words

21. The pupil is <u>alert</u> in class.
22. Do you have a <u>license</u> to drive?
23. Please <u>select</u> the color you like.
24. She flew with the use of <u>radar</u>.
25. We will <u>feature</u> him in the play.

• SELECTION •

Lou Gehrig: The Luckiest Man

Technology

Spelling Spree!™

Students may use the **Spelling Spree!™** for extra practice with the spelling principles taught in this lesson.

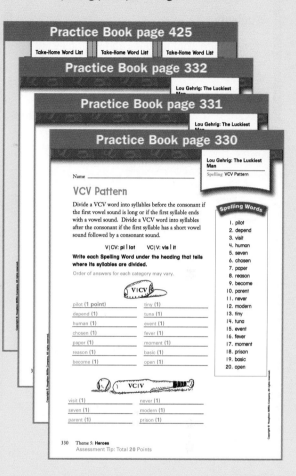

Practice Book page 425

Practice Book page 332

Practice Book page 331

Practice Book page 330

VCV Pattern

Divide a VCV word into syllables before the consonant if the first vowel sound is long or if the first syllable ends with a vowel sound. Divide a VCV word into syllables after the consonant if the first syllable has a short vowel sound followed by a consonant sound.

V|CV: pi | lot   VC|V: vis | it

Write each Spelling Word under the heading that tells where its syllables are divided.

Order of answers for each category may vary.

V|CV

pilot (1 point)	tiny (1)
depend (1)	tuna (1)
human (1)	event (1)
chosen (1)	fever (1)
paper (1)	moment (1)
reason (1)	basic (1)
become (1)	open (1)

VC|V

visit (1)	never (1)
seven (1)	modern (1)
parent (1)	prison (1)

Spelling Words
1. pilot
2. depend
3. visit
4. human
5. seven
6. chosen
7. paper
8. reason
9. become
10. parent
11. never
12. modern
13. tiny
14. tuna
15. event
16. fever
17. moment
18. prison
19. basic
20. open

330 Theme 5: Heroes
Assessment Tip: Total 20 Points

--- **Houghton Mifflin Spelling and Vocabulary** ---
Correlated instruction and practice

 **Challenge**

Challenge Word Practice Have students write each Challenge Word. Then, for each Challenge Word, have them write another word they associate with it, and write a sentence using both words.

Example: radar–police

The <u>police</u> use <u>radar</u> to catch speeders.

OBJECTIVES

Students

- recognize word histories and what they tell
- use word histories to enrich their understanding of words

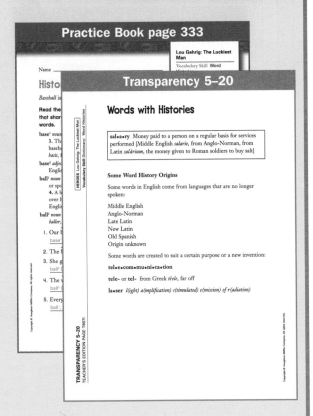

Practice Book page 333

Transparency 5–20

Words with Histories

sal•a•ry Money paid to a person on a regular basis for services performed [Middle English *salarie*, from Anglo-Norman, from Latin *salārium*, the money given to Roman soldiers to buy salt]

Some Word History Origins

Some words in English come from languages that are no longer spoken:

Middle English
Anglo-Norman
Late Latin
New Latin
Old Spanish
Origin unknown

Some words are created to suit a certain purpose or a new invention:

tel•e•com•mu•ni•ca•tion

tele- or tel- from Greek *tēle*, far off

la•ser l(ight) a(mplification) s(timulated) e(mission) of r(adiation)

Vocabulary Skills

Dictionary: Word Histories

▶ Teach

Display **Transparency 5–20,** blocking out all but the dictionary entry for *salary.* Read the entry aloud. Explain that many dictionary definitions include a *word history,* or an explanation of where a word came from. Tell students that learning about word histories can enrich a reader's understanding of language. For example, the sample word history makes a connection between two everyday words, *salt* and *salary.* Readers might not make this connection without a word history.

Uncover the next section of the transparency, *Some Word History Origins.* Read aloud the six terms. Explain that these are just a few of the sources of words in English. Explain that English, like most languages, has borrowed or adapted words from other languages over hundreds of years. Point out that people coming to the United States from other countries brought their native languages as well as customs and traditions. Many words from those languages found their way into English.

Uncover the last section of the transparency. Explain that some words are created to describe things that did not exist previously, such as new inventions. Tell students that the new words may use word parts that are ancient, such as the Greek *tele-.* The word part *tele-* has been used to make the words *telephone, television,* and *telecommunication.* Other words, like *laser,* are made up of the first letters of a much longer technical term.

Modeling Read aloud this sentence from page 593 of *Lou Gehrig: He was suffering from amyotrophic lateral sclerosis.* Model how knowing more about the history of a word or term can enrich the reader's knowledge.

Think Aloud

When I read this sentence, I realize I need to learn more about this disease by looking it up in the dictionary. I learn that it is often called ALS for short. The entry goes on to explain the symptoms. The entry also says that this is known as Lou Gehrig's disease. This is another way that something gets a new name and adds to a word's history.

▶ Practice

Working in pairs or small groups, have students choose one of the following words to look up in a dictionary containing word histories: *radar, submarine, ranch, bagel, raccoon.* Point out that for some words (such as *submarine*), they may have to look up the parts of the word (*sub-* + *marine*). Ask students to share their work with the class.

▶ Apply

Have students complete **Practice Book** page 333.

Teacher's Note

Word Histories One of the most interesting things about word histories is the fact that scholars do not always know how a word developed. That does not stop people from making their own guesses. An example is the word *Yankees.* One story says that the word comes from the boy's name *Janke,* a Dutch nickname for *Jan.* In the 1700s, *Yankee* was used derisively by the British for New Englanders. But through their bravery at the Battle of Lexington in 1775, the "Yankees" gave a new dignity to the name.

⋯ **Houghton Mifflin Spelling and Vocabulary** ⋯
Correlated instruction and practice

Expanding Your Vocabulary
Sports Terminology

Point out to students that every sport has its own vocabulary. Sometimes terms are the same in different sports, such as *umpire* and *foul.* Suggest that students select a sport they are familiar with and create a glossary of ten words. Have them create a chart with those words and their definitions. Students might also draw and label a diagram of the field on which the game is played.

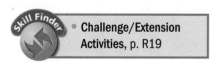

• Challenge/Extension Activities, p. R19

 English Language Learners

Begin a discussion of borrowed words by providing some examples many students will be familiar with, such as *plaza, café,* and *karate.* Explain that these words came from other languages and are now widely used and understood as English terms. Encourage students to offer suggestions of other borrowings.

<table>
<tr><td colspan="2">Writing and Language Instruction</td></tr>
<tr><td>DAY 1</td><td>• Daily Language Practice
• Grammar Instruction
• Journal Writing</td></tr>
<tr><td>DAY 2</td><td>• Daily Language Practice
• Writing a Problem/Solution Paragraph
• Journal Writing
• Grammar Practice</td></tr>
<tr><td>DAY 3</td><td>• Daily Language Practice
• Grammar Instruction
• Write a Book Jacket Summary</td></tr>
<tr><td>DAY 4</td><td>• Daily Language Practice
• Listening/Speaking/Viewing
• Writing: Improving Your Writing
• Grammar Practice</td></tr>
<tr><td>DAY 5</td><td>• Daily Language Practice
• Grammar: Improving Your Writing</td></tr>
</table>

OBJECTIVES

Students

- identify possessive pronouns
- use possessive pronouns
- proofread and correct sentences with grammar and spelling errors
- proofread for *its* and *it's* to improve writing

Wacky Web Tales

Students may use the **Wacky Web Tales** floppy disk to create humorous stories and review singular and plural possessive pronouns.

Grammar Skills

Singular and Plural Possessive Pronouns

Day 1

Display the chart at the top of **Transparency 5–21,** and go over the examples of possessive pronouns. Then display the sentences at the bottom of the transparency. Have students read the sentences. Ask volunteers to replace each possessive noun with a possessive pronoun and read the corrected sentence aloud. Then go over the following rules and definitions:

■ A possessive pronoun may be used in place of a possessive noun to show ownership.

■ These possessive pronouns appear before nouns: *my, your, her, his, its, our, their.*

■ These possessive pronouns stand alone: *mine, yours, hers, his, its, ours, theirs.*

Ask students to look at *Lou Gehrig: The Luckiest Man* to find examples of possessive pronouns and to share the examples they find. Then have them correct the Day 1 Daily Language Practice sentences in **Transparency 5–23.**

Day 2

Practice/Homework Have students correct the Day 2 Daily Language Practice sentences. Then assign **Practice Book** page 334.

Day 3   Whose Is It?

Divide the class into groups of four or five students. Have one member of each group take an object such as a book or a pen and show it to the other members of the group, describing the object in two ways: "This is my book. This book is mine." Then have another member of the group describe the same object in two ways: "That is her book. That book is hers." or "That book is your book. It is yours." The other members of the group then repeat the activity for their own object and the objects of the other members of the group. Then have two members present an object as their own and describe it in two ways: "This book is our book. This book is ours." Other pairs then repeat that activity for their own object and for the objects of the other pairs: "That book is their book. It is theirs." or "That book is your book. That book is yours." Then have students correct the Day 3 Daily Language Practice sentences.

Day 4

Practice/Homework Have students correct the Day 4 Daily Language Practice sentences. Assign **Practice Book** page 335.

Day 5   Improving Your Writing

Proofreading for *its* and *it's*: Point out that good writers are careful to use the possessive pronouns *its* and the contraction *it's* correctly in sentences. Have students read the sentences on **Transparency 5–22.** Ask students to correct any errors in the use of *its* or *it's* and then rewrite the sentences using the correct form.

Then have students review a piece of their own writing to see if they can improve it by proofreading for the correct use of *its* and *it's*.

Practice/Homework Have students correct the Day 5 Daily Language Practice sentences. Then assign **Practice Book** page 336.

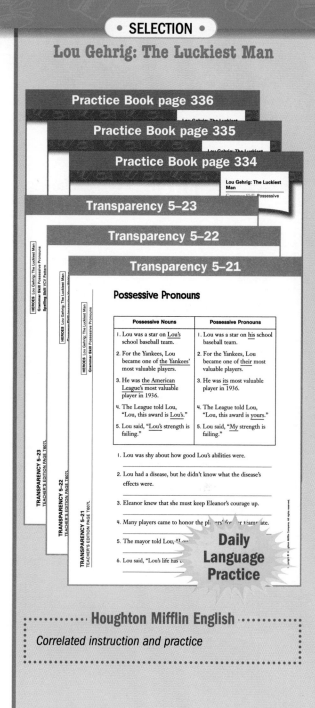

Practice Book page 336
Practice Book page 335
Practice Book page 334
Transparency 5–23
Transparency 5–22
Transparency 5–21

Possessive Pronouns

Possessive Nouns	Possessive Pronouns
1. Lou was a star on Lou's school baseball team.	1. Lou was a star on his school baseball team.
2. For the Yankees, Lou became one of the Yankees' most valuable players.	2. For the Yankees, Lou became one of their most valuable players.
3. He was the American League's most valuable player in 1936.	3. He was its most valuable player in 1936.
4. The League told Lou, "Lou, this award is Lou's."	4. The League told Lou, "Lou, this award is yours."
5. Lou said, "Lou's strength is failing."	5. Lou said, "My strength is failing."

1. Lou was shy about how good Lou's abilities were.

2. Lou had a disease, but he didn't know what the disease's effects were.

3. Eleanor knew that she must keep Eleanor's courage up.

4. Many players came to honor the players' former teammate.

5. The mayor told Lou, "Lou..."

6. Lou said, "Lou's life has..."

Daily Language Practice

········· **Houghton Mifflin English** ···········
Correlated instruction and practice

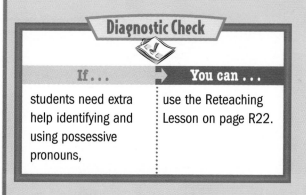

Diagnostic Check

If . . .	You can . . .
students need extra help identifying and using possessive pronouns,	use the Reteaching Lesson on page R22.

Grammar Skills   **607L**

Writing Skills
Writing a Magazine Article

Transparency 5–25

Combining Sentences Using

Transparency 5–24

A Magazine Article

Hammerin' Hank Hammers Home

The baseball world held its breath. Would today be the day? To most of the world, April 8, 1974, was an ordinary day. To the baseball fans, sports reporters, and family who packed the Atlanta Stadium in Atlanta, Georgia, that day turned out to be anything but an ordinary day.

The third game of the baseball season was under way. Just four days before, Hammerin' Hank, as Hank Aaron was known, had hit his 714th home run. That tied Babe Ruth's record set almost fifty years before. Would today be the day Aaron beat Ruth's home run record?

In Hank's first at bat, he walked. In the fourth inning, Aaron came to bat for the second time. The first pitch was outside the strike zone. Ball one! The next pitch was a fast ball, and Aaron swung. The ball rose, and sailed farther and farther, up and over the left field fence. Hammerin' Hank had done it. The new home run king had hammered home run number 715.

▶ Teach

In *Lou Gehrig,* students read about a baseball hero from the 1930s. Point out that this story could have appeared as an article in a baseball or sports magazine.

Tell students that magazine articles can be longer than news articles and usually include more details. Most newspaper stories focus on what's new, especially current events. Remind students that both kinds of stories answer the questions Who? What? Where? When? Why? and How?

▶ Practice

Display **Transparency 5–24.** Have students read the magazine article. Ask:

- Who is the magazine article about? (Hank Aaron)

- What is the article about? (Aaron breaking Ruth's home run record)

- When and where does the article's story take place? (April 8, 1974, Atlanta, Georgia, Atlanta Stadium)

- What other information is given? Who? What? Where? When? Why? How? (The article explains what happened his first at bat and why, when, and how Aaron beat Ruth's record.)

- How did the opener or title grab your attention? (Answers will vary.)

Discuss with students the guidelines for writing a magazine article.

Guidelines for
Writing Magazine Article

- Begin with an attention-grabbing opener or topic sentence.
- Use facts and details that answer the questions Who? What? Where? When? Why? and How?
- Use quotations to make the article come alive.
- Write a catchy, interesting title.

▶ Apply

Students can use **Practice Book** page 337 to help them plan and organize their writing. Have them use it to plan a magazine article about a sports hero or other person they admire. Remind students to begin with an attention-grabbing opener or topic sentence and to write a catchy, interesting title. Tell them their articles should include facts and details that answer the questions *Who? What? Where? When? Why?* and *How?* If possible, suggest they use quotations to make their magazine articles come alive.

Improving Your Writing
Combining Sentences with Possessive Pronouns

Teach Review possessive nouns with students. Remind them that possessives show ownership. Explain that possessive pronouns can be used in place of possessive nouns. Then review singular and plural possessive pronouns.

> ### Possessive Pronouns
>
> Singular: my, your, hers, his, its
>
> Plural: our, your, their

Practice To model how to use possessive pronouns to combine sentences, display **Transparency 5–25**. Have students read the examples at the top of the transparency. Explain that the possessive noun has been replaced with a possessive pronoun that refers to a previous noun to avoid repetition. Then have students practice combining sentences by using possessive pronouns.

Apply Assign **Practice Book** page 338. Then have students review their magazine articles to see if they can improve their articles by using possessive pronouns.

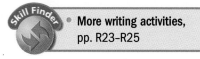
More writing activities, pp. R23–R25

The Writer's Resource Library

Students may use this set of reference tools as they work on their own writing.

©Sunburst Technology Corporation, a Houghton Mifflin Company. All Rights Reserved.

Type to Learn™

Students may use **Type to Learn™** to learn proper keyboarding technique.

©Sunburst Technology Corporation, a Houghton Mifflin Company. All Rights Reserved..

.... **Houghton Mifflin English** ....

Correlated instruction and practice

Portfolio Opportunity

Save students' magazine articles as samples of their writing development.

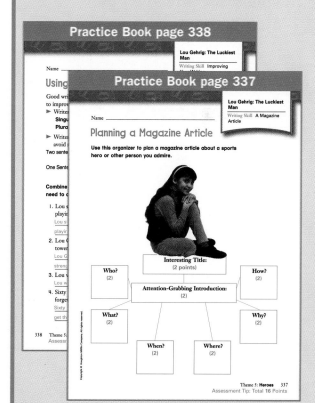

Writing & Language

Present an Oral Book Report

▶ Teach

Explain to students that in an oral book report, the speaker should share with the audience information about the book that they would be interested in. Explain that a good approach would be to summarize the book and then evaluate it. For example, students might tell why they liked the book and recommend the book to audience members. Students might also tell what they didn't like about the book, explain how the book might have been better, and give their opinion as to whether it is still worth reading or not. Have students brainstorm guidelines for preparing and presenting a good oral book report. List their ideas on the board, guiding them to include the following:

- Make sure to state the author and title of the book.

- Tell enough about the book to make it interesting, but not too much. Don't give away the ending!

- Describe what you think the book's strong points are and explain why you think so.

- Make notes on index cards so that you remember to include everything you want to say.

- Practice saying your report without reading it word for word.

- Speak loudly and clearly and look at the audience.

English Language Learners

Most English language learners will be better able to practice and master the skills needed for a successful oral report if they work with a selection that they have read and discussed thoroughly as a group. Consider allowing students to present a report on one of the selections read earlier.

Practice

Tell students that since they have been reading about heroes, their book report should be about someone they admire. Recommend that they look in their school or public library for a biography about a person they have selected. (You may also wish to preselect biographies for students to read or to request assistance from your school library media specialist.) Suggest that students' reports include both information about that person and an explanation of why he or she is to be admired. Set a time length for each report. Tell students to time their reports as they practice them. Before students deliver their reports in class, have them practice in pairs so that each partner can listen to the other's report and offer feedback.

▶ Apply

Set up a chart of times for each student to deliver his or her report, spacing them out over several days.

Improving Presentation Skills

Have students brainstorm tips to get the audience more involved in their book reports. Guide them to include the following:

- Invite comments from the audience. For example, if others have read the same book, they might want to add something everyone would be interested in. Perhaps another student has read a different book or seen a movie about the person being reported on. Or, perhaps someone has read another book by the same author.

- Use visuals. If you don't have the book to show, present your own drawing.

- Tell the audience where they can get the book if they are interested.

Theme Assessment Wrap-Up

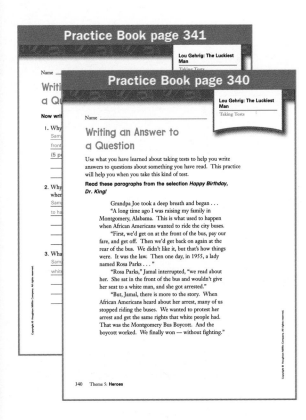

Practice Book page 341

Lou Gehrig: The Luckiest Man

Practice Book page 340

Lou Gehrig: The Luckiest Man

Taking Tests

Name _____

Writing an Answer to a Question

Use what you have learned about taking tests to help you write answers to questions about something you have read. This practice will help you when you take this kind of test.

Read these paragraphs from the selection Happy Birthday, Dr. King!

Grandpa Joe took a deep breath and began . . .
"A long time ago I was raising my family in Montgomery, Alabama. This is what used to happen when African Americans wanted to ride the city buses.
"First, we'd get on at the front of the bus, pay our fare, and get off. Then we'd get back on again at the rear of the bus. We didn't like it, but that's how things were. It was the law. Then one day, in 1955, a lady named Rosa Parks . . ."
"Rosa Parks," Jamal interrupted, "we read about her. She sat in the front of the bus and wouldn't give her seat to a white man, and she got arrested."
"But, Jamal, there is more to the story. When African Americans heard about her arrest, many of us stopped riding the buses. We wanted to protest her arrest and get the same rights that white people had. That was the Montgomery Bus Boycott. And the boycott worked. We finally won — without fighting."

340   Theme 5: **Heroes**

▶ ## Preparing for Testing

Remind students that they can use test-taking strategies to help them do well on important tests.

Writing an Answer to a Question Tell students that today they will learn strategies for writing answers to comprehension questions. Have them read Taking Tests on Anthology pages 608–609.

Discuss the tips and the model student think aloud on Anthology pages 608–609 with students. Mention these points:

■ Plan your answer before you start to write.

■ Check to make sure you respond to what the question asks.

■ Write in complete sentences.

■ Even if you can only answer part of the question, write it down. You will get some points for correct, but incomplete, answers.

More Practice The **Practice Book,** pages 340–341, contains additional written-response comprehension questions for more practice.

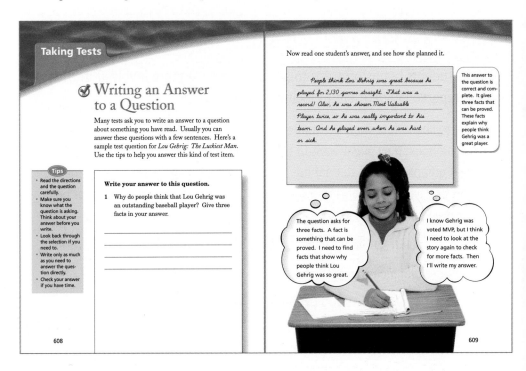

Taking Tests

✓ Writing an Answer to a Question

Many tests ask you to write an answer to a question about something you have read. Usually you can answer these questions with a few sentences. Here's a sample test question for *Lou Gehrig: The Luckiest Man.* Use the tips to help you answer this kind of test item.

Tips
• Read the directions and the question carefully.
• Make sure you know what the question is asking. Think about your answer before you write.
• Look back through the selection if you need to.
• Write only as much as you need to answer the question directly.
• Check your answer if you have time.

Write your answer to this question.

1 Why do people think that Lou Gehrig was an outstanding baseball player? Give three facts in your answer.

_____
_____
_____

608

Now read one student's answer, and see how she planned it.

People think Lou Gehrig was great because he played for 2,130 games straight. That was a record! Also, he was chosen Most Valuable Player twice, so he was really important to his team. And he played even when he was hurt or sick.

This answer to the question is correct and complete. It gives three facts that can be proved. These facts explain why people think Gehrig was a great player.

The question asks for three facts. A fact is something that can be proved. I need to find facts that show why people think Lou Gehrig was so great.

I know Gehrig was voted MVP, but I think I need to look at the story again to check for more facts. Then I'll write my answer.

609

▶ Assessing Student Progress

Formal Assessment The **Integrated Theme Test** and the **Theme Skills Test** are formal group assessments used to evaluate student performance on theme objectives. The **Theme Skills Test** may be used as a pretest or may be administered following the theme.

The **Integrated Theme Test** assesses students' progress as readers and writers in a format that reflects instruction. Authentic literary passages test reading skills in context.

The **Theme Skills Test** assesses students' mastery of specific reading and language arts skills taught in the theme. Individual skill subtests can be administered separately.

■ Integrated test of reading and writing skills: Comprehension strategies and skills, word skills, spelling, grammar, and writing

■ Tests discrete skills: Comprehension skills, word skills, spelling, grammar, writing, and information and study skills

Spelling Review/Assessment

Practice Book
Practice Book: pp. 342–344 Take-Home Word Lists: Practice Book Handbook

5-Day Spelling Plan

See p. 555G

Review with students the Spelling Words and, if appropriate, the Challenge Words from the spelling lessons on pages 555G, 581G, and 607G. Have volunteers summarize each spelling principle and explain how the words in each lesson illustrate the principle.

Pretest/Test

1. We studied maps of different cities.
2. The empty prison was an uninviting place to visit.
3. My dad is happiest when he has a daily paper to read.
4. Practicing kindness is a powerful way to make friends.
5. Having a fever is a good reason to stay home.
6. He had to redo seven words on the spelling exercise.
7. He was angriest when his friend copied his work.
8. Do they dislike fishing for tuna?
9. The clown's movement was crazier than anything else.
10. You may become a parent someday.
11. It is never useless to try your best.
12. It is peaceful to reread a favorite book.
13. Having to cancel our trip will displease our families.
14. In the earlier part of the day I was worried.
15. I was unsure which job would be easier to do.

Challenge Words

1. A look at the radar screen helped the pilot select the best airport.
2. Most companies discontinue unpopular products.
3. We have to be alert when we drive on the iciest roads.
4. My aunt has a license to fly unusual airplanes.
5. A resourceful sailor can navigate well on the breezier spring days.

 MEETING INDIVIDUAL NEEDS

Challenge

Challenge Words Practice Have students use the Challenge Words from the Take-Home Word List to write a character sketch of a modern-day hero.

Theme 5

Oral Reading Fluency

Early Grade 4	99–125 words per min.
Mid-Grade 4	112–133 words per min.
Late Grade 4	118–145 words per min.

For some students in Grade 4, you may want to check the oral fluency rate three times during the year. For students who appear to be having difficulty learning to read, this assessment may need to be done more often. The rates above are approximate.

Decoding and comprehension should be considered together in evaluating students' reading development. For information on how to select appropriate text, administer fluency checks, and interpret results, see the **Teacher's Assessment Handbook.**

For more information on assessing fluency, also see the Back to School section of this **Teacher's Edition.**

Assessing Fluency Oral reading fluency is a useful measure of a student's development of rapid automatic word recognition. Students who are reading on level in Grade 4 should be able to read, accurately and with expression, in appropriate level text at the approximate rates shown in the table to the left. In this theme, an appropriate selection to be used with most students is *Lou Gehrig: The Luckiest Man.*

Using Multiple Measures Student progress is best evaluated through multiple measures, which can be collected in a portfolio. The portfolio provides a record of student progress over time and can be useful in conferencing with the student, parents, or other educators. In addition to the tests mentioned on page 609, portfolios might include the following:

■ Observation Checklist from this theme

■ Personal Essay writing from the Reading-Writing Workshop

■ Other writing, projects, or artwork

■ One or more items selected by the student

Using Assessment for Planning Instruction You can use the results of theme assessments to evaluate individual students' needs and to modify instruction during the next theme. For more detail, see the test manuals or the **Teacher's Assessment Handbook.**

Customizing Instruction

Student Performance Shows:	Modifications to Consider:
Difficulty with Decoding or Word Skills	**Emphasis:** Word skills, phonics, reading for fluency; check for phonemic awareness **Resources:** Teacher's Edition: *Phonics Review, Structural Analysis Reteaching lessons;* Phonics Screening Test; Lexia Quick Phonics Assessment CD-ROM; Lexia Phonics CD-ROM: Intermediate Intervention
Difficulty with Oral Fluency	**Emphasis:** Reading and rereading of independent level text; vocabulary development **Resources:** Teacher's Edition: *Leveled Books;* Reader's Library; Theme Paperbacks; Houghton Mifflin Classroom Bookshelf; Book Adventure Website
Difficulty with Comprehension	**Emphasis:** Oral comprehension; strategy development; story comprehension; vocabulary development **Resources:** Teacher's Edition: *Extra Support notes, Comprehension Reteaching lessons;* Get Set for Reading CD-ROM; SOAR to Success
Overall High Performance	**Emphasis:** Independent reading and writing; vocabulary development; critical thinking **Resources:** Teacher's Edition: *Think About the Selection questions, Challenge notes;* Theme Paperbacks; Houghton Mifflin Classroom Bookshelf; Book Adventure Website; Education Place Website; Challenge Handbook

Theme Resources
Resources for Heroes

Contents

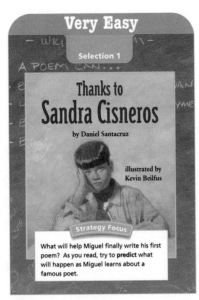

Thanks to Sandra Cisneros
by Daniel Santacruz

Selection Summary
Miguel's assignment is to write a poem. He thinks poems are about flowers and sunsets that have little to do with his life. He is stumped until his sister Flora introduces him to the work of poet Sandra Cisneros, whose background (Chicago-born, Mexican-American) is identical to Miguel's. Her poetry helps him write a poem to Flora, who has helped him in many ways: with homework, with spelling, by giving him baseball cards and by being his sister.

Key Vocabulary
garbage: pail bucket used for trash

flipped: quickly moved

widely: as wide as possible

Thanks to Sandra Cisneros

Reader's Library for Happy Birthday, Dr. King

▶ Preparing to Read

Building Background Talk about poetry: How is a poem different from a story or an article? What do poets write about? Be sure students realize that rhymed lines *may* be a feature of a poem and that poetry is often about the poet's personal feelings. Have students discuss favorite poets and poems. You might also read aloud the Cisneros poem "Good Hot Dogs," mentioned in this story.

Developing Key Vocabulary Make sure students understand the meanings of the Key Vocabulary words listed at the left. Remind them to use the Phonics/Decoding Strategy when they come to a word they don't know. For students who need more help with decoding, use the review on the next page.

▶ Strategy/Skill Focus

Refer students to the Strategy Poster. Review when and how to use the Predict/Infer Strategy.

Cause/Effect Alert students to be on the lookout for cause-effect relationships in the story and explain that when they make predictions about what will happen as they read, they may use a cause to predict an effect or an effect to predict a cause.

On the board, write two sentences from a poem by a brother to his sister.

> *But to you my sister Flora I write*
> *Because you help me do homework at night.*

Point out that these two ideas are related, as shown by the signal word because. His sister's helping him causes a brother to write a poem, thanking her. Explain that signal words like *because* and *so* are not always present; sometimes readers must figure out for themselves how ideas are connected.

▶ Guided Preview

After reading aloud the title and introduction to students, invite them to browse through the story art and to use the title, introduction, and artwork to make predictions about the story.

▶ Guiding the Reading

Have students read silently or with a partner. If needed, use these prompts:

pages 4–10

- *What is Miguel's assignment? How does he feel about this assignment?*

- *What does he think poems are about? Do you agree with him? Explain.*

- *What is the relationship between Flora and Miguel? How can you tell?*

pages 11–16

- *What does Flora do to help Miguel with his assignment?*

- *What effect does Sandra Cisneros's poem have on Miguel?*

- *How is Cisneros's background like Miguel's? How does this affect him?*

- *What do you predict Miguel will do next?*

pages 17–20

- *What is Miguel's poem about? Do you like it? Why or why not?*

- *How does Miguel feel about his poem? How does Flora feel?*

▶ Responding

After students have finished reading *Thanks to Sandra Cisneros*, begin a discussion of the story by helping them answer the questions on page 21. Then have students complete the cause-effect chart on page 21 and use it to summarize the story.

Sample Answers Questions **1)** "Good Hot Dogs" **2)** He realizes poems can be about anything that is part of his life. **3)** She wants to help Miguel with his assignment. **Chart:** (cause) He starts to think about writing a poem. (effect) She decided to write such books herself. (cause) Flora introduces Miguel to Sandra Cisneros and her poems.

English Language Learners

Building Background Invite students to recite lines of poetry from their culture, so the rest of the class can enjoy the sounds and rhythms of poetry in other languages.

Key Vocabulary The poem Miguel hears is about hot dogs and french fries. Make sure students are familiar with these foods.

Strategy Review
Phonics/Decoding

Model using the Phonics/Decoding Strategy. Write part of Miguel's poem on the board and point to the word *composition*.

> You know I'd rather do addition
> Than sit and write this <u>composition</u>.

💭 Think Aloud

When I look at this word, I see another word I already know—"position." The letters /c-o-m/ must be a prefix added to the base word /position/. When a vowel is surrounded by two consonants, it usually has a short sound. So I'll pronounce /c-o-m/ using the most common sound for /c/ and the short /o/ sound: /kom + position/. The word is "composition," a piece of writing.

Diagnostic Check

If ...	➤ You can ...
students need help with decoding,	use the lesson above to review the Phonics/Decoding Strategy.
students have difficulty understanding cause-effect relationships,	use the Reteaching lesson on page R8.

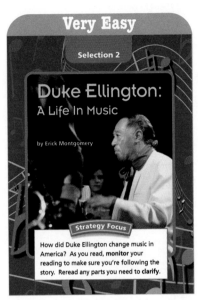

Very Easy

Selection 2

Duke Ellington: A Life In Music

by Erick Montgomery

Strategy Focus

How did Duke Ellington change music in America? As you read, **monitor** your reading to make sure you're following the story. Reread any parts you need to **clarify**.

Duke Ellington: A Life in Music
by Erick Montgomery

Selection Summary
Edward "Duke" Ellington, born in 1899, began playing the piano at age 7 and composing at age 14. After moving to New York, he formed an orchestra, playing a new kind of improvisational music. He wrote with Billy Strayhorn, and played with Louis Armstrong and Ella Fitzgerald. Duke Ellington entertained millions and served as an inspiration to generations of musicians.

Key Vocabulary
soda fountain: a lunch counter serving soda and ice-cream treats

indigo: dark blue

beige: ight tan

sophisticated: experienced, worldly-wise

Duke Ellington: A Life in Music

Reader's Library for Gloria Estefan

▶ Preparing to Read

Building Background Ask volunteers to name their favorite musicians and tell why they enjoy their music. Then explain that the person in the story, Duke Ellington, was a very famous musician and song writer in his day. Point out that he pioneered a new kind of music that still influences musicians today. You might also have students listen to some big-band music, such as Duke Ellington's *Take the 'A' Train.*

Developing Key Vocabulary Make sure students understand the meanings of the Key Vocabulary words listed at the left. Remind them to use the Phonics/Decoding Strategy when they come to a word they don't know. For students who need more help with decoding, use the review on the next page.

▶ Strategy/Skill Focus

Refer students to the Strategy Poster. Review when and how to use the Monitor/Clarify Strategy.

Making Judgements Remind students that good readers make judgments as they read. Remind students to monitor and clarify their judgments as they read.

Display these sentences about Ellington's composition "Black, Brown, and Beige."

> *This was not music to dance to. It was a serious work for a big concert hall. Not everyone liked it.*

Point out the judgments expressed here: The second sentence expresses the author's judgment. The third expresses the judgment of some listeners.

▶ Guided Preview

Ask a volunteer to read aloud the title and introduction. Invite students to browse through the photographs, note the captions, and discuss what the pictures seem to show. What do they think they will learn about Duke Ellington?

▶ Guiding the Reading

Have students read silently or with a partner. If needed, use these prompts:

pages 22–27

- *When did Duke start composing music? What does this tell you?*
- *What happened after Duke moved to New York City?*
- *What was different about Duke's music? How did people respond to it?*

pages 28-32

- *What judgment does the author make about Duke working with others?*
- *Who was Billy Strayhorn? What was his and Duke's best-known song?*
- *Why was the Carnegie Hall show important? What did Duke play?*

pages 33–38

- *What did Duke mean by saying his favorite song was "the next five"?*
- *Why did Duke receive the Presidential Medal of Freedom?*

▶ Responding

After students finish *Duke Ellington: A Life in Music*, begin a discussion of the selection by helping them respond to the questions on page 39. Then have students complete the judgment charts on page 39.

Sample Answers **Questions 1)** He was born in Washington D.C. in 1899. **2)** That's where his music really took off; he formed his own band; became famous. **3)** They played a fun, fresh kind of music that still makes people want to listen, tap their feet, and dance.
Chart: He cared deeply about the struggle of African Americans. His music made soldiers and their families happy.

English Language Learners

Building Background Students may need help with the New York City references: *Harlem* (an area in northern Manhattan), *'A' Train* (a subway train that goes from Harlem to downtown Manhattan).

Key Vocabulary Tell students that a *duke* is a member of royalty; as a nickname, it is a sign of respect. Help students understand *took off, at his best, dream come true,* and *like no other.*

Strategy Review
Phonics/Decoding

Model using the Phonics/Decoding Strategy. Write this sentence on the board and point to the word *orchestra*.

In New York, Duke started his own band, The Duke Ellington <u>Orchestra</u>.

Think Aloud

When I look at this word from left to right, I see the words "or" and "chest." I don't know any word that starts with /orchest/. I know that /ch/ sometimes has the /k/ sound, as in "echo." Maybe it's /or-kest/. Then I'll try the long /a/ sound for /ra/. I'll blend the parts together: /or kest ray/. That doesn't sound quite right. I'll try a short a sound at the end: /or kest rah/. That sounds like a word I've heard, but I'll look it up in the dictionary to be sure: orchestra. I was pretty close.

Diagnostic Check

If . . .	You can . . .
students need help with decoding,	use the lesson above to review the Phonics/Decoding Strategy.
students have difficulty making judgments,	use the Reteaching lesson on page R10.

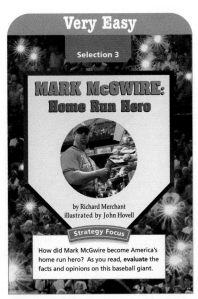

Mark McGwire: Home Run Hero
by Richard Merchant

Selection Summary

On September 8, 1998, Mark McGwire of the St. Louis Cardinals hit his 62nd home run and made history. McGwire had battled problems with his vision, injuries, public pressure, and hitting technique to become, with Sammy Sosa of the Cubs, a contender for the home-run record first held by Babe Ruth and then by Roger Maris. His 1998 record of 70 homers may never be broken.

Key Vocabulary

fixed: looked at steadily

screamed: moved so fast that it made a shrill, piercing noise

hounded: went after and pestered

Mark McGwire: Home Run Hero

Reader's Library for Lou Gehrig

▶ Preparing to Read

Building Background Begin a discussion about professional baseball. Ask volunteers to name their favorite players, why they like them, and what they know of the home run race between Mark McGwire and Sammy Sosa in 1998.

Developing Key Vocabulary Make sure students understand the meanings of the Key Vocabulary words listed at the left. Remind them to use the Phonics/Decoding Strategy when they come to a word they don't know. For students who need more help with decoding, use the review on the next page.

▶ Strategy/Skill Focus

Refer students to the Strategy Poster. Review when and how to use the Evaluate Strategy.

Fact and Opinion Remind students that good readers need to know the difference between a fact, which can be proved, and an opinion, which is what someone believes. As they read this article, they should evaluate the statements made to decide if they state opinions or facts.

On the board, write these sentences from the selection.

> *Everyone in the crowd jumped to their feet and started cheering wildly. It was the most exciting day of the 1998 season.*

Point out that the first sentence states a fact, something that could be seen and proven. The second states the author's opinion.

▶ Guided Preview

Read aloud the title and introduction. Then walk students through the various photographs, noting any captions and inviting students to speculate as to what they will learn about Mark McGwire and why he might be a hero.

▶ Guiding the Reading

Have students read silently or with a partner. If needed, use these prompts:

pages 40–45

- *How did Mark McGwire make baseball history on September 8, 1998?*

- *What did he do after crossing home plate? What does this tell you about him?*

pages 46–51

- *Did Mark hit well his first year in the major leagues? Explain.*

- *Mark said to reporter, "You'll always have a chance to hit 50 home runs." What did he mean?*

- *How did things get hard after Mark's first season? How did he react?*

pages 52–56

- *Mark's career improved after 1995. What, in his opinion, helped him?*

- *Describe the relationship between Mark and Sammy Sosa in 1998.*

- *The author says Mark's 1998 record may not be broken. Do you agree?*

▶ Responding

When students have finished reading, begin a discussion of the selection by helping them answer the questions on page 57. Then have students complete the fact/opinion charts on page 57.

Sample Answers Questions**1)** on September 8, 1998 **2)** He gave up a chance to hit 50 or more home runs in his first full season, so it must have been really important for him to be there. **3)** Fact. **Chart:** Opinion, Opinion, Fact.

English Language Learners

Building Background Make sure students know what a toothpick is so that they understand the simile on page 41.

Key Vocabulary Develop meanings for these idioms: *grinning from ear to ear, paid off, from bad to worse,* and *came out on top.*

MEETING INDIVIDUAL NEEDS

Strategy Review
Phonics/Decoding

Model using the Phonics/Decoding Strategy. Write this sentences on the board and point to the word *concentrate.*

> He had learned how to focus and <u>concentrate</u>.

⬭ Think Aloud

I'll look at this word from left to right. I see /con/ at the beginning, which I know from "contest" and "concert." Then I see the word "cent," as in one penny. That leaves /r-a-t-e/, which looks like the word "rat," but the final /e/ probably makes the /a/ a long /a/, as in "late." Now I'll blend the sounds of the parts together: /con sent rate/. Concentrate. I think I know this word. I'll check the dictionary

Diagnostic Check

If . . .	➤ You can . . .
students need help with decoding,	use the lesson above to review the Phonics/Decoding Strategy.
students have difficulty distinguishing fact from opinion,	use the Reteaching lesson on page R12.

Comprehension Skills: Cause and Effect

Reteaching

Teach

Remind students that cause and effect exists when one event makes another event happen. We can find an effect by asking the question, *What happened?* We can find the cause by asking the question, *Why did this happen?*

Write these sentences on the board:

> The school was closed last Thursday.
> Last Thursday was Thanksgiving, a holiday.

Have students identify which sentence is a *cause* and which sentence is an *effect*. If they are having trouble, guide them through the process. First ask, *What happened?* (School was closed on Thursday.) Then ask, *Why did this happen?* (Thursday was a holiday.)

Point out that identifying causes and effects can help us better understand what we read. Knowing why things happen helps us understand how events are related to each other. Use this example to illustrate the point. Have students silently read the first paragraph of the introductory material on page 532. Ask, *What happened to Mrs. Parks?* (The police arrested her.) *Why did this happen?* (Mrs. Parks refused to move to the back of the bus.) Have students identify the cause and the effect and explain their reasoning.

Practice

Have students create a two-column chart with the heads *Cause* and *Effect*. Tell them to complete this organizer as they read *Happy Birthday, Dr. King!* They can record events in the *Effect* column. They should summarize why each event happened in the *Cause* column. Model this example. Direct students back to page 539 of the story. Ask, *What happened to Jamal in school?* (His teacher gave him a pink slip.) Ask, *Why did this happen?* (He fought with another boy over a seat in the back of the bus.)

If students are having trouble, work through the story with them. Point out important events. Ask students to explain why these events happened.

Apply

Have students keep track of cause and effect, with an eye to identifying what happens and why it happens, in the **Reader's Library** selection *Thanks to Sandra Cisneros* by Daniel Santacruz. Then have them complete the questions and activity on the Responding Page.

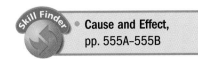

Cause and Effect, pp. 555A–555B

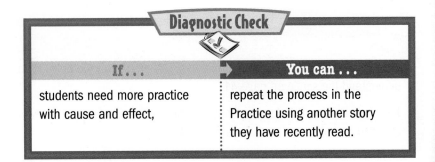

Diagnostic Check

If . . .	You can . . .
students need more practice with cause and effect,	repeat the process in the Practice using another story they have recently read.

Challenge/Extension

Challenge
Writing
Write a Tribute

Independent Activity Ask students to imagine that they are participating in a celebration of Martin Luther King Day. Have them write a tribute that they might deliver at a school assembly. Once they have researched information about Dr. King's life and achievements, have them use a word map to list ideas they want to include. Encourage them to look for cause-and-effect relationships between events in Dr. King's life and progress in civil rights. Remind students that they should add a conclusion that summarizes his importance in American history.

Speaking
Deliver an Oral Tribute

Independent Activity Invite students to present their Dr. King tributes to the class. Allow students time in class to rehearse their presentations. Partners might work together during the rehearsal stage.

Discuss the following tips for an oral presentation. Post the list of tips on a bulletin board so that students can refer to it.

- Rehearse by reading your tribute at home to family members or in front of a mirror.
- Remember to speak slowly and clearly. Pronounce each word carefully.
- Stress important ideas. You can do this by changing the pitch, tone, and volume of your voice and the speed at which you speak.
- Use gestures and facial expressions to show emotions.
- Look at your audience as you speak.

Social Studies
A Civil Rights Time Line

Small Group Activity Form small groups. Provide each group with reference materials that discuss important events in the history of civil rights. Then give each group a large sheet of butcher paper. Have them draw a time line that lists milestones in the crusade for equal rights. They should print the year *1950* at the left border of the time line and the current year at the right border. In between, students can enter events in the correct chronological order. Examples might include *the Montgomery Bus Boycott (1955), Title IX of the Education Act of 1972, the Americans with Disabilities Act of 1990.* Ask groups to present their findings to the class. Encourage them to explain the effect each event had on people.

Duke Ellington: A Life in Music

Reader's Library

Comprehension Skills: Making Judgments

Reteaching

Students

- weigh pros and cons to make judgments
- understand that there is no one correct judgment

Teach

Remind students that a judgment is an opinion based on personal values. Point out that readers make various judgments when they read. In some cases, we judge the actions of people who are the subjects of a written work. Some readers may decide that a person behaved wisely or was right in a certain situation. Other readers may think that the person behaved foolishly or was wrong. Because a judgment is based on personal values, there is no one correct judgment. However, readers should consider all the facts before making a judgment.

One way to consider the facts is by listing the pros and cons of a person's behavior. *Pros* are facts that support the way a person behaved. *Cons* are facts that do not support the way a person behaved. Direct students back to pages 564–566 of *Gloria Estefan.* Use the information on those pages to model using pros and cons to make a judgment.

Use a Think Aloud to model making a judgment about the fact that Gloria did not begin singing full time until she graduated from college.

Think Aloud

Pros: A full-time singing career would have interfered with Gloria's studies. Gloria had promised her mother that she would graduate from college. It is very hard to become a successful singer. Musicians are wise to get an education in case their music career does not go well.

Cons: Gloria had great talent. She loved to perform. She believed music was her true calling. Staying in college delayed her opportunity to pursue a music career. She loved Emilio, whose passion was music.

Ask students, *Do you think Gloria's decision to stay in college was wise?* Hold a class discussion. Encourage students to add other facts, pro or con, that they think should be considered. Afterwards, remind them that there is no one correct judgment.

Practice

Have students form opinions about other situations discussed in the selection. Remind them to consider all the facts. Tell them to list each fact as a pro or con before making a judgment. You might suggest that they think about the following situations: *Emilio quits his full-time job shortly after their first child is born. Record company officials decide to release the band's albums only in South America. Gloria decides to undergo a risky operation. Gloria turns down roles in movies.*

Hold class discussions. Encourage students to share their judgments with their classmates. Ask them to identify the facts they considered as pros and cons before forming an opinion.

Apply

Have students keep track of making judgments, with an eye to weighing pros and cons, in the **Reader's Library** selection *Duke Ellington: A Life in Music* by Erick Montgomery. Ask students to complete the questions and activity on the Responding Page.

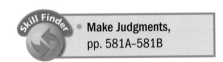

Skill Finder • Make Judgments, pp. 581A–581B

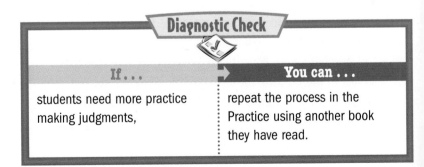

Diagnostic Check

If . . .	You can . . .
students need more practice making judgments,	repeat the process in the Practice using another book they have read.

Challenge/Extension

Challenge
Speaking/Listening
How to Help Our School

Small Group Activity Explain that students are going to make judgments about ways in which the class, as a whole, can contribute to the school.

First, have students brainstorm a list of activities. Examples might include *planting flowers around the building, designing banners that can be displayed in hallways,* or *tutoring younger students.* Select the two activities that you think would be most appropriate for your students.

Have students work in small groups, discussing the pros and cons of each activity. Then each member should decide which activity can best benefit the school and tell why he or she came to this conclusion. When all students have made a decision, conduct a poll to learn which activity most students judged the best.

Music Appreciation
A Favorite Tune

Independent Activity Have students listen as you play two songs by Gloria Estefan. Then tell students that you are going to play each song again. This time students should make judgments about each one. Tell them to consider melody, rhythm, and lyrics as well as any other facts they think are important. As you play each song, they should jot down their impressions.

Afterward, they should use their notes to list pros and cons of each song. Then they should write short reviews, explaining why they liked or did not like each song. Ask students to share their judgments and reasons with classmates.

Writing
Write a Fan Letter

Independent Activity Have students select one fact that they admire about Gloria Estefan. Ask them to write a fan letter to the singer. In their letter, they should state their opinion of something they learned about her in the biography. Then they should explain why they admire her action or the choice she made.

Dear Gloria,

I think it's great that you helped people after Hurricane Andrew. You're my hero!

Your fan,
Rose

Reader's Library

Comprehension Skills: Fact and Opinion

Reteaching

OBJECTIVES

Students

* understand the meaning of facts and opinions
* can distinguish between fact and opinion

Teach

Remind students that a fact is a statement that can be proved right or wrong. A fact usually can be checked in a reference source, such as an encyclopedia or an almanac. Often facts include statistical information, such as numbers and dates. An opinion states what someone thinks, feels, or believes. Mention that clue words sometimes appear before opinions. These clue words include *I think, everyone,* and *all the time.* You may agree or disagree with an opinion. However, you cannot prove it is true or false.

Write these sentences on the board:

> Lou Gehrig played baseball. Baseball is the best sport.

Point out that the first sentence is a fact. You can prove it is right by checking the information in a reference book, such as an encyclopedia or a book of baseball facts. The second sentence is an opinion. Some people may agree; others may disagree. However, the statement cannot be proved right or wrong.

Use the first paragraph in *Lou Gehrig: The Luckiest Man* to model identifying facts.

Think Aloud

I can check a reference work and find that Henry Ford sold his first automobile in 1903. This is a fact. Reference books also will tell me when the Wright Brothers made their first flight. This is a fact.

Practice

Have students identify other facts as they skim the selection. Discuss with them how they know that particular statements are facts. You might focus on the following information:

> *Lou never missed a day of school.*
> *Lou played in 2,130 consecutive games.*
> *He won Most Valuable Player Awards in 1927 and 1936.*

Ask students whether they think the following statements are facts or opinions, and have them explain their answers.

> *Lou's mother thought games and sports were a waste of time.*
> *She was convinced that [Lou] was ruining his life.*
> *Fiorello La Guardia… said, "You are the greatest prototype of good sportsmanship and citizenship."*

Apply

Have students keep track of fact and opinion, with an eye to identifying what can be proven right or wrong, in the **Reader's Library** selection *Mark McGwire: Home Run Hero* by Richard Merchant. Then have them complete the questions and activity on the Responding Page.

Skill Finder • Fact and Opinion, pp. 607A–607B

Diagnostic Check

If . . .	You can . . .
students need more practice with fact and opinion,	have them look for examples of facts and opinions in newspaper or magazine articles.

Comprehension Skills: Fact and Opinion
Challenge/Extension

Speaking/Listening
Recognizing Facts and Opinion in Conversation

Partner Activity Have partners work together to practice distinguishing between facts and opinions. Tell each student to write five sentences about favorite athletes, entertainers, or other famous people. At least three sentences should be facts. One or two must be opinions. Partners should take turns reading sentences aloud to each other. The listener should tell whether each sentence is a fact or an opinion, and then explain why.

Challenge
Math
Figuring Out a "Slugging Average"

 Independent Activity Remind students that a batting average is calculated by dividing a player's number of hits by number of at bats. Explain that slugging average is calculated by dividing a player's total number of *bases* by number of at bats. Have students figure out Lou Gehrig's slugging average for 1927 by providing them with the following information.

Lou Gehrig 1927	
584 at bats	18 triples (3 bases)
218 hits	47 home runs (4 bases)
101 singles (1 base)	Total bases = (447 bases)
52 doubles (2 bases)	Slugging Average = (.765)

Writing
Write a Newspaper Article

Independent Activity Imagine that you are a sports reporter covering Lou Gehrig Appreciation Day on July 4, 1939. Write an article for a newspaper telling readers about the event. Remember that most of your readers were not in the stadium. Therefore, you must provide enough details so that they can get a "mental picture" of the scene. Use details from the selection to help you. Organize your facts by writing answers to these questions: *Who? What? When? Where? Why?* and *How.* Then add two opinions about Lou Gehrig as a player and as a person.

Structural Analysis Skills: Words with a Prefix/Suffix

Reteaching

(margin) Theme Resources · Word Work

Teach

Review that prefixes are word parts added to the beginnings of words and suffixes are word parts added to the ends of words. Remind students that adding a prefix or a suffix changes the meaning of a word and makes a new word.

Write the prefixes *re-*, *dis-*, and *un-* and the words *like, write,* and *happy* on the board and model how to combine the words and prefixes to make new words.

> *I can add these prefixes to words to make new words. If I add re- to write, I get rewrite. When I add dis- to like, I get dislike. When I add un- to happy, I get unhappy. In each case, the prefix changes the meaning of the word.*

The prefix *re-* means "again." The prefix *dis-* means "opposite." The prefix *un-* means "opposite" or "not."

Write *-ness, -ment, -ful,* and *-less* and the words *spot, improve, wonder,* and *sad* on the board and model how to combine the words and suffixes.

> *I know that suffixes are added to the ends of words. I can combine sad and -ness to make sadness, a word I know. I can also combine improve and -ment to make improvement, wonder and -ful to make wonderful, and spot and -less to make spotless. These are words I know. I can also see that the suffix changes the meaning of the word or how I can use it.*

The suffixes *-ment* and *-ness* both mean "state or quality of." The suffix *-ful* means "full of." The suffix *-less* means "without."

Practice

Have students skim the selection to find one or more words with the following prefixes and suffixes: *re-, dis-, un-, -ment, -ful*. Ask them to write a definition for each word.

Apply

Give students the following words and have them use the prefixes *re-, dis-,* and *un-* and the suffixes *-ful, -less, -ment,* and *-ness* to make new words. They may use some words twice. Ask them to explain the meanings of the words they make.

govern	ability	comfort	cooked
courteous	paint	cheer	bold
thank	run	opened	power
calm	light	clever	arrange
type	slow	require	weak

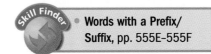

Skill Finder · Words with a Prefix/Suffix, pp. 555E–555F

Diagnostic Check

If...	You can ...
students need more practice with reading words with prefixes and suffixes,	suggest that they look through other stories for words with the prefixes and suffixes *re-, dis-, un-, -ful, -less, -ment, -ness.*

Heroes
Vocabulary Activities

Challenge
Dictionary: Prefixes *re-, un-, dis-*

Partner Activity Provide each pair with a dictionary and the following list of words. One partner looks at the word and uses its prefix to give its meaning, while the other partner looks it up in the dictionary to check the first partner's answer. They take turns decoding and using the dictionary until they have the meanings of all the words.

rebound	disapproval	unavoidable
reclamation	disobedient	uncharitable
recharge	discontinued	unconcerned
refreshment	disagreement	unfailing
relocate	distasteful	unexceptional

Vocabulary Expansion

Small Group Activity Have small groups work together to look back at the story and find words that have to do with the civil-rights movement. Students can record the words in a word web and add other words that have to do with civil rights. Have students use the words from their webs to give a short report on civil rights.

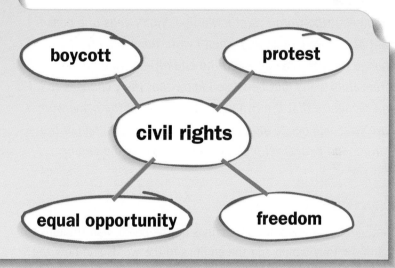

Structural Analysis Skills: Changing Final *y* to *i*

Reteaching

OBJECTIVES

Students change final *y* to *i* when adding endings and suffixes.

Teach

Review that when an ending or a suffix is added to a word that ends in a consonant plus *y*, the *y* changes to *i*. Explain to students that knowing how the spelling of the word changes will help them recognize words to which endings have been added.

Write the word *worry* and this sentence on the board and model changing the *y* to *i* before adding the ending: *Gloria was _____ that she would not have enough time to study.*

Think Aloud

I know that the word I want is worried. Worry *ends in a consonant plus* y. *So I know that when I write the word, I have to change the* y *to* i *before I add the ending* -ed. Worried *looks different from* worry, *but because I know that the* y *changes to* i, *I can recognize that the two words are forms of the same word. I have to remember to look closely at the words, though. If the word ended in a vowel plus* y, *I would just add the ending.*

Practice

Write the following words and endings on the board. Ask students to explain how they would add the endings to the words and how the new word would be spelled.

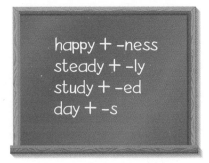

happy + -ness
steady + -ly
study + -ed
day + -s

Apply

Write the following sentences. Have students copy the underlined words and write the base words and endings from which they were made.

That is the <u>silliest</u> hat I've ever seen.
Several <u>families</u> came to the party.
Do you know any <u>remedies</u> for poison ivy?
He finished the job <u>easily</u>.
The mayor <u>replied</u> to my letter.
Yesterday was a <u>glorious</u> day.

Skill Finder
- Changing final *y* to *i*, pp. 581E–581F

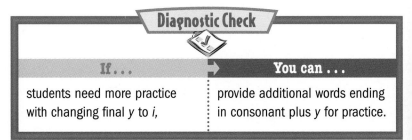

Diagnostic Check

If . . .	You can . . .
students need more practice with changing final *y* to *i*,	provide additional words ending in consonant plus *y* for practice.

Heroes
Vocabulary Activities

Challenge
Homophones

Small Group Activity Give students the following list of homophones. Have them take turns providing definitions for the words on the list while one group member acts as recorder. The first group to get correct definitions of all the words on the list wins.

1. aisle   I'll   isle
2. doe   dough
3. break   brake
4. flour   flower
5. allowed   aloud
6. meddle   medal
7. haul   hall
8. scent   sent
9. steal   steel
10. beat   beet
11. waist   waste
12. pair   pare   pear

Partner Activity Give pairs of students the following list of words. Have them work together to come up with a homophone for each word. Challenge them to use each one in a sentence that shows its meaning.

be   sighed
so   billed
ate   its
ceiling   chili

Vocabulary Expansion

Independent Activity Remind students that the selection they just read is about music and the music business. Ask them to recall the music words they found and add others of their own.

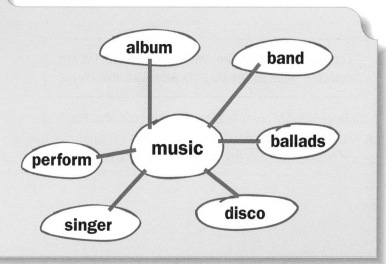

Structural Analysis Skills: VCV Pattern

Reteaching

Theme Resources · *Word Work*

Teach

Review that many words have a VCV (Vowel/Consonant/Vowel) pattern. Remind students that when they come to a word with the VCV pattern, they can try to pronounce the word by giving the first vowel a long sound. If they do not recognize the word, they can then try the short sound.

Write this sentence on the board: *The scout offered Lou Gehrig a good underline{salary}.*

Think Aloud

When I look at the underlined word, I see that it has a VCV pattern. The first vowel might have a long sound, so I'll try that first. SALE-uh-re—no, that's not a word I recognize. Next I'll try the short sound of a, / a /. I recognize the word salary, and it makes sense in the sentence.

Practice

Write the following sentences on the board and ask students to identify the words with a VCV pattern. Have volunteers pronounce them and explain how they decided whether the first vowel was long or short.

> *Lou Gehrig compiled an outstanding record. He was selected twice as the league's Most Valuable Player.*

Help students identify *compiled, record, selected,* and *Player* as words with the VCV pattern. Call on volunteers to pronounce the words and tell whether the first vowel is long or short.

Apply

Write the following words on the board. Ask students to copy the words and underline the VCV pattern. Have them put a check next to the words in which the first vowel is long, and an x next to the words in which the first vowel is short.

remember	material
money	melody
decided	electrical
government	similarly

Skill Finder • VCV Pattern, pp. 607E–607F

Diagnostic Check

If...	You can ...
students need more practice with reading words with the VCV pattern,	suggest that they look for other words in the selection with the VCV pattern.

Heroes

Vocabulary Activities

Challenge
Dictionary: Word Histories

Small Group Activity Provide each group with a dictionary. Give the groups the following list of words and ask them to take turns using the dictionary to find their histories. Call on a member of each group to present one of the word histories to the class.

pasteurize	California
sandwich	millipede
forsythia	lawn
school	hippopotamus
volcano	dandelion

Vocabulary Expansion

Independent Activity Remind students that Lou Gehrig played for the Yankees. Have them research the word *yankee* and find out its origins as well as its other uses.

Grammar Skills: Subject Pronouns

Reteaching

Teach

Encourage students to discuss what they learned from the story *Happy Birthday, Dr. King!* Then display the following sentences:

> *The students learned a lot about Dr. King.*
> *We learned a lot about Dr. King.*

Ask students how the sentences differ. Then underline *We* in the second sentence. Explain that *We* is a pronoun that can take the place of the subject *The students.* Review that a subject is who or what a sentence is about.

Have students write the following subject pronouns on index cards: *I, we, you, he, she, it, they.* Read aloud the following sentences and identify the subject. Ask students to hold up a card to show the pronoun that can take the place of each subject.

> Jamal and Arthur were in trouble. (They)
>
> Mrs. Gordon gave them both a note from the principal. (She)
>
> Jamal took the note home. (He)
>
> The note said Jamal had been fighting. (It)

Practice

Ask students to look at the first sentence in the fourth paragraph on page 536. Then model how to replace subjects with subject pronouns.

Think Aloud

The first thing I do when I look at this sentence is try to figure out the subject. Jamal *is who the sentence is about, so* Jamal *must be the subject. Then I ask myself, Which subject pronoun can take the place of* Jamal? *The pronoun* He *might work. I'll try the pronoun in the sentence:* He decided to go in the front door... *That makes sense.* He *must be the correct subject pronoun.*

Encourage students to use this thinking process as they identify the subjects in these story sentences and replace them with pronouns:

p. 536 Maybe <u>Mom</u> won't ask me about school. (she)
p. 541 <u>Grandpa Joe</u> took a deep breath and began... (He)
p. 544 <u>That man</u> was Dr. King. (He)
p. 547 <u>Our class</u> could do something to show that fighting is not the way to get things done. (We)

When finished, review by asking: *What words are subject pronouns?* (I, we, you, he, she, it, they) *What does a subject pronoun do?* (It replaces the subject of a sentence.)

Apply

Ask students to write five sentences about the story. At least three sentences should contain subject pronouns. Have students exchange papers, underline the subject pronouns in each other's sentences, and name the subject for which each pronoun stands.

Skill Finder • Subject Pronouns, pp. 555K–555L

Diagnostic Check

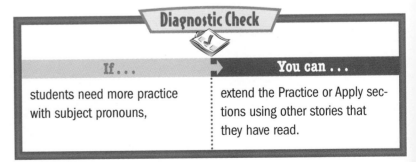

If...	You can ...
students need more practice with subject pronouns,	extend the Practice or Apply sections using other stories that they have read.

Grammar Skills: Object Pronouns

Reteaching

Teach

Ask students to name three facts that they learned from the story about Gloria Estefan. Then write the following sentence on the chalkboard:

> The story gave the students facts about Gloria Estefan.

Ask students to change the sentence to make it tell about what happened to them. Have them replace the underlined words with a pronoun. (us) Then explain that the pronoun *us* is an object pronoun. Review that object pronouns come after action verbs.

Have students write the following object pronouns on index cards: *me, us, you, him, her, it, them.* Ask students to listen carefully as you read the following sentences. Identify the object in each sentence. Have students hold up a card to show the pronoun that can replace each object.

> *A tour bus carried <u>Gloria, Emilio, and Nayib</u>.* (them)
> *A truck hit <u>the bus</u>.* (it)
> *The crash threw <u>Nayib</u> under a mountain of stuff.* (him)
> *The accident hurt <u>Gloria</u>.* (her)

Practice

Have students look at the sentence on page 561 that begins, *By the time Gloria was two...* Then model how to replace objects with object pronouns.

Think Aloud

To figure out which object pronoun to use, I must first find the object of the sentence. The words the family *come after the verb* had settled. *The object of the sentence must be* the family. *Then I ask myself, Which object pronoun can take the place of* the family? *I'll try* them *in the sentence.* By the time Gloria was two years old, José Fajardo had settled them in Miami, Florida. *That makes sense. The object pronoun* them *must be the correct.*

Have students use this thinking process as they identify the objects in these sentences from the story and replace them with pronouns:

p. 564 A few weeks after that, Emilio asked <u>Gloria</u> to join the band permanently. (her)

p. 566 Three months later, on September 1, 1978, she married <u>Emilio</u>. (him)

p. 567 The couple named <u>the boy</u> Nayib. (him)

p. 569 These two albums made <u>Gloria and the Miami Sound Machine</u> a success all over English-speaking America. (them)

When finished, review by having students name object pronouns. (me, us, you, him, her, it, them) Ask what an object pronoun does. (It replaces the object of a sentence.)

Apply

Have students use object pronouns in a brief written summary of the story. Students can exchange papers, underline each object pronoun, and name the object for which it stands.

Object Pronouns, pp. 581K–581L

Diagnostic Check

If...	You can ...
students need more practice with object pronouns,	extend the Practice or Apply sections using another story from this theme.

Theme Resources

Writing & Language

Grammar Skills: Possessive Pronouns

Reteaching

OBJECTIVES

Students

- identify possessive pronouns
- use possessive pronouns in sentences

Teach

Discuss Lou Gehrig's early life with students. Ask them to recall how his mother felt about him joining the Yankees. Then display these sentences:

> *Lou's mother wanted him to stay in college.*
> *His mother wanted him to stay in college.*

Ask students what they notice about the proper noun *Lou's* in the first sentence. Help them recognize that the word ends with *'s*. The word is possessive. It tells whose mother. Then ask students to name the word in the second sentence that replaces *Lou's*. (His) Point out that *His* is a possessive pronoun.

Have students write these possessive pronouns on index cards: *my, our, your, his, hers, its, their*. Ask them to listen carefully as you read the following sentences. Identify the possessive in each sentence. Have students hold up a card to show the pronoun that can replace it.

The young boy's home was New York City. (His)
Christina Gehrig's dreams for Lou did not come true. (Her)
The players' manager sent Lou to bat for the shortstop. (Their)
Lou was one of baseball's most valuable players. (its)

Practice

Have students look at the second sentence on page 590. Then model how to use possessive pronouns.

Think Aloud

I know that words that end with 's are possessive. The name Lou's ends with 's. It tells whose. I know that I can replace a possessive noun with a possessive pronoun. The pronoun His might work. I'll try it in the sentence: His constant play earned him the nickname Iron Horse. That makes sense. The pronoun His must be the correct pronoun to use.

Encourage students to use this process as they identify possessives in the story and replace them with possessive pronouns:

> p. 590 He was selected again as the league's MVP in 1936. (its)
> p. 592 On June 19, his thirty-sixth birthday, they told Lou's wife, Eleanor, what was wrong. (his)

Have students identify the possessive pronoun in each of these story sentences and name the noun for which it stands.

> p. 586 Christina Gehrig had great hopes for her son Lou. (Christina Gehrig)
> p. 594 Many of the players from the 1927 Yankees. . . came to honor their former teammate. (Yankees)

Review by asking students: *What words are possessive pronouns?* (my, our, your, his, hers, its, their.) *What does a possessive pronoun do?* (It replaces a possessive noun.)

Apply

Ask students to write a paragraph about Lou. Have them use at least three possessive pronouns in the paragraph. Students can exchange papers, underline each possessive pronoun, and name the possessive noun for which it stands.

Possessive Pronouns, pp. 607K–607L

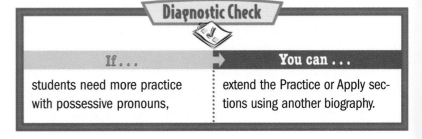
Diagnostic Check

If . . .	You can . . .
students need more practice with possessive pronouns,	extend the Practice or Apply sections using another biography.

Heroes
Writing Activities

What Is a Hero?

Write the word *survey* on the board. Explain that this word means asking different people what they think about a specific topic. Then ask one or two students to brainstorm which qualities they associate with being a hero.

Show students how to set up a survey sheet to record questions and responses. Have students set up their own survey questions as well as a chart for recording responses.

Organize students into groups. One person can conduct the survey while the others answer. Students can take turns being the surveyor within the same group or move around to work with different groups.

Encourage students to share their findings with the rest of the class. Discuss what students have learned from their surveys.

Write a Profile

Show students some age-appropriate examples of magazine or newspaper profiles of people. Ask them to think of someone they would like to profile. The person can be someone from their life or someone who represents a particular cause or profession. Students should read about and research their subject so that their profile focuses on one event or aspect of the person's life.

Remind students that an effective profile helps readers feel like they have gotten to know the subject. Encourage students to try to include some personal details such as the how the person looks or sounds, or what some of their favorite things are.

Heroes

Writing Activities

Create an Award

Display for students some plaques or awards that are given in honor of someone's achievements. Then invite students to create an award in honor of someone they admire. The person can be someone in their own life or a well-known person. Guide students to design the award with a logo or a picture that symbolizes what they admire about the person. Below the design have students write a caption that explains what the award means, and what the person has done to deserve this honor.

Challenge
Conduct an Interview

Have students work in pairs. Each partner can prepare a set of interview questions that he or she would like to ask of a personal hero. Students can take turns posing their interview questions to their partner, who can stand in as the "hero" and answer the questions.

Scene from A Hero's Life

Invite students to write a short play scene (including dialogue and stage directions) that focuses on an event in someone's life that they admire. Encourage students to think about which characters need to be included in the scene, where it takes place, and where the scene begins and ends. Students can act out the scenes they wrote.

Heroes

Writing Activities

Challenge
Write a Proposal

Encourage students to think about community projects where they could make a difference. Mention that people write proposals to explain how their idea can help others. A proposal has to include different sections that help describe how the idea could be put into action. Ask students to write a proposal suggesting something they could do to help others. Encourage students to:

- Explain their idea, including how it would help others
- Include a schedule
- Describe steps needed to make their idea happen
- List names of groups who would be involved
- List resources that would be needed
- Predict challenges that would have to be worked out

Write a Poem

Have students think about a time when they tried something new for the first time or had to do something that was difficult. Brainstorm some words that express some of those feelings. For students who may have difficulty starting, put all the words in a poetry box and ask students to pull out a few words to build their poems around.

Students can use the **Student Writing Center** for all their writing activities.

Portfolio Opportunity

Save responses to activities on these three pages for writing samples.

Theme Resources

Writing & Language

Cross-Curricular Activities

Health and Safety
Make a "What If" Poster

Remind students that sometimes ordinary people can become heroes just by knowing what to do in an emergency. Brainstorm with students some of the things they can do if they are with somebody who gets hurt and needs help. Guide students to think about things they can do safely such as staying calm, finding an adult to help, or calling 911. You may wish to organize students into small groups and assign them a specific "what if" situation. Ask students to come up with three things they should do and put them on a safety poster.

- What if you see a fire?
- What if a friend gets hurt when you are playing?
- What if you see a rabid or dangerous animal?
- What if you are near water?
- What if you see an elderly person fall down?

Social Studies
Create a Magazine Cover

Explain that various magazines choose a person or persons of the year. Tell students that these people are chosen because they made a difference that year. Ask students to think of a person or persons from their own lives who made a difference during the last year. Have them design a magazine cover about that person. Students can use or their own drawings and include a caption about why they are honoring the person.

Heroes

Cross-Curricular Activities

Math
Create a Bar Graph

Have children brainstorm categories of heroes, such as: sports heroes, professional heroes, and animal heroes. Have a large piece of paper available and record the different categories. Ask each student to think of heroes and decide which categories they belong to. Have a volunteer record the responses on a large bar graph. When the graph is completed, have the students compare and contrast their findings. Discuss which category has the largest number of heroes and which categories have the smallest number of heroes.

Science
Animal Heroes

Have small groups choose an animal hero to research, such as a seeing eye dog, a helper monkey, or a rescue dog. Students can also look for local animal heroes to report on. Make sure students include any special attributes or skills their animal has. Encourage groups to share what they have learned once their research is complete.

Challenge

Listening/Speaking
Listen to a Speech

Ask students if they have ever heard a speech read. Read either a specific speech such as Martin Luther King's "I Have a Dream" speech or play a tape recording of a famous speech or poem from an important event. Play the speech or a portion of it twice for students. Ask them which words or sentences stood out. Discuss how the tone and expression of a speech can affect the way people feel.

Invite students to read part of a speech or a poem and vary their expression.

Technology Resources

American Melody
P. O. Box 270
Guilford, CT 06437
800-220-5557

Audio Bookshelf
174 Prescott Hill Road
Northport, ME 04849
800-234-1713

Baker & Taylor
100 Business Court Drive
Pittsburgh, PA 15205
800-775-2600

BDD Audio
1540 Broadway
New York, NY 10036
800-223-6834

Big Kids Productions
1606 Dywer Ave.
Austin, TX 78704
800-477-7811
www.bigkidsvideo.com

Blackboard Entertainment
2647 International
Boulevard
Suite 853
Oakland, CA 94601
800-968-2261
www.blackboardkids.com

Books on Tape
P.O. Box 7900
Newport Beach, CA 92658
800-626-3333

Filmic Archives
The Cinema Center
Botsford, CT 06404
800-366-1920
www.filmicarchives.com

Great White Dog Picture Company
10 Toon Lane
Lee, NH 03824
800-397-7641
www.greatwhitedog.com

HarperAudio
10 E. 53rd St
New York, NY 10022
800-242-7737

Houghton Mifflin Company
222 Berkeley St.
Boston, MA 02116
800-225-3362

Informed Democracy
P.O. Box 67
Santa Cruz, CA 95063
831-426-3921

JEF Films
143 Hickory Hill Circle
Osterville, MA 02655
508-428-7198

Kimbo Educational
P. O. Box 477
Long Branch, NJ 07740
900-631-2187

The Learning Company (dist. for Broderbund)
1 Athenaeum St.
Cambridge, MA 02142
800-716-8506
www.learningco.com

Library Video Co.
P. O. Box 580
Wynnewood, PA 19096
800-843-3620

Listening Library
One Park Avenue
Old Greenwich, CT 06870
800-243-45047

Live Oak Media
P. O. Box 652
Pine Plains, NY 12567
800-788-1121
liveoak@taconic.net

Media Basics
Lighthouse Square
PO Box 449
Guilford, CT 06437
800-542-2505
www.mediabasicsvideo.com

Microsoft Corp.
One Microsoft Way
Redmond, WA 98052
800-426-9400
www.microsoft.com

National Geographic Society
1145 17th Street N. W.
Washington, D. C. 20036
800-368-2728
www.nationalgeographic.com

New Kid Home Video
1364 Palisades Beach Road
Santa Monica, CA 90401
310-451-5164

Puffin Books
345 Hudson Street
New York, NY 10014
212-366-2000

Rainbow Educational Media
4540 Preslyn Drive
Raleigh, NC 27616
800-331-4047

Random House Home Video
201 E. 50th St.
New York, NY 10022
212-940-7620

Recorded Books
270 Skipjack Road
Prince Frederick, MD 20678
800-638-1304
www.recordedbooks.com

Sony Wonder
Dist. by Professional Media
Service
19122 S. Vermont Ave
Gardena, CA 90248
800-223-7672

Spoken Arts
8 Lawn Avenue
P. O. Box 100
New Rochelle, NY 10802
800-326-4090

SRA Media
220 E. Danieldale Rd.
DeSoto, TX 75115
800-843-8855

Sunburst Communications
101 Castleton St.
P. O. Box 100
Pleasantville, NY 10570
800-321-7511
www.sunburst.com

SVE & Churchill Media
6677 North Northwest
Highway
Chicago, IL 60631
800-829-1900

Tom Snyder Productions
80 Coolidge Hill Road
Watertown, MA 02472
800-342-0236
www.tomsnyder.com

Troll Communications
100 Corporate Drive
Mahwah, NJ 07430
800-526-5289

Weston Woods
12 Oakwood Avenue
Norwalk, CT 06850-1318
800-243-5020
www.scholastic.com

Pourquoi
Tales

OBJECTIVES

During this Focus on Pourquoi Tales, students

- identify and define *pourquoi tales*
- recognize and identify the elements of a pourquoi tale
- compare and contrast pourquoi tales
- write their own pourquoi tale

Introducing the Genre

Explain to students that pourquoi tales tell why or how something happens. Invite students to choose one title from the contents on page 611 and to predict what they think will happen or what question it will answer.

▶ **Building Background**

Pourquoi tales are folktales that tell why or how something happens in nature.

■ Invite a volunteer to read the first paragraph under *Focus on Pourquoi Tales.*

■ Then read aloud the list of the elements of pourquoi tales.

■ Ask the class if they have read any pourquoi tales in the past. How do they know? Have them refer to the list of elements.

 Journal Writing Encourage students to use their journals to make notes and list possible ideas for their own pourquoi tales.

 **Teacher's Note**

Tell students that folk legends and tales have survived to this day thanks to the ancient tradition of oral storytelling. For hundreds of years, before there was any means of writing, people passed stories down from one generation to the next through the tradition of storytelling.

610

Focus on

Pourquoi Tales

Why do dogs bark? Why is it dark at night? How did the elephant get its trunk? Folktales that answer these kinds of questions are called pourquoi tales. Pourquoi [poor-kwa] is the French word for "why," but these entertaining tales are found all over the world.

Pourquoi tales
* explain how something in nature came to be
* can be about animal traits, nature, or people's customs
* feature animals or natural forces that have personalities and can speak
* often take place in the distant past
* sound as if they are being told aloud.

Contents

611

▶ ## Suggestions for Using
Focus on Pourquoi Tales

■ Students note key elements of a pourquoi tale.

■ Students study Writer's Craft.

■ Students practice implementation of various reading strategies.

■ Students gain a basis of comparison for writing their own pourquoi tale.

▶ ## Genre Connections

Use **Practice Book** pages 345 and 346 to review and reinforce the pourquoi tale genre. Students can complete the **Practice Book** pages either after finishing the first two selections or all the selections. Use the **Practice Book** pages when students most need review and reinforcement.

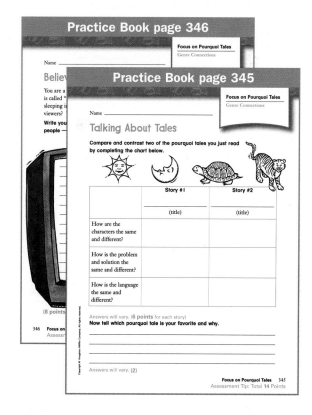

Reading "Why the Sun and the Moon Live in the Sky"

pages 612–614

▶ Preparing to Read

■ Read the title aloud and ask students how they know that the story they are about to read is a pourquoi tale. (The story tells *why* something happens.)

■ Ask students who they think the main characters might be. (Sun and Moon)

▶ Supporting Comprehension

1 What does the author do that makes you feel as though Sun, Moon, and Water are real people? (The author gives them human traits, such as having friends and feeling hurt.)

2 How does the author let you know that Water may have trouble visiting Sun and Moon? (Water says that Sun and Moon's house would have to be very, very, very big for him to visit them.)

 Journal Writing Encourage students to list characters that might appear in a pourquoi tale. They can use this list when they write their own tale.

Vocabulary *(page 612)*

stroll: a relaxed walk

chatting: talking easily

company: friendship

WHY THE SUN AND THE MOON LIVE IN THE SKY

by Julius Lester

IN THE TIME OF THE BEGINNING of beginnings, everything and everyone lived on earth. If you had been living in those times, you could've sat on your porch in the evening and watched the Sun, the Moon and the Stars taking a stroll and chatting with all the neighbors.

The Sun had many friends, but his best friend in all the universe was Water. Every day Sun visited Water and they talked about this and that and enjoyed each other's company, which is what friends do.

There was one thing wrong with their friendship, however. Water never came to visit Sun at his house. That hurt Sun's feelings.

He could've held onto his hurt feelings and gotten angry. But that's not the way to treat your feelings when they're hurt. You feel better if you talk to the one who hurt them. Maybe Water didn't know that he had hurt Sun's feelings. **1**

"Why don't you ever visit me?" Sun asked Water.

"I would love to visit you," Water replied, "but your house might not be big enough for me and all of my relatives. I wouldn't want to force you out of your house. If you want me to visit, you must build a very, very, very, very, very large house. I need a lot of room." **2**

612

 English Language Learners

Multiple Meanings

Invite students to keep a list of words with more than one meaning. The word *company*, for example, has two meanings; it can refer to friends or to a business.

Sun went home and told his wife, the Moon, that they had to build a very, very, very, very, very large house. His friend, Water, was coming to visit.

They set to work immediately. He sawed. She nailed. He hammered. She measured, and they built a very, very, very, very, very large house indeed.

The house was so large that it took a whole day to walk from the front door to the back door. The house was so wide that when you stood on one side, you couldn't see the other side.

Sun went and told Water that he could come visit now.

The next morning Water flowed up the road. "Is it safe to come in?" he asked when he got to the house.

"Please enter," said Sun and Moon, opening the door to the house they had built.

Water began flowing in. With him came the fish and all the other water creatures.

613

Revisiting the Text

Genre Lesson
Pourquoi Tales

OBJECTIVES

Students identify the elements of a pourquoi tale.

Review the elements of pourquoi tales:

- They explain why or how something in nature came to be.

- They can be about animal traits, nature, or people's customs.

- They feature animals or natural forces that have personalities and can speak.

- They often take place in the distant past.

- They sound as if they are being told aloud.

Remind students that pourquoi tales are simple stories and easy to read. Ask students to find examples of each element in *Why the Sun and the Moon Live in the Sky* that make it a pourquoi tale. Encourage them to refer to the list if they need to. (The tale explains why the sun and the moon are in the sky; it's about nature; the characters are natural forces that speak; it takes place long ago; it sounds as if it were being told aloud.)

Challenge

Science Connection

In this pourquoi tale, it takes a whole day to walk from the front door to the back door of Sun and Moon's new house. Have students make this science connection: What takes a whole day for Earth to do? (to spin once all the way around its axis)

Wrapping Up "Why the Sun and the Moon Live in the Sky"

pages 612–614

Comprehension/Critical Thinking

1 Why do you think the author made the Sun and Moon husband and wife? (Answers will vary, but could include that they both share the sky in a kind of partnership.) **Making Inferences**

2 Why did the author choose Water as Sun's friend in this tale? (When Water visits his friend, Sun, he forces Sun and Moon into the sky.) **Drawing Conclusions**

3 What elements of a pourquoi tale has the author used? (The tale answers a *why* question; natural forces are the main characters; nature takes on human characteristics; the tale takes place in the distant past.) **Noting Details**

 Journal Writing Invite students to brainstorm a list of things that happen in nature, such as the sun rising or snow falling, and think of explanations for these natural things that could make a pourquoi tale.

Soon the water was knee-deep. "Is it still safe for me to come in?"

"Of course," Sun and Moon said.

More water flowed in. Soon it was halfway to the ceiling. "Do you want more of me to come in?"

"Of course," said Sun and Moon, rising to the ceiling so they wouldn't get wet and have their lights put out.

More water and more water and more water flowed in. Sun and Moon had to go sit on the roof.

"Do you want more of me to come in?" asked Water.

Sun and Moon said yes, not knowing what they were saying.

More and more Water poured in. With him came more and more fish and whales and sharks and seaweed and crabs and lobsters. Water covered the roof of the house and got higher and higher.

The higher Water rose, the higher in the sky Sun and Moon had to go to stay dry.

Finally Sun and Moon were so high in the sky they weren't sure how to get down. But they liked being so high up and looking down on the world.

And that's where they've been ever since.

614

 Challenge

Introducing Personification

Review the main characters of the story with students. Ask them to tell how the author has personified these elements of nature. (They talk, they walk, and they feel and act like humans.) Invite students to choose one element of nature, such as the wind, a mountain, or a river, and to describe it in a way that personifies it. They can use this element in their own tale.

Focus on
Pourquoi
Tales

Tiger

by Michael Rosen

A meeting is taking place on Great Mountain.

Tiger says Tiger's the best, the strongest, the fastest on earth. Thunder says Thunder's the best, the loudest, the fiercest on earth. Echo says Echo's the best, the toughest, the cleverest on earth. Dragon says Dragon's the best, the mightiest, the hottest on earth.

"Yes, yes, yes," says Tiger. "I know all about you. But the thing that makes me the best is I'm not afraid of anything."

Tiger, Thunder, Echo, and Dragon cannot decide who is the greatest.

"Let us have a contest," says Tiger. "In this contest we will see which of us is the most terrifying. Whoever can make the other three cry, 'Stop, no more!' is the winner."

They all agree, and Tiger laughs.

"Now I'll show them."

3

615

Reading "Tiger"
pages 615–619

▶ **Preparing to Read**

Ask students what they think this pourquoi tale might tell them about tigers. What would they like to know about tigers? (Answers will vary, but might include how tigers got their stripes or why they live where they do.)

▶ **Purpose Setting**

The four main characters in this pourquoi tale are Thunder, Echo, Dragon, and Tiger. Have students read to see what the character traits of each are and how the characters interact.

 Journal Writing Invite students to list animals that they would enjoy writing about as characters in a tale. They can use this list of characters in their own pourquoi tale.

 English Language Learners

Demonstration

For better understanding, help students act out the sounds Thunder and Echo might make in nature.

Reading "Tiger," continued
pages 615–619

• •

▶ **Supporting Comprehension**

3 What is the result of each animal saying that he is the best? (They have a contest.)

4 Why do you think Tiger loses right away? (Answers might include because he was the first to say he's the best.)

5 What makes the contest interesting? (Each of the four characters have different qualities that they use in clever ways to try to defeat the others.)

Vocabulary *(pages 616–617)*

horrendous: terrible

deafening: so loud that it hurts your hearing

coils: winds into a circle

squirms: twists and turns

mad: crazy

Tiger paws the ground, opens his jaws, shows every tooth in his head, and roars. Thunder vanishes into thin air and sits among the clouds. Echo rolls down Great Mountain, across Blue River, up Little Mountain and is gone. Dragon coils and twists her long body and tail and squirms her way up into the sky, out of reach of Tiger's claws.

No one cries, "Stop, no more!" Tiger is left pawing the ground and roaring to himself until no roar is left. Thunder, Echo, and Dragon come back.

4

"Tiger loses," they say.

"I know, I know, I know," says Tiger.

Now Thunder comes forward, looks around at the clouds, and flies off to the deepest, darkest one in sight. From that cloud come the most horrendous drumming and deafening rolls.

Tiger can't bear it and shouts, "Stop, no more!"

But Echo listens to Thunder's rolls, waits for them at the top of Little Mountain, and rolls them back at Thunder. And Dragon just coils and twists her long body and tail and squirms her way up into the sky, up above Thunder's clouds where it is all quiet.

616

 Cross-Curricular Connection

Science Wild tigers live only in Asia. The stripes on a tiger are as unique as our fingerprints. No two tigers have the same markings. A tiger's roar can be heard from as far away as 2 miles (3.2 kilometers).

Thunder, Echo, and Dragon come back.
"Thunder loses," they say.
"I'm better than Tiger," says Thunder.
"I know, I know, I know," says Tiger.
Now Echo comes forward and waits.
"Well, aren't you going to start?" says Tiger.
"Going to start?" says Echo.
"Well, don't hang about," says Tiger.
"Don't hang about," says Echo.
"It's not me that's hanging about, you fool," says Tiger.
"You fool," says Echo.
"Who are you calling a fool?" asks Tiger angrily.
"Who are you calling a fool?" asks Echo angrily.
"You," says Tiger.
"You," says Echo.
"Just get on with it," roars Tiger.
"Get on with it," roars Echo.
"It's not my turn," says Tiger.
"It's not my turn," says Echo.
"It is," shouts Tiger.
"It is," shouts Echo.
"You're driving me mad," says Tiger.
"You're driving me mad," says Echo.
"Stop, stop, no more!" cries Tiger.
"Stop, stop, no more!" cries Echo.
"I agree," says Thunder.
"I agree," says Echo.
"Stop, no more!" says Thunder. **5**

617

Revisiting the Text

Writer's Craft Lesson
Personification

OBJECTIVES

Students identify personification and its use in writing a pourquoi tale.

Explain that authors of pourquoi tales personify their characters. They give an animal or an object qualities like a person has. Animals, objects, or even natural forces become beings that speak and act just like us. Ask students to explain how each item below is an example of personification.

- An alarm clock shouts at a sleeping child to wake up.

- A hurricane worries aloud about the damage it causes.

- A dog complains about dirty water in his drinking bowl.

Ask students how the characters in this pourquoi tale are true to their nature. (Tiger roars; Thunder makes a lot of noise; Dragon breathes fire; Echo repeats.) Ask if pourquoi tales would be possible without the use of personification. (No, because pourquoi tales always involve animals or natural forces that can speak and have personalities.)

Have small groups tell how the author uses personification in this pourquoi tale. Allow time for students to share their work.

Reading "Tiger," *continued*
pages 615–619

....

▶ **Supporting Comprehension**

6 What hints are given in the tale to indicate who the winner of the contest will be? (The characters compete in the same order as their introduction in the story, which suggests that Dragon will win.)

7 What is the result of Dragon's starting a forest fire? (Flaming branches fall on Tiger, burning and striping his fur.)

Vocabulary *(page 619)*

jet: a strong, steady stream

crackles: makes a series of sharp, popping sounds

Echo looks around for Dragon, but Dragon has coiled and twisted up her long body and tail and squirmed away up into the sky, where not even an echo can reach. Sometime later, Dragon comes back.

"Echo loses," they say.

"Echo was better than Thunder," says Dragon.

"Better than Thunder," says Echo.

"That's true," says Thunder.

"Echo was better than Tiger," says Dragon.

"Better than Tiger," says Echo.

"I know, I know, I know," says Tiger.

6 Now it's Dragon's turn. Dragon coils and twists her long body and tail and pours fire out of her mouth. Thunder flees to a cloud, but Dragon follows and breathes fire on the cloud and dries it up until there is nowhere for Thunder to sit.

"Stop, no more!" shouts Thunder.

Dragon chases Echo down Great Mountain, across Blue River, and up Little Mountain until they meet going down the other side.

"Do you want to give up?" asks Dragon.

"Give up," says Echo.

"Stop, no more?" asks Dragon.

618

 Extra Support

Words that end in -est

Point out the superlatives used in the beginning of *Tiger: best, strongest, fastest, loudest, fiercest, toughest, cleverest, mightiest, hottest, greatest.* Ask students what kind of words these are (adjectives). Tell students that an adjective's ending shows degree of comparison. Adjectives ending in *-est* are comparing three or more things. Adjectives comparing just two things end in *-er.*

"Stop, no more," says Echo.

"And now for Tiger," says Dragon. But Tiger is hiding in the forest on the side of the Great Mountain. So Dragon coils and twists up her long body and tail and lets fly a huge jet of flame, setting that forest on fire. But Tiger is ready, and he runs from the fire that races through the trees. And Tiger could have escaped, but for the wind in the treetops that flies even faster. Just as Tiger is leaving the forest, the fire crackles overhead. Flaming branches of a tree fall on Tiger, just as he thinks he is free.

"Stop, no more!" shouts Tiger.

"I've won," says Dragon.

"That's true," say Thunder and Echo.

"Never mind that," says Tiger, "look at my coat, the branches have burned my fur."

"Yes," says Dragon. "You're all *stripy*."

"I know, I know, I know," says Tiger.

619

Wrapping Up "Tiger"
pages 615–619

Comprehension/Critical Thinking

1. What natural event does this pourquoi tale explain? (how tigers got their stripes) **Story Structure**

2. What elements of the pourquoi tale does this author use? (The animal characters have personalities and can talk; the tale explains something in nature; it takes place in the past; it's easy to read aloud.) **Noting Details**

3. How is this tale alike and different from the other tale? (Both tales explain something in nature; in both tales the characters are personifications; the characters in *Tiger* are animals while in the first tale they were nonliving elements of nature.) **Compare and Contrast**

✏ **Journal Writing** Invite students to write a new ending to this tale. They can use their ending for their own pourquoi tale.

Challenge

Sequel

Invite students to turn Great Mountain, featured in this pourquoi tale, into a character. Add a new chapter to this tale explaining what Great Mountain might do after Dragon sets a forest fire where Tiger is hiding.

Reading "How Turtle Flew South for the Winter"

pages 620–623

▶ **Preparing to Read**

Refer to the title. Ask students how they know this story is a pourquoi tale.

▶ **Purpose Setting**

Have students identify what aspect of nature is explained in this pourquoi tale.

 Journal Writing Encourage students to think about how pourquoi tales explain things and entertain the reader at the same time. Invite students to write about something they would like to explain in a pourquoi tale.

▶ **Supporting Comprehension**

8 Why do the birds tell Turtle that they are going to fly south? (Birds really do fly south and Turtle can't fly. They will try to solve this problem.)

9 What makes Summer seem like a person? (Summer has human characteristics: it lives down south and has plenty of food.)

Vocabulary *(page 621)*
pleaded: begged; asked

NATIVE AMERICAN
STORIES *by Joseph Bruchac*

How Turtle Flew South for the Winter

by Joseph Bruchac

IT WAS THE TIME OF YEAR when the leaves start to fall from the aspens.

Turtle was walking around when he saw many birds gathering together in the trees. They were making a lot of noise and Turtle was curious. "Hey," Turtle said. "What is happening?"

"Don't you know?" the birds said. "We're getting ready to fly to the south for the winter."

"Why are you going to do that?" Turtle asked.

"Don't you know anything?" the birds said. "Soon it's going to be very cold here and the snow will fall. There

620

English Language Learners

Animal Characteristics

Use the illustration on page 620 to prompt a discussion of a turtle's characteristics. Ask questions such as the following:

- Are turtles fast or slow?

- Do turtles walk or fly?

- What does a turtle have on its back? Is it hard or soft?

won't be much food to eat. Down south it will be warm. Summer lives there all of the time and there's plenty of food."

As soon as they mentioned the food, Turtle became even more interested. "Can I come with you?" he said.

"You have to fly to go south," said the birds. "You are a turtle and you can't fly."

8

But Turtle would not give up. "Isn't there some way you could take me along?" He begged and pleaded. Finally the birds agreed just to get him to stop asking.

"Look here," the birds said, "can you hold onto a stick hard with your mouth?"

"That's no problem at all," Turtle said. "Once I grab onto something no one can make me let go until I am ready."

"Good," said the birds. "Then you hold on hard to this stick. These two birds here will each grab one end of it in their claws. That way they can carry you along. But remember, you have to keep your mouth shut!"

"That's easy," said Turtle. "Now let's go south where Summer keeps all that food." Turtle grabbed onto the middle of the stick and

9

621

Writer's Craft Lesson
Problems and Solutions

OBJECTIVES

Students identify how problems and solutions are used in a pourquoi tale.

Remind students that every pourquoi tale has a problem and a solution. By telling a solution to the problem, the author gives an explanation of an aspect of nature. Point out the main problem in this tale, that turtle cannot fly, and then ask how the birds solve it. (They have Turtle bite on a stick, which they carry.) Ask students what other problem arises while Turtle is flying. (He wants to talk, but he's holding on to the stick; he opens his mouth to talk and then he falls to the ground.) Point out that the solution to this final problem provides the explanation for why turtles have cracked shells and why they sleep through the winter.

Invite groups of students to review the other two tales to find their problems and solutions. Have students list these problems and solutions in their journals as reference for when they write their own tales.

Reading "How Turtle Flew South for the Winter," *continued*

pages 620–623

▶ **Supporting Comprehension**

10 How does the birds' solution lead to a problem later on? (Turtle has to hold onto a stick and can't talk, but he likes to talk.)

two big birds came and grabbed each end. They flapped their wings hard and lifted Turtle off the ground. Soon they were high in the sky and headed toward the south.

    Turtle had never been so high off the ground before, but he liked it. He could look down and see how small everything looked. But before they had gone too far, he began to wonder where they were. He wondered what the lake was down below him and what those hills were. He wondered how far they had come and how far they would have to go to get to the south where Summer lived. He wanted to ask the two birds who were carrying him, but he couldn't talk with his mouth closed.

10

622

 Cross-Curricular Connection

Science Many birds migrate, while many reptiles hibernate. As recently as the late 18th century many educated people, even scientists, believed that swallows did what turtles do in the winter: dive into the water and burrow deep into the warm mud at the bottom of a pond, stream, or marsh until spring. When the ice thawed, people believed, the swallows would take to the air again!

Turtle rolled his eyes. But the two birds just kept on flying. Then Turtle tried waving his legs at them, but they acted as if they didn't even notice. Now Turtle was getting upset. If they were going to take him south, then the least they could do was tell him where they were now! "Mmmph," Turtle said, trying to get their attention. It didn't work. Finally Turtle lost his temper.

"Why don't you listen to . . ." but that was all he said, for as soon as he opened his mouth to speak, he had to let go of the stick and he started to fall. Down and down he fell, a long, long way. He was so frightened that he pulled his legs and his head in to protect himself! When he hit the ground he hit so hard that his shell cracked. He was lucky that he hadn't been killed, but he ached all over. He ached so much that he crawled into a nearby pond, swam down to the bottom and dug into the mud to get as far away from the sky as he possibly could. Then he fell asleep and he slept all through the winter and didn't wake up until the spring.

So it is that today only the birds fly south to the land where Summer lives while turtles, who all have cracked shells now, sleep through the winter.

623

Wrapping Up

Comparing and Contrasting Pourquoi Tales

1 How are Turtle and Tiger alike? (They are both animals that act like people; they have similar personalities, bossy show-offs; they create problems for themselves that lead to the solution of the story.) **Compare and Contrast**

2 Of the three pourquoi tales you have read, which ones sound to you as if someone is telling them aloud? What about these tales creates this effect? (Answers will vary.) **Making Judgments**

3 Which of the pourquoi tales has characters that are personifications of elements of nature and aren't animals? (*Why the Sun and the Moon Live in the Sky:* Sun, Moon, Water; *Tiger:* Thunder, Echo; *How Turtle Flew South for the Winter:* Summer.) **Noting Details**

4 What do you think makes a good pourquoi tale? (Answers will vary.) **Making Generalizations**

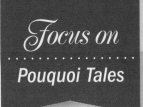
Extending

Before students begin writing their own pourquoi tale, you can teach the following brief writing lesson.

Writing Skill Lesson
Writing a Pourquoi Tale

OBJECTIVES

Students write a pourquoi tale.

Review the elements of a pourquoi tale with students. Remind students that they can use their journals to get ideas for their tales. Write the following questions on the board to help students decide what they will write their pourquoi tale about, and how:

■ What aspect of nature will you write about, explaining how or why it came to be?

■ What animal trait, natural event, or people's custom will you write about?

■ Who will the main characters be—animals, natural forces, or other things found in nature?

■ When will the story take place?

■ How will you write your pourquoi tale so that it is fun and can easily be told aloud?

Have students brainstorm and outline their pourquoi tales before they write. Give students time to draft and rewrite their stories. As you assign the writing, consider the following:

■ Read aloud "Write Your Own Pourquoi Tale."

■ Share other pourquoi tales as models.

Creating

Write Your Own Pourquoi Tale

Become a storyteller. Think of something in nature that would be fun to explain in a creative way. It could be an animal, a geographical feature, or a force of nature. Decide how your "character" came to be the way it is. Write your story so that it sounds as if you were telling it aloud.

Tips

• Give your "character" an interesting personality.
• Use dialogue as well as action to show the personalities of all the characters.
• You might include a lesson in your tale: the character gets what it deserves in the end.
• Read your tale aloud to see if it has the effect you want.

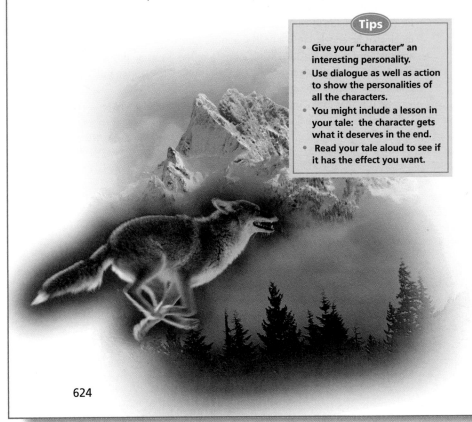

624

More Pourquoi Tales

How Rabbit Lost His Tail
by Ann Tompert (Houghton)
This Seneca tale explains why Rabbit no longer has a long, beautiful tail.

Days of the Blackbird
by Tomie de Paola (Putnam)
Find out why the last three days of January are called the Days of the Blackbird in northern Italy.

Misoso: Once Upon a Time Tales from Africa
by Verna Aardema (Knopf)
These twelve stories explain animal traits, such as Elephant's tusks and Antelope's cough.

Cat and Rat: The Legend of the Chinese Zodiac
by Ed Young (Holt)
This legend explains why there is no Year of the Cat on the Chinese calendar.

625

Presentation Activities

Use one or more of these activities to extend the *Focus on Pourquoi Tales.*

Storytelling

Give students a chance to carry on the oral storytelling tradition by having volunteers read their pourquoi tales aloud. Remind them that reading with expression and emphasizing the humor of the story helps keep listeners interested.

Books on Tape

Invite students to record their pourquoi tales so that others can hear them. Offer a collection of class cassettes to the school or local library.

Comic Books

Students who enjoy drawing can turn one of the pourquoi tales into a comic book and share it with the class. Remind them that comic books focus on dialogue and action scenes. Invite them to brainstorm how to portray a force of nature such as Echo or Thunder.

Glossary

This glossary contains meanings and pronunciations for some of the words in this book. The Full Pronunciation Key shows how to pronounce each consonant and vowel in a special spelling. At the bottom of the glossary pages is a shortened form of the full key.

Full Pronunciation Key

Consonant Sounds

b	**bib**, ca**bb**age	kw	**ch**oir, **qu**ick	t	**t**igh**t**, s**t**opped
ch	**ch**urch, sti**tch**	l	li**d**, nee**dl**e, ta**ll**	th	ba**th**, **th**in
d	**d**ee**d**, maile**d**, pu**ddl**e	m	a**m**, **m**an, du**mb**	th	ba**the**, **th**is
f	**f**ast, **f**i**fe**, o**ff**, **ph**rase, rou**gh**	n	**n**o, su**dd**en	v	ca**ve**, **v**al**ve**, **v**ine
g	**g**a**g**, **g**et, fin**g**er	ng	thi**ng**, i**nk**	w	**w**ith, **w**olf
h	**h**at, **wh**o	p	**p**o**p**, ha**pp**y	y	**y**es, **y**olk, on**i**on
hw	**wh**ich, **wh**ere	r	**r**oa**r**, **rh**yme	z	ro**se**, **s**ize, **x**ylophone, **z**ebra
j	**j**u**dge**, **g**em	s	mi**ss**, **s**au**ce**, **sc**ene, **s**ee	zh	gara**ge**, plea**s**ure, vi**s**ion
k	**c**at, **k**i**ck**, s**ch**ool	sh	di**sh**, **sh**ip, **s**ugar, ti**ss**ue		

Vowel Sounds

ă	p**a**t, l**au**gh	ŏ	h**o**rrible, p**o**t	ŭ	c**u**t, fl**oo**d, r**ou**gh, s**o**me
ā	**a**pe, **ai**d, p**ay**	ō	g**o**, r**ow**, t**oe**, th**ough**		
â	**a**ir, c**a**re, w**ear**	ô	**a**ll, c**au**ght, f**o**r, p**aw**	û	c**i**rcle, f**u**r, h**ear**d, t**er**m, t**ur**n, **ur**ge, w**or**d
ä	f**a**ther, k**oa**la, y**ar**d	oi	b**oy**, n**oi**se, **oi**l		
ĕ	p**e**t, pl**ea**sure, **a**ny	ou	c**ow**, **ou**t	yōō	c**ure**
ē	b**e**, b**ee**, **ea**sy, p**ia**no	ŏŏ	f**u**ll, b**oo**k, w**o**lf	yōō	ab**u**se, **u**se
ĭ	**i**f, p**i**t, b**u**sy	ōō	b**oo**t, r**u**de, fr**ui**t, fl**ew**	ə	**a**go, sil**e**nt, penc**i**l, lem**o**n, circ**u**s
ī	r**i**de, b**y**, p**ie**, h**igh**				
î	d**ear**, d**eer**, f**ier**ce, m**ere**				

Stress Marks

Primary Stress ´: bi·ol·o·gy [bī **ŏl**´ ə jē]
Secondary Stress ´: bi·o·log·i·cal [bī´ ə **lŏj**´ ĭ kal]

Pronunciation key and definitions © 1998 by Houghton Mifflin Company. Adapted and reprinted by permission from *The American Heritage Children's Dictionary.*

710

A

a·blaze (ə **blāz**´) *adj.* On fire: *One match set the fire ablaze.*

a·bun·dance (ə **bŭn**´ dəns) *n.* A large amount: *The hikers saw an abundance of wildlife in the forest.*

ad·ven·tur·er (ad **vĕn**´ char ər) *n.* A person who takes part in bold, dangerous, or risky activities: *The adventurers were the first to reach the mountaintop.*

af·fect (ə **fĕkt**´) *v.* To cause a change in; have an effect on: *Hot, dry weather affected the crops.*

ag·gres·sive·ly (ə **grĕs**´ ĭv lē) *adv.* Very actively and forcefully: *She worked aggressively to get elected.*

al·le·giance (ə **lē**´ jəns) *n.* Loyalty to one's country, a person, or a cause: *The player showed her allegiance to the team by playing her best.*

am·pli·fi·er (**ăm**´ plə fī´ ər) *n.* An electronic device that makes sound stronger or louder: *The amplifiers allowed everyone in the large room to hear the speech.*

an·ces·tor (**ăn**´ sĕs´ tar) *n.* A person in one's family who lived many years ago.

ar·range·ment (ə **rānj**´ mənt) *n.* Planning done beforehand; preparation: *The family made arrangements for their vacation.*

at·ten·tive·ly (ə **tĕn**´ tĭv lē) *adv.* With attention or alertness: *We listen attentively to our teacher.*

au·tumn (**ô**´ təm) *n.* The season of the year between summer and winter.

B

be·wil·der (bĭ **wĭl**´ dər) *v.* To puzzle greatly: *The city's busy streets bewildered the young boy.*

blare (blâr) *v.* To make a loud harsh noise, as of a horn: *The car horn was blaring in the street.*

bliz·zard (**blĭz**´ ərd) *n.* A very long, heavy snowstorm with strong winds.

bor·row (**bŏr**´ ō) *v.* To take something with the understanding that it will be returned: *Matt let his friend borrow his book.*

boy·cott (**boi**´ kŏt´) *n.* A refusal to use, buy from, or deal with a store, company, person, or nation: *Many people joined the boycott against the store's unfair policy.*

bunk·house (**bŭngk**´ hous´) *n.* A building in a ranch or camp where a group of people sleeps: *The bunkhouse had twenty beds.*

blizzard

C

ca·reer (kə **rîr**´) *n.* A profession or occupation that a person follows as a life's work: *Raul chose a career as a teacher.*

cham·ber (**chām**´ bər) *n.* A hall or room used by a group of lawmakers or judges: *The mayor spoke in the crowded chamber.*

chamber
Chamber comes from the Latin word for "room." Now it can refer to a room, like a bedroom, or to a small space, like the chamber of a heart.

ōō **boot** / ou **out** / ŭ **cut** / û **fur** / hw **which** / th **thin** / th **this** / zh **vision** / ə **ago, silent, pencil, lemon, circus**

711

---

char·ac·ter (**kăr**´ ĭk tər) *n.* A symbol, such as a letter or number, used in printing or writing: *Joe painted red characters on a sign for the Chinese New Year.*

charred (chärd) *adj.* Burned or scorched by fire: *Only a few charred walls were left after the house fire.*

check out (chĕk out) *v.* To sign out and take: *You can check out books from the library.*

check·point (**chĕk**´ point´) *n.* A place along a route where a check or count is made: *The runners were counted at each checkpoint.*

cit·i·zen (**sĭt**´ ĭ zən) *n.* A person who is an official member of a country: *American citizens vote for a president every four years.*

cit·i·zen·ship (**sĭt**´ ĭ zən shĭp´) *n.* The legal position of a citizen of a country, with the duties, rights, and privileges of this position: *The judge granted citizenship to all the people at the ceremony.*

civ·il rights (**sĭv**´ əl rīts) *adj.* Relating to the legal privileges of a citizen, as in the civil rights movement: *The civil rights movement supported fairness for all.*

clas·si·cal (**klăs**´ ĭ kal) *adj.* Of or relating to a musical style developed in Europe in the 1700s: *The orchestra played classical music.*

con·duc·tor (kən **dŭk**´ tər) *n.* The person in charge of a railroad train or subway: *The conductor collected our tickets on the train.*

corral
Corral is a Spanish word that means a "an enclosed area for cattle." It comes from an old Latin word for "circle" or "ring."

conductor

con·sec·u·tive (kən **sĕk**´ yə tĭv) *adj.* Following one right after the other: *Chad hit a home run in three consecutive games.*

con·sume (kən **sōōm**´) *v.* To destroy by burning: *The house was consumed by the fire.*

con·tract (**kŏn**´ trăkt´) *n.* A written agreement that the law can enforce: *The band signed a contract to record two CDs.*

cord (kôrd) *n.* A measure for a stack of cut wood. A cord is eight feet long, four feet wide, and four feet high: *The men cut and stacked two cords of wood.*

cor·ral (kə **răl**´) *n.* A fenced-in area for cattle or horses.

cou·ra·geous (kə **rā**´ jəs) *adj.* Having or showing courage; brave: *The courageous policeman saved the child from drowning.*

coy·o·te (kī ō´ tē) *or* (**kī**´ ōt´) *n.* An animal similar to a wolf that lives in western North America.

crest (krĕst) *n.* Something that grows out of an animal's head, such as a cluster of feathers: *There was a crest of bright blue feathers on the bird's head.*

cross·ly (**krôs**´ lē) *adv.* In a grumpy or grouchy way: *Evie looked crossly at Gabe when he sat in her favorite chair.*

cy·cle (**sī**´ kal) *n.* A series of events that is regularly repeated in the same order: *The cycles of seasons are the same each year.*

ă **rat** / ā **pay** / â **care** / ä **father** / ĕ **pet** / ē **be** / ĭ **pit** / ī **pie** / î **fierce** / ŏ **pot** / ō **go**, ô **paw, for** / oi **oil** / ōō **book**

712

D

de·but (dā´ byōō´) *or* (dā **byōō**´) *n.* A first performance in public: *Rosa made her musical debut at the school concert.*

dem·on·strate (**dĕm**´ ən strāt´) *v.* To show clearly; reveal: *This race demonstrated his speed.*

de·pot (**dē**´ pō) *or* (**dĕp**´ ō) *n.* A railroad or bus station.

de·ter·mined (dĭ **tûr**´ mĭnd) *adj.* Having or showing firmness in sticking to a goal: *Dave was determined to become a doctor.*

dis·ap·point·ed (dĭs´ ə **point**´ əd) *adj.* Made unhappy because hopes or wishes were not satisfied: *Chris was disappointed that she wasn't picked for the soccer team.*

draft (drăft) *n.* A flow of air: *A cold draft made the boy shiver.*

drought (drout) *n.* A period of little or no rain: *The drought dried up the farmer's crops.*

E

ea·ger (**ē**´ gər) *adj.* Full of strong desire; excited: *Ramón was eager to learn to swim.*

el·e·gant (**ĕl**´ ĭ gant) *adj.* Marked by good taste; stylish and graceful: *The people at the fancy party looked very elegant.*

em·ber (**ĕm**´ bər) *n.* A piece of glowing coal or wood in the ashes of a fire: *The log burned until only an ember remained.*

en·rich (ĕn **rĭch**´) *v.* To improve the quality of by adding certain parts, qualities, or ingredients: *Music can enrich your life.*

etch (ĕch) *v.* To make a drawing or design by cutting lines: *Lynn etched her name in the soft clay.*

e·ven·tu·al·ly (ĭ **vĕn**´ chōō əl lē) *adv.* At the end; finally: *After a long delay, the train eventually arrived at the station.*

ex·pe·ri·enced (ĭk **spîr**´ ē ənst) *adj.* Possessing skill or knowledge from having done a particular thing in the past: *The experienced workers solved the problem quickly.*

F

fare (fâr) *n.* The money a person must pay to travel, as on a plane, train, or bus: *The bus driver collected my fare.*

field (fēld) *v.* In baseball, to catch or pick up a ball and throw it to the correct player: *The outfielder had difficulty fielding the ball.*

fierce (fîrs) *adj.* Wild and mean; dangerous: *The lion sounded fierce when it roared.*

first base·man (fûrst **bās**´ mən) *n.* The baseball player who fields from a position near first base.

flam·ma·ble (**flăm**´ ə bal) *adj.* Easy to set fire to and able to burn rapidly: *Old wooden buildings are very flammable.*

fare

ōō **boot** / ou **out** / ŭ **cut** / û **fur** / hw **which** / th **thin** / th **this** / zh **vision** / ə **ago, silent, pencil, lemon, circus**

713

front·ier (frŭn tîr´) *n.* A remote or distant area beyond which few or no people live: *The family went west and settled on the frontier.* ♦ *adj.* Relating to the frontier: *Frontier life was difficult.*

frost (frôst) *n.* A very thin covering of ice: *The cold weather coated the windows with frost.*

frost

G

gath·er·ing (găth´ ər ĭng) *n.* A coming together of people: *The party was a family gathering.*

gear (gîr) *n.* Equipment, such as tools or clothing, used for a particular activity: *We bought camping gear for our hike.*

glare (glâr) *v.* To stare angrily: *After the argument, Mark was glaring at his brother.*

god·moth·er (gŏd´ mŭth´ ər) *n.* A woman or girl who acts as parent or guardian of a child, in the event that the child's parents are unable to: *Leah was asked to be the baby's godmother.*

H

hom·age (hŏm´ ĭj) *n.* Special public honor or respect: *The crowd paid homage to the famous artist at the awards ceremony.*

home·land (hōm´ lănd´) *n.* The country in which one was born or has lived for a long time: *Seema returned to her homeland after many years in a foreign country.*

home·stead (hōm´ stĕd´) *n.* A house with the land and buildings belonging to it: *The homestead has belonged to his family for generations.* ♦ In the 1800s, land given by the government to a person who settled on and farmed it: *Finally, the covered wagon reached the family's homestead.*

hon·or (ŏn´ ər) *v.* To show special respect for: *People came to honor the heroes at the parade.*

ho·ri·zon (ha rī´ zan) *n.* The line along which the earth and the sky appear to meet: *I watched the sun rise over the horizon.*

I

im·mense (ĭ mĕns´) *adj.* Of great size, scale, or degree: *The immense building seemed to touch the clouds.*

J

jazz (jăz) *n.* A type of music with a strong rhythm which developed in the United States from work songs, hymns, and spirituals: *When the pianist plays jazz, she sometimes invents the song as she goes along.*

jolt (jōlt) *v.* To move, ride, or cause to move in a jerky way: *The bus was jolting along the bumpy road.*

ă rat / ā pay / â care / ä father / ĕ pet / ē be / ĭ pĭt / ī pĭe / î fierce / ŏ pot / ō go / ô paw, for / oi oil / ōō book

714

L

land·scape (lănd´ skāp´) *n.* A stretch of land: *Emily admired the landscape of rolling hills.*

lap (lăp) *v.* To take up with the tip of the tongue: *Have you ever watched a cat lap up water?* ♦ *n.* The front part of a sitting person's body from the waist to the knees: *The cat slept on Yoshi's lap.*

long (lông) *v.* To wish or want very much: *My mother longed to see her childhood home again.*

lum·ber·jack (lŭm´ bər jăk´) *n.* A person who chops down trees and hauls the logs to a sawmill.

lurch·ing (lûrch´ ĭng) *adj.* Sudden, heavy, unsteady movements to one side or forward: *The lurching boat made Roslyn sway back and forth.*

lure (lōōr) *n.* Fake bait used to attract and catch fish: *The fisherman tied a silver lure to his line.*

M

mar·vel (mär´ vəl) *v.* To be filled with surprise, amazement, or wonder: *Don marveled at the beautiful waterfall.*

mer·cu·ry (mûr´ kyə rē) *n.* A silvery-white metal that is a liquid at room temperature; used in thermometers.

mis·cal·cu·late (mĭs kăl´ kyə lāt´) *v.* To plan or figure incorrectly; make a mistake: *Amy miscalculated how much money she needed.*

mis·un·der·stand·ing (mĭs´ ŭn dər stăn´ dĭng) *n.* A failure to understand: *Carl's feelings were hurt because of a misunderstanding over whose turn it was.*

mod·est (mŏd´ ĭst) *adj.* Having a quiet, humble view of one's own talents, abilities, or accomplishments; not boastful: *The piano player was modest even though he was very talented.*

mur·mur (mûr´ mər) *n.* A low, constant sound: *We often hear the murmur of running water from the nearby stream.*

mush·er (mŭsh´ ər) *n.* The driver of a dog sled team.

N

ner·vous·ly (nûr´ vəs lē) *adv.* With concern, worry, or fear: *He nervously walked onto the stage to deliver his speech.*

O

oath (ōth) *n.* A pledge or promise to act in a certain way: *The new citizens pledged an oath to obey the laws of the United States.*

op·por·tu·ni·ty (ŏp´ ər tōō´ nĭ tē or ŏp´ ər tyōō´ nĭ tē) *n.* A good chance to advance oneself: *Joining the school band was an opportunity to make new friends.*

or·phan (ôr´ fan) *n.* A child whose parents are dead.

landscape

lumberjack
Lumberjack is a compound word made up of *lumber*, meaning trees used for wood, and *jack*, meaning "man." *Jack* originally comes from the Hebrew name for Jacob.

P

peas·ant (pĕz´ ənt) *adj.* Of or relating to a poor farmer or farm worker: *The couple lived a simple peasant life in the country.*

pe·cu·liar (pĭ kyōōl´ yər) *adj.* Unusual; strange or odd: *The warm weather was peculiar for January.*

per·sist (pər sĭst´) *v.* To continue repeatedly to say or do something: *My sister persisted in asking me to read to her.*

phonograph

pho·no·graph (fō´ nə grăf´) *n.* An old-fashioned record player: *Jenna danced to a happy song playing on the phonograph.*

pi·o·neer (pī´ ə nîr´) *n.* A person who settles in an unknown, unclaimed region: *The pioneers made their new homes in the valley.*

pioneer
Pioneer comes from the Italian word for "foot soldier," the first kind of soldier to go into battle. Today, *pioneer* refers to the settlers of the American West or to anyone who leads the way for others.

pitch in (pĭch ĭn) *v.* To start working with other people to get a job done: *Everyone on the farm pitches in to finish the work.*

plaque (plăk) *n.* A flat piece of wood, metal, or stone with writing on it that usually honors a person or event: *Plaques on the sunken ship honor the people who lost their lives.*

plat·form (plăt´ fôrm´) *n.* A raised floor or surface, for example, by a track at a train station: *They stood on the platform, waiting for the train.*

prai·rie (prâr´ ē) *adj.* Of the plains, a wide area of flat or rolling land with tall grass and few trees: *The prairie winds covered everything with dust.*

pro·test (prə tĕst´ or prō´ tĕst´) *v.* To express strong objections to something: *Many people came to protest the plan to build a new airport.*

proud (proud) *adj.* 1. Thinking too highly of oneself: *The boy was proud because he thought he was better than anyone else.* 2. Full of self-respect: *Li felt proud to be marching in the parade.*

R

re·mind (rĭ mīnd´) *v.* To make someone remember something: *The song reminded him of home.*

re·new (rĭ nōō´) or (rĭ nyōō´) *v.* To make new again; to bring new life to: *Each spring the forest renews itself with green leaves.*

re·un·ion (rē yōōn´ yən) *n.* A gathering of members of a group who have not seen each other for a while: *The school holds its yearly reunions in the gym.*

rhythm (rĭth´ əm) *n.* 1. A movement, action, or condition that repeats in a regular pattern: *Everyone's walk has a special rhythm.* 2. A musical pattern with a series of regularly accented beats: *We sang songs with many different rhythms.*

rug·ged (rŭg´ ĭd) *adj.* Having a rough, uneven surface: *The rugged trail was hard to climb.*

ă rat / ā pay / â care / ä father / ĕ pet / ē be / ĭ pĭt / ī pĭe / î fierce / ŏ pot / ō go / ô paw, for / oi oil / ōō book

716

S

satch·el (săch´ əl) *n.* A small bag used for carrying books, clothing, or other small items: *The two satchels held all she owned.*

sat·is·fac·tion (săt´ ĭs făk´ shən) *n.* The condition of being pleased and contented: *Her satisfaction with her family showed in her big smile.*

scale (skāl) *n.* 1. One of the small, thin, flat parts that cover a fish or reptile: *The lizard was covered with shiny green scales.* 2. An instrument used for weighing: *Anton weighed a bunch of bananas on the scale.*

scav·en·ger (skăv´ ĭn jər) *n.* An animal that feeds on dead animals or plants: *Scavengers often eat dead fish.*

set·tler (sĕt´ lər) *n.* A person who settles, or makes a home, in a new region: *The settlers traveled west to find a better life.*

ship·wreck (shĭp´ rĕk´) *n.* 1. A wrecked ship: *The Titanic is the most famous of all shipwrecks.* 2. The destruction of a ship, in a collision or because of a storm: *A shipwreck may happen during a storm at sea.*

short·stop (shôrt´ stŏp´) *n.* The baseball player who plays the position between second and third bases.

singe (sĭnj) *v.* To burn slightly; scorch: *Celia saw that the fire was about to singe her sweater.*

slump (slŭmp) *v.* 1. To sink down suddenly: *The woman slumped to the ground and cried.* 2. To experience a period of poor performance, especially in a sport: *Our best hitter always slumps in hot weather.*

snake (snāk) *v.* To move like a snake: *The line of children snaked through the playground.*

snow·shoe (snō´ shōō´) *n.* A rounded wooden frame with leather strips stretched across it, attached to the shoe; used for walking on top of the snow.

spawn (spôn) *v.* To lay eggs and reproduce, as fish and some other water animals do: *Salmon return to spawn in the same river where they were born.*

spe·cial·ize (spĕsh´ a līz) *v.* To be involved in a particular activity or branch of study: *This bookstore specializes in children's books.*

sports·man·ship (spôrts´ mən shĭp´) *n.* The quality of someone who acts with dignity in difficult situations, especially used with people who play sports: *It was good sportsmanship to clap for the other team.*

sto·ry·tel·ler (stôr´ ē tĕl´ ər) *n.* A person who tells stories.

stride (strīd) *v.* To walk with long steps: *The boy strides quickly down the street.*

stu·pen·dous (stōō pĕn´ das) *adj.* Amazing; marvelous: *The falling star was a stupendous sight.*

scale
Scale comes from the Old Norse word for "bowl," or a drinking vessel made from a shell. Scales used to have two plates or bowls to hold the objects that were being weighed.

sur·round (sə round´) *v.* To put all around: *He surrounded his desk with pictures of his family.*

sur·vi·vor (sər vī´ vər) *n.* Someone or something that has stayed alive: *The rescue ship picked up the survivors from the lifeboats.*

T

teem·ing (tēm´ ing) *adj.* Full; crowded: *The parade moved through the teeming city streets.*

thermometer
Thermometer comes from two Greek words: thermē, meaning "heat," and metron, meaning "measure." A thermometer measures heat.

tem·per·a·ture (tĕm´ pər ə chər) *n.* Hotness or coldness as measured on a standard scale: *The temperature outside was low, so we put on our warmest clothes.*

ther·mom·e·ter (thər mŏm´ ĭ tər) *n.* An instrument that measures temperature, usually by the height of a liquid that expands or contracts inside a slender glass tube.

tim·ber (tĭm´ bər) *n.* **1.** Trees that can be used as wood: *They used timber from their own land to build their house.* **2.** A long, heavy piece of wood for building; a beam: *Only a few blackened timbers of the barn remained after the fire.*

tim·id (tĭm´ ĭd) *adj.* Easily frightened; shy: *The timid squirrel sat still until everyone had left.*

tire·less (tīr´ lĭs) *adj.* Capable of working a long time without getting tired: *She was a tireless worker who always stayed late.*

weathervane

trou·ble·some (trŭb´ əl səm) *adj.* Causing trouble or difficulty: *Ben felt he was in a troublesome situation when he couldn't find the movie tickets.*

U

un·sink·a·ble (ŭn´ sĭngk´ ə bəl) *adj.* Not capable of being sunk: *The ship was so big that people thought it was unsinkable.*

V

voy·age (voi´ ĭj) *n.* A long journey to a distant place, usually made by ship or airplane.

W

weath·er·vane (wĕth´ ər vān´) *n.* A moveable pointer that shows which way the wind is blowing: *The weathervane on top of the barn pointed north.*

woods·man (wŏŏdz´ mən) *n.* A person who works or lives in the forest: *The young woodsman walked to the forest every day.*

world·wide (wûrld´ wīd´) *adj.* Extending or spreading throughout the world: *Several songs became worldwide hits.*

wreck·age (rĕk´ ĭj) *n.* The remains of something that has been damaged or destroyed: *The wreckage of the ship was found on the ocean floor.*

å rat / ā pay / â care / ä father / ĕ pet / ē be / ĭ pit / ī pie / î fierce / ŏ pot / ō go / ô paw, for / oi oil / ŏŏ book

Acknowledgments

(acknowledgments text, permissions, Links and Theme Openers, Focus Selections — small print)

Credits

Photography

Assignment Photography

Illustration

Index

Boldface page references indicate formal strategy and skill instruction.